EXPLORATIONS IN DIFFERENCE:
LAW, CULTURE, AND POLITICS
Edited by Jonathan Hart and Richard W. Bauman
Foreword by The Honourable Jules Deschênes

How do current debates over identity and difference come into play within the workings of our cultural, legal, and political institutions? *Explorations in Difference* addresses this question, gathering together a range of perspectives on the meanings and implications of difference in the context of postmodern theory.

This collection mirrors the postmodern challenge to notions of unity and consensus, presenting disparate, often contrasting viewpoints, and varying attitudes to postmodernism itself. Within individual essays, contributors express their ambivalence towards postmodernism as, on the one hand, lamentable reality, reflecting and maintaining political stasis, or alternatively, a liberating, potentially subversive realm of discourse. Amidst this multiplicity of perspectives, *Explorations in Difference* sustains a focus on the political, asserting the ideological dimension of all representations within our social structure.

The volume is divided into two sections: 'Theoretical Accounts,' which establishes a context for postmodern inquiries into difference, and 'Instances,' which provides application to particular issues. This format allows both a broadly suggestive analysis of the underpinnings of identity and community, and an exploration of particular sites of conflict. The contributions in 'Instances' range from an examination of the tension between European-derived and aboriginal laws in British Columbia, to an analysis of feminist theories of connectedness and the discourse of abortion rights. The first Canadian study of its kind, *Explorations in Difference* offers a timely inquiry into postmodern difference and its implications, both within Canada and beyond.

JONATHAN HART is a professor in the Department of English, University of Alberta.

RICHARD W. BAUMAN is an associate professor in the Faculty of Law, University of Alberta.

THEORY/CULTURE

General Editors:
Linda Hutcheon, Gary Leonard,
Janet Paterson, and Paul Perron

EDITED BY JONATHAN HART
AND RICHARD W. BAUMAN

Explorations in Difference:
Law, Culture, and Politics

Published in association with the Centre for Constitutional Studies,
University of Alberta, by

UNIVERSITY OF TORONTO PRESS
Toronto Buffalo London

© University of Toronto Press Incorporated 1996
Toronto Buffalo London
Printed in Canada

ISBN 0-8020-0693-0 (cloth)
ISBN 0-8020-7645-9 (paper)

Printed on acid-free paper

Canadian Cataloguing in Publication Data

Main entry under title:

Explorations in difference : law, culture, and politics

(Theory/culture)
Co-published by the Centre for Constitutional
Studies, University of Alberta.
ISBN 0-8020-0693-0 (bound)
ISBN 0-8020-7645-9 (pbk.)

1. Culture and law. 2. Sociological jurisprudence.
3. Law – Canada. I. Hart, Jonathan. II. Bauman,
Richard W. III. University of Alberta. Centre for
Constitutional Studies. IV. Series.

K487.C8E9 1996   340'.115'0971   C95-931995-6

University of Toronto Press acknowledges the financial assistance to its
publishing program of the Canada Council and the Ontario Arts Council.

Ad Mariam
JLH

Contents

Foreword

THE HONOURABLE JULES DESCHÊNES, C.C.

In 1945 Hugh MacLennan wrote about our Canadian *Two Solitudes* and, after having magnificently described the course of the Saint Lawrence and Ottawa Rivers and their merging at Montréal, he was led to conclude his very first chapter on a rather melancholic note:

But down in the angle at Montréal, on the island about which the two rivers join, there is little of this sense of new and endless space. Two old races and religions meet here and live their separate legends, side by side. If this sprawling half-continent has a heart, here it is. Its pulse throbs out along the rivers and railroads; slow, reluctant and rarely simple, a double beat, a self-moved reciprocation.[1]

Half a century later, the situation has only grown more complex: exploring our differences has proven to be the main Canadian pastime. Yet the task is never achieved. Indeed, from what we now know of our differences, we may have reached that critical point when we genuinely fear we will never be able to bridge the gap.

Now what brings together this collection is a most salutary and typically Canadian reaction: we may quarrel and differ, but at least we talk to each other. We have learned to live generally in civilized peace among ourselves in this blessed land. This result, however, does not seem to come to us, if I may say, naturally. The differences always surge back to the surface, and the first one that comes to mind is the 'distinct society' difference: between Québec and the rest of the country, between French and English and neo-Canadians.

In 1867 the Parliament at Westminster enshrined in the Canadian Constitution the distinction between Protestants and Catholics: a decision fraught with danger, as appears from the fate of many other countries where religious feuds have torn apart whole nations and societies. Fortunately, outside of a few incidents, we have avoided religious clashes. In this country, language, not religion, is the spark which ignites passions.

We must broaden our view of linguistic difference in Canada beyond that between the two official languages, French and English. I will not dwell on the foreign languages which our large population of immigrants have brought with them: they have usually chosen to rally to one of our official languages as their main vehicle of communication. But we are now witnessing the phenomenon of the rebirth of aboriginal languages. Fifty-three of these have been identified in 1988 by a study carried out at the request of the Assembly of First Nations. The aboriginals themselves acknowledge that the majority of these traditional languages are destined to disappear, but they insist on the future of Cree, Obidjue, and Inuktituk at least.

This movement will gather strength from the *Universal Declaration on the Rights of Indigenous Peoples*, which is reaching its final drafting stage in the United Nations. Part 2 of the *Declaration* spells out expressly the right of indigenous peoples to 'develop and promote and transmit to future generations their own languages and writing systems and literature' and 'to revive and practise their cultural identity and traditions.'[2] As a matter of fact and of law, an Ordinance of the Northwest Territories issued in 1984 and amended in 1991 now recognizes as official, together with English and French, no less than six aboriginal languages.[3] In the Yukon, as of 1 January 1993, eight aboriginal languages benefit from what I may call semi-official status. This is a difference that is only emerging, but it is likely to gain importance as the aboriginal claims to autonomy grow in strength.

Understandably, foreigners, and many Canadians also, get lost in this *quid pro quo* where, within the same borders, a language may or may not be official depending upon the level of authority within which it is used, and may even be totally prohibited provincially, as in commercial advertising, even though it is official federally in the country at large. Nothing like this situation can be found anywhere else in the world.

Of course, the stubborn presence of two legal systems within Québec's borders does nothing to soothe the temper of those whom it irritates. This time, however, when we deal with federal law, Canadian common lawyers emerge from this situation the poorer, even though many of them will refuse to admit it. Now where and what is the difference? Since the *Quebec Act, 1774*, property and civil rights (such is the sacrosanct phrase) are governed by civil law.[4] This includes, for instance, status, contracts, and torts. On the other hand, law inspired by the English tradition rules the public domain and the Constitution, and the federal law applicable to Québec covers, to name but a few popular topics, divorce, bankruptcy, banks, unemployment insurance, criminal law, and defence.

Now the preservation of the civil law system is precious for the culture and institutions of French Canada, although it means the persistence of a difference. It also renders necessary an exacting intellectual gymnastics on the part of those who have to make both legal systems a part of their daily life. But where the difference becomes striking is in the treatment given to federal law which, as the truism goes, applies throughout the country.

Traditionally, Québec judges and lawyers have shown a keen interest in the way courts and writers from other parts of the country construe and apply those laws which are also binding in Québec. The converse proposition, however, has not found much favour. Probably because of the language barrier, rarely does it happen that courts outside Québec quote from Québec sources in matters of federal law. Yet such sources are not wanting, far from it. That is where common lawyers get the poorer end of the deal, but that result is not due to any ill will on the part of Québec's legal profession.

Should we turn to an exploration of our political differences? I will not touch on this here, not so much because of the subject matter, but because such matters are dealt with extensively in the following collection of essays. This country still has to come to grips with the problems which those differences are exacerbating. Some of the contributors to this collection may wish to discuss them and contribute to an exciting debate on these timely subjects. I do not have the heart to open up those wounds again.

NOTES

1 Hugh MacLennan, *Two Solitudes* (Toronto: Collins, 1945), 4.
2 See 'Draft Universal Declaration on the Rights of Indigenous Peoples,' reprinted in [1992] 2 C.N.L.R. 1 at 3.
3 Official Languages Ordinance, S.N.W.T. 1984 (2d Sess.), c. 2, s. 5, as am. by Official Languages Act (Amendment), S.N.W.T. 1990, c.7, s. 4.
4 *Quebec Act, 1774*, 14 Geo. III, c. 83 (U.K.) reprinted in R.S.C. 1985, App. II, No. 2.

Acknowledgments

Earlier versions of the essays in this collection were originally presented at the conference 'Explorations in Difference: Law, Culture, and Politics,' held at the University of Alberta in March 1992 and organized by the editors of this volume. We are grateful for the generosity of the Royal Society of Canada, the Centre for Constitutional Studies, the Alberta Law Foundation, and the office of the vice-president (academic), University of Alberta, which helped ensure the success of the conference and the publication of this book. We are also grateful to the following individuals for their unstinting support of the venture: Mr Justice Jules Deschênes (then president of the Royal Society of Canada); David Schneiderman (executive director of the Centre for Constitutional Studies); Anne McLellan (then acting dean of law); Dean Patricia Clements; Dean Timothy J. Christian; J. Peter Meekison (then vice-president [academic] of the university); and Shirley Neuman. For their aid and assistance, our gratitude is also due various departments at the University of Alberta, including the Departments of Anthropology, Comparative Literature, English, and Sociology, and the Women's Studies Programme. We are also indebted to Annalise Acorn, Alain Bissonnette, Barbara Johnson, and Sharon Venne for their presentations at, and other contributions to, the conference. Our thanks also to the individuals who served as chairs and commentators, including Michael Asch, Ronald Ayling, Don Carmichael, Terence Cave, Larry Chartrand, Patricia Clements, Ray Morrow, Lynn Penrod, Victor Ramraj, and Daphne Read; as well as to Martin Lefebvre. To those who attended the conference, we thank you for contributing to its success. Finally, we are thankful for the valuable comments of the three anonymous readers at University of Toronto Press, the general editors of this series, Linda Hutcheon, Paul Perron, Janet Paterson, and Gary Leonard, and our editor, Suzanne Rancourt.

Revised versions of some of the following materials appear by permission:

Jennifer Nedelsky, 'Reconceiving Rights as Relationship,' *Review of Constitutional Studies* 1 (1993).

Christopher Norris, 'Getting at Truth: Genealogy, Critique, and Postmodern Scepticism' in *The Truth about Postmodernism* (Oxford: Blackwell 1993).

Christine Sypnowich, 'Some Disquiet about "Difference,"' *Praxis International* 13 (1993).

EXPLORATIONS IN DIFFERENCE

Introduction

JONATHAN HART AND RICHARD W. BAUMAN

This book arises out of debates in postmodern theories of culture and law. At the core of these debates are notions of 'difference' and 'identity.' The meaning and consequences of these concepts are surrounded by controversy. This collection offers a range of views about the nature of difference and how it operates in relation to law, culture, and politics. The dimensions of difference, as well as its implications for our cultural, political, and legal institutions, are pressing issues, both in Canada and elsewhere. The collection brings together a variety of contrasting perspectives. They vary in their assumptions, their methods, and their conclusions. But the authors also connect in important ways. Both the variations and connections are outlined in this Introduction. First, we suggest a context within which the essays are set.

To speak effectively about difference requires a background acquaintance with postmodernist movements. *Postmodernism*, a notoriously complex term, has been around for more than three decades. During its history, postmodernism has assumed various forms and had significant impact on a wide array of fields. The *postmodern*, along with other terms connoting supersession, such as *post-structuralism, post-industrialism,* and *post-Marxism,* has been evoked in philosophy, the arts, social sciences, and popular culture.[1] It has arrived belatedly in legal studies, where it is only during the last ten years or so that law as a discipline has begun to show traces of postmodern themes.[2] Linda Hutcheon has distinguished between the postmodernism of the 1960s and that of the 1970s and 1980s. Sixties postmodernism challenged authority and developed a general historical consciousness. It was particularly aware of the role of women and of ethnic and racial minorities in history. The sixties version combined despair and celebration.[3] Postmodernism in the 1970s and 1980s has been more ambivalent and less oppositional and idealistic than its sixties counterpart. It has tended to question and demystify key values in modern culture. Among the self-conscious achievements of postmodernism have been the rejection of hierarchy, suspicions about authority and textual closure, and the impossibility of representation and consensus. Yet it has also had to come to grips with its own complicity with those values and with its sequestration from social and political engagement.[4] Hutcheon herself is a prominent advocate of the political resonance of postmodernism. This collection has been structured with the politics of postmodernism in the foreground. The question of difference and thus of identity should be viewed in this context. All representations, whether legal, cultural, or political, possess an ideological dimension that bears exploring. The very questions of identity politics and the diversity and difference of gender, race, and ethnicity within nations, which took hold in the 1960s, continue in the new phases of our ineluctably postmodern world. Postmodernism intersects with other movements, such as feminism, but whether they can be combined or not is a vexed question.[5]

There are, then, many postmodernisms. While Hutcheon suggests that postmodernism consists of numerous points of view and polarized camps (at one extreme, self-reflexive and parodic, while at the other, worldly postmodernism), she notes that some of its characteristics are commonly agreed on. Hutcheon lists the various types of boundary tensions in postmodernism. These are 'created by the transgression of the boundaries between genres, between disciplines or discourses, between high and mass culture, and most problematically, perhaps, between practice and theory.'[6] Among the cruxes of the debate on difference within a postmodernist context are its practical implications. Do the cultural indeterminacies of postmodernism end up unsettling or revising the world or, as the opponents of postmodernism argue, do they lead to the opposite? Ihab Hassan has suggested the former.[7] In support, Jean Baudrillard has argued that the power of capitalism operates in social reproduction or the cultural domain and should be opposed there. Therefore, by implication the work that postmodern theorists and artists do through aesthetics, linguistics, and texts is political.[8] Rather than elaborate this vast web of postmodern theory, we would like to concentrate on an aspect of the work of Jean-François Lyotard on postmodernism, especially his continuing dispute with Jürgen Habermas over legitimation and consensus in the production and reception of knowledge. This debate applies specifically to this collection, because some writers, like Lyotard, celebrate the difference and dissension of postmodernism and others, like Habermas, are wary of a movement that depreciates the possibility of communication and common ground.

Lyotard's *The Postmodern Condition: A Report on Knowledge* was originally commissioned by the Conseil des Universités of the government of Quebec and appeared in 1979. The report was translated into English in 1984.[9] This example of *dirigiste* or state-sponsored research has since become a seminal text in universities throughout the West. Lyotard begins the body of his report in the understated and impersonal language of contemporary social science: 'Our working hypothesis is that the status of knowledge is altered as societies enter what is known as the postindustrial age and cultures enter what is known as the postmodern age' (3). Lyotard's introduction, however, speaks in a more personal vein. He notes that he has chosen to use 'postmodern,' a term current among American sociologists and critics, to designate the condition of our entire culture.

Since the Second World War, according to Lyotard, this culture has undergone great transformations that have changed the rules of the game for science, the arts, and literature (xxiii). In Lyotard's view, science has always been in conflict with narratives. Science itself implies a narrative about itself – a consensus between the sender and receiver of a statement on its truth based on agreement between rational minds. Lyotard calls this the Enlightenment narrative and describes its plot as one in which 'the hero of knowledge works toward a good ethico-political end – universal peace' (xxiv). In his scheme, the postmodern stresses incredulity about such meta-narratives. The Enlightenment meta-narrative, which legitimates itself through a philosophy of history that underwrites social institutions and the bonds within them, is now obsolete. The obsolescence of this self-legitimation, according to Lyotard, corresponds to the crisis of metaphysics and the university, which relied on this meta-narrative quest-myth. Philosophy is supposed to demonstrate the justice of the social consequences of science and its historical teleology. Lyotard is led to proclaim a revolution of 'language particles,' as opposed to the language systems of modernity, of heterogeneity and localism, rather than homogeneity and universality. The postmodern condition is a place of contradictions: for example, we are urged both to work less in order to cut costs and to assume more responsibility for social services and programs that governments are abandoning. But we cannot gather solace from such a situation as Marx did. At the heart of Lyotard's disagreement with Habermas is the possibility of achieving legitimation through discursive consensus. According to Lyotard:

Such consensus does violence to the heterogeneity of language games. And invention is always born of dissension. Postmodern knowledge is not simply a tool of the authorities; it refines our sensitivity to differences and reinforces our ability to tolerate the incommensurable. Its principle is not the expert's homology, but the inventor's paralogy. (xxv)

Paralogy should not be confused with innovation. Paralogy is not under the command of the system, but is a move made in the pragmatics of knowledge (60–1). Lyotard contends that science succeeds in fitting the world into a system (homologies), but it uses flexible means (the plurality of languages) and is a pragmatic game (43). In place of grand narratives, Lyotard favours small narratives.[10]

Habermas takes a different approach to questions of knowledge and legitimation. His work follows a Kantian pattern. Kant tried to differentiate autonomous areas of pure reason, practical reason, and judgment and to find formal, rational grounds appropriate to each area of activity. Similarly, Habermas holds that social systems, such as economic, legal, and aesthetic systems, separate themselves from the life-world or social whole – the horizon of shared social interactions. Within the context of modernity, the major intellectual task is to identify the fundamental principles underlying these systems or edifices of thought without resorting to external values or truths. Modernity requires a normative quest for a society's own self-generated principles. Therefore, the conflicts that do arise derive from among these social systems: for example, art may be treated as 'pure supplementarity,' a marginal preoccupation with affective, but not cognitive or political, meaning.[11] For Habermas, the life-world is a web of presuppositions common to a speech community.[12] The a priori nature of this life-world disturbs Lyotard. Habermas has claimed that postmodernism repudiates modernism by means of a bourgeois philistinism and conservatism.[13] He remains interested in redeeming the emancipatory potential of the systems of rationality.[14] He has warned against abandoning the 'unfulfilled project of modernity.'[15] What appears a crisis in community and communication for Habermas is, for Lyotard, an opportunity.[16] In their discussion of the constituent features of postmodern jurisprudence, Douzinas, Warrington, and McVeigh have expressed a similar position. They interpret Lyotard as arguing that 'the radical split and the multiplying incommensurable language games in which we find ourselves rather than being a cause for lament must be retained and protected in their separate identities. Lyotard turns this injunction into a postmodern theory of justice.'[17]

In his introduction to the English translation of Lyotard's *The Postmodern Condition*, Fredric Jameson elaborates on a difference between Lyotard and Habermas to which we have alluded. Lyotard belongs to the French Enlightenment. He shares a revolutionary view of philosophy as the politics of commitment and sees psychology as based on a decentred subject (the illusion of the self). By contrast, Habermas belongs to the German Hegelian tradition, which involves the contemplation of totality and the autonomy of the self. These presuppositions reflect Habermas's Frankfurt School credentials.[18] Lyotard sees narrative as a means of characterizing and opposing scientific method. Thus, postmodernism reminds us that stories will not go away and that arguments are made up of stories: this is comparable to Northrop Frye's insistence on the priority of myth over ideology.[19] Although Jameson embraces postmodernism more than Frye did, he thinks, as Frye did, that the master narratives never go away although they may be repressed or submerged.[20] Jameson is a good example of a writer who is confident about the total narratives in the tradition of German philosophy (which Nietzsche criticized from within). Other writers deplore such confidence. The narrative turn in postmodernism has been attributed to a loss of confidence in an epistemological and ontological grounding for theory or metaphysics.[21] Jameson begins his own recent *Postmodernism, or the Cultural Logic of Late Capitalism* by suggesting that the philosophy of history is remote from the contemporary mind: 'It is safest to grasp the concept of the postmodern as an attempt to think the present historically in an age that has forgotten how to think historically in the first place.'[22]

Within the postmodern debate, difference occupies an important place. Otherness, alterity, or difference did not begin with Derrida and deconstruction, but Derridean eloquence and influence have led to great interest in this subject. Michel de Certeau and Tzvetan Todorov have also discussed the heterologies of the other, and their work, which looks at the relation between Europeans and other cultures, has been important in discussions of the relation of the postcolonial and the postmodern.[23] In his study of desire and difference, Raoul Mortley has reminded us that alterity or difference is a problem in discourse and life that Plato addresses. Diaphora is a key aspect for a philosopher who insists on unity in life as well as a philosophical scheme. Difference in Plato, but not in Derrida, creates a crisis as it disaggregates the system. The importance of difference can first be seen in Plato's *The Sophist*. In Derrida, difference supplants desire.[24] In fact, Mortley argues that difference begins in Plato and is found in Aristotle, Plotinus, Aquinas, and Heidegger before it occurs in Derrida. But 'difference' as we use it has more to do with the disjunction between the modern desire for national and personal identity, on the one hand, and the postmodern celebration of heterogeneity and multiplicity, on the other.[25] The desire for different individuals and groups to be represented in history, where for ethnic, racial, class, gender, and other pretexts they have been excluded, is the difference addressed throughout this collection. Although life and discourse are not identical, a kind of reading against the grain, or an alternative and pluralistic cultural poetics or semiotics, should help produce a greater understanding of the complexity of postmodern societies and the texts and images that represent them. How postmodernism is best interpreted remains an open question even after the difference between Habermas and Lyotard.

In *Explorations in Difference,* many of the contributors follow the example of such writers as Linda Hutcheon and Barbara Johnson by both considering the important implications of postmodernism and also expressing their disquiet over its assumptions.[26] They frequently examine the ambivalence of difference with some ambivalence. The collection is divided into two sections. The first, 'Theoretical Accounts,' situates the concept of difference in postmodernism. The second, 'Instances,' provides applications to specific topics. 'Theoretical Accounts' begins with Ross Chambers's essay, which outlines some of the issues of cultural and individual identity that have important implications for the rest of the essays in the collection. Chambers analyses difference from a historical perspective that goes beyond deconstructive difference while making some use of deconstructive method in that analysis. The post-deconstructive aspects of Chambers's essay lie in its postmodern attributes of questioning authority and setting up oppositional or alternative discourses and moves. Jennifer Nedelsky's essay complements Chambers's essay as they both provide an account of the construction of community. In discussing postmodernist scepticism, Christopher Norris also wonders about community and communication, about the possibility of truth-seeking discourse through evidence and reason, which are legacies of the Enlightenment. Like Norris, Christine Sypnowich observes the origins of postmodern difference in the Enlightenment. She, too, hopes for common ground behind the politics of difference.

The second part, 'Instances,' includes theoretical essays, but these contributions especially develop specific applications of that theory. Each essay represents an aspect of postmodern politics in law and in literature. Sheila Noonan analyses feminist theories of connectedness and the discourse of abortion rights. Looking at the connection between the ancient Brehon Laws and the Irish hunger strikes, Richard Devlin deconstructs the political rhetoric of the Irish resistance to British rule. Claude Denis also gives an account of the conflict of rights between cultures. He examines the tension between European and aboriginal laws, especially as it arises out of the British Columbia Supreme Court decision in *Thomas* v. *Norris*.[27] Like the previous essays in 'Instances,' Pamela McCallum's interprets postmodern difference in light of, if not in opposition to, the Enlightenment. She reads the history and politics in Alejo Carpentier's *El Siglo de las luces* through the rhetoric of baroque allegory. In the process, she views the historical through the literary and so concludes the collection with the kind of postmodern border-crossing that the other essays have deployed.

Although this is the rationale behind their division and order, the essays of *Explorations in Difference* present other common aspects in their discussion of heterogeneity. All the essays have important implications for Canada and the international community. Several are concerned with aspects of difference and cultural identity that apply to Canada specifically (particularly to the relations between Quebec and Canada, and between the aboriginal peoples and European society). The essays also resonate more generally, and internationally. Jennifer Nedelsky, for instance, explores the role of relationship in rights, and Sheila Noonan, the relation between abortion and feminism, and both use international as well as Canadian examples.

In Canada, we continue to have differences over self-government for aboriginal peoples, over feminism, over multiculturalism, over the dispossessed, and over sexual preference. Such tensions are manifest in legal disputes under the *Canadian Charter of Rights and Freedoms*.[28] They have also shaped the long and difficult constitutional debates from the *Quebec Act, 1774* through the *Constitutional Act, 1791* and the *Constitution Act, 1867* to the repatriation of the Constitution in 1982 and the deaths of the Meech Lake Accord in 1990 and of the Charlottetown Accord in 1992.[29] Canada, like the former states of the Soviet Union, the Czech Republic and Slovakia, and other countries, is undergoing political crisis.[30] So far, as in the former Czechoslovakia, the political and constitutional tensions in Canada have remained non-violent. We have not witnessed the daily bloodshed that has marked the disintegration of the former Yugoslavia, where political, religious, and ethnic divisions have been tragic. Nor do Canadians, despite the nagging issues of difference, face the formidable job of having to rebuild their economic, legal, and educational infrastructure that dominates such countries as South Africa.[31] In Canada, we have become closely attuned to questions about legal and political recognition of minority cultures to a degree that has been more peaceful and more articulate than elsewhere.[32] Whether the problems are urgent or just persistent, there is an existential and political edge to matters of difference that the contributors in this collection address.

The diverse contributions to the collection raise many questions about the way things are in the fields of law, culture, and politics, but we want to concentrate on a few concerns. One of the central concerns in the essays is the relation of power to powerlessness and of individual (self or subject) to the state or community. Whether power is male, European, judicial, political, or all of these, and whether the powerlessness is aboriginal, female, minority, or imprisoned, the contributors look at the configurations of power in Western, Canadian, and aboriginal societies. Several essays examine questions of identity – the relation of the liberal autonomous self to the needs of the community. They also focus on the role of reason and the Enlightenment in creating the dilemmas facing people now. Or they explore the possibility of solving these problems, taking into account the incommensurability of different individuals, groups, or cultures in communicating and in constructing community. Especially as a result of feminist and aboriginal critiques of the prevailing order, the contributors have sought new ways to look at these complex issues. They seek remedies to our present predicament through law, culture, and politics.

The question of cultural identity runs throughout the collection. To begin the first part of the volume, 'Theoretical Accounts,' Ross Chambers offers a possible way out of the traps of cultural identity. He discusses this identity, concentrating on mediators and symbolic scapegoats, in terms of discourse theory. All differences, Chambers argues, are ideologically produced, and these differences give meaning to communities and provide them with the grounds of negotiation. He claims that there are scapegoats among the community of scapegoaters. Chambers reminds us that there are no boundaries without overlap or leakage. Using a politics of invitation, the scapegoats, Chambers contends, should invite some of the scapegoaters to join with them to search for a 'possible communitarian dialogue.' In Chambers's scheme, culture, which is a principle of identity, precedes communication, which is the negotiation of differences. Chambers also asks why stereotyping is decried while cultural identity, a similar practice of the politics of sameness, is affirmed as necessary to emancipatory politics. He uses Michel Serres's description of the mediator as the excluded third, the person who makes a dialogue possible by his or her exclusion not from culture but the exercise of discursive power. Each discursive community relies on an excluded third. Chambers argues that differences should become qualifying, a means of constituting 'differential positions without which there is no communication.' Community, according to Chambers, is the mediator of communication and not a family of people that has in common something essential, which is, in his view, the definition of fascistic discourse. Chambers provides an acute analysis of scapegoating, which builds on the work of René Girard and Eve Sedgwick, especially the latter's observation of the basic law of scapegoating – it takes one to know one.[33] Differences that do not make a difference, Chambers says, must begin to make a difference in the positive sense and cease to make a difference as a means of disqualification. Like Trinh T. Minh-ha, Chambers is optimistic about the ways people are now finding differences within cultural identities rather than yielding to stereotypes and generalizations about identity, for instance, of 'woman.' Boundaries are there to be crossed. Chambers looks, for example, at recognition, at the historical difference of cruising in the gay community, at how the reader of Neil Bartlett's *Who Was That Man?*, gay or straight, can be cruised, can share a recognized context.[34] The marginal or scapegoated group invites the dominant group to be in a community of which it is already a member. Chambers says ideological blindness prevents people from seeing that the evidence shows 'that today's cultural other is tomorrow's companion in dialogue.'

Jennifer Nedelsky shares with Chambers an interest in community. The focus of her essay is the reconception of rights as relationship, an idea that Richard Devlin and Claude Denis also raise. She observes the paradoxical nature of rights: she sees relationship, not separation, as making autonomy possible. Nedelsky thereby reconceives of the liberal notion of autonomous selves in the law. There are, she argues, more values than those associated with democracy that must be taken into account. Relationships turn our attention to context. Nedelsky examines the critique of rights. She says that what is wrong with liberal individualism 'is that it fails to account for the ways in which our essential humanity is neither possible nor comprehensible without the network of relationships of which it is a part.' Like Sheila Noonan, Nedelsky finds it incomplete to look at the relation between women and children essentially as 'one of competing interests to be mediated by rights.' For Nedelsky, humans are individual and social. The relationships that rights constructs are of power, trust, obligation, and responsibility. Recognizing rights as relationship, she says, brings to consciousness what already exists. Like Christine Sypnowich,

Nedelsky sees the point of rights in a democracy as furthering the goal of equality. Nedelsky advocates an equitable structuring of relationships by way of equal constitutional rights. The ordinary law, she says, determines what differences matter, which will be the source of power, privilege, and advantage, and which the source of powerlessness, subordination, and disadvantage. Nedelsky asserts that property should be held accountable to equality. She draws attention to the *Alternative Social Charter*, an idea promoted during the last round of constitutional reform, which sets out a practical vision of equality in Canadian society. It also illustrates what Nedelsky means by 'dialogue of democratic accountability' – a democratic tribunal that would hear complaints alleging infringements against groups that experience systemic disadvantage. She concludes that recasting rights as relationships and viewing the constitution as a dialogue of democratic accountability would help Canadians move beyond their current problems and to deal with future ones.

The desire for dialogue in a community similarly is a strong theme in Christopher Norris's essay. Norris shares Habermas's misgivings about certain aspects of postmodernism. Reason is one of our main tools for cultural critique, Norris argues, and should not be put aside as an unfortunate legacy of the Enlightenment. Norris provides a critique of Michel Foucault, especially as Foucault sees analogies between instruments of torture and Christian, psychoanalytical, or Marxist attempts at the truth. Norris looks at the debate over truth in the context of postmodernism and post-structuralism and their critics. He shares with duBois and de Man their suspicions that any revelation of truth can be used to discriminate against others on the grounds of economics, gender, and race, and also agrees with duBois in her critique of irrationalist doctrines, claiming that radical interpretive theory today needs to be scrutinized insofar as it follows Heidegger's irrationalist and anti-Enlightenment turn. Norris parts ways with duBois, however, over how she sometimes tends to imply that any type of 'truth-seeking discourse' – any project that is indebted to values of truth claims, proper understanding, or certain knowledge in contrast to opinion or belief – must participate in the same bad legacy as Heidegger's thinking. Norris's position also differs from Richard Rorty's aversion to truth-seekers and his preference for poets over philosophers. Like duBois, Rorty has embraced the idea that knowledge is an instrument of power, a matter of rhetoric, a means of the will-to-power to silence or marginalize opposing voices. Norris defends evidence and reason, and the Enlightenment that gave them such a crucial place. For Norris, although postmodernism's talk of plurality and difference sounds radical, it amounts to the same thing as Rorty's neo-pragmatist message, that we should pursue the private virtues. In Norris's view, which he distinguishes from Catherine Belsey's, it has been a perversion of Enlightenment values, and not the Enlightenment itself, that has led to strategies of harmful policies against women, minorities, and dissidents. Unlike Ross Chambers, Norris is not willing to adopt the view that reality is wholly a construct of discursive, textual, or linguistic representation. Evidence, reason, and other legacies from the Enlightenment will better serve as a defence against arbitrary or violent forms of the imposition of doctrine than will relativism. Norris seeks to demonstrate the difference between Jacques Derrida and Paul de Man and the proponents of what Norris calls 'postmodern-pragmatist thought' in that however difficult, deferred, improbable, or unstable truth is, the rules of argument and the theme of truth are inescapable. This kind of philosophical rigour, this 'truth,' must be used to oppose the torturing truth that duBois examines. Derrida is, after all, the philosopher of *différance*. Norris concludes his defence of Enlightenment reason by praising Kant's separation of private beliefs from public values, arguments, principles, and reasons, all of which are openly accountable. This legacy should not be rejected.

Christine Sypnowich also records some disquiet about difference. She sums up the challenge of difference to the modern state: 'The claims of various ethnic and regional identities have put into question the modern idea of citizenship in a collective, universal entity which subsumes diversity and the particular.' Sypnowich argues that difference is an antidote to 'the false universalism of many theories of emancipation' (something that Pamela McCallum also examines), but that the importance of difference beyond that contribution is hard to discern. Sypnowich agrees with Norris that the postmodern world of difference owes its existence to the Enlightenment. Nonetheless, Sypnowich also notes some homogenizing elements in the Enlightenment, what she calls the metaphysics of sameness, especially as they appear in liberalism and Marxism. In particular, feminists 'have taken issue with the Enlightenment model of personal identity, although their critiques have implications for issues of race, ethnicity, and a number of other cultural differences.' Feminists and Marxists suggest 'that the idea of a universal human nature is ideological, camouflaging unequal relations of power.' Other differences have called into question the universal nature of Marxism and feminism as well as liberalism. Like Noonan in a subsequent essay, Sypnowich claims that cultural feminisms have been guilty of the very universalism for which they have criticized liberalism: the caring woman is like the atomistic individual. Grand narratives of emancipation have splintered into fragmentary freedoms. The postmodern, according to Sypnowich, is a critique of unity, certainty, and fixity. Like Norris, Habermas, Donna Haraway, and others, Sypnowich wonders whether the postmodern view is compatible with projects of liberation. Sypnowich also shares with Iris Marion Young, Ernesto Laclau, Chantal Mouffe, Ross Chambers, Claude Denis, and others a vision in which dominated social groups are empowered, not with the goal of assimilation, but as a means of recognizing their difference and thereby allowing them to challenge social institutions. But, compared with the other critics mentioned, Sypnowich is less optimistic about the results of recognizing difference. She thinks that difference will defeat political theories that want to stress and resolve it because in the postmodern view of difference, politics can only aspire to, but not achieve, the coexistence of plural identities. Differences are ultimately irreconcilable. In the contemporary nation-state, despite its partiality and bigotry, Sypnowich sees the germ of a promise of liberation, of unity in diversity and a universal order, which through citizenship is open to everyone. She stresses a paradox that relates to the positions taken by Chambers and Denis in their essays in this volume: 'If differences are born out of oppression, then it is not clear how liberatory the recognition of them can be.' Sypnowich also sets out the ontological differences among differences. She wonders whether universalism of some kind is unavoidable and worries whether 'difference unleashes an endless cycle of accusations and inclusions.' Behind the various politics of difference, Sypnowich sees a hope of commonality. She also observes that the local identities of postmodernism can lead to a neo-foundationalism. There are reasons to be cautious, Sypnowich says, because 'a focus on the inclusion of difference per se is problematic; philosophically, the project risks incoherence, and politically, the project risks an impotence in the face of oppression.' Norris has made a similar point. Sypnowich also considers problems of rights. She concludes: 'The challenge of our differences cannot be met by subsuming them within a new, multifarious "we"; rather, the only viable response must be a modest one, that of working towards a culture of openness.' For Sypnowich, people must focus on inequality, and not difference, if they are 'to live diversely in common.'

The second part of the collection, 'Instances,' shares with 'Theoretical Accounts' an interest in the relation between difference and identity. The theme of emancipation, which represents a concern of both modernity and postmodernity, but with a difference, reappears in its Enlightenment and post-Enlightenment guises. In her contribution, Sheila Noonan explores feminist views of emancipation. Like Ross Chambers, she locates her argument in a body of works that contains visions of justice. Those visions promise that the difference of oppressed groups will become affirmative and not devaluing. More specifically, she explores woman's difference. How do the differences among women 'intersect with the universalizing properties of law itself'? Noonan criticizes 'Robin West's cartography of feminist legal theory,' which 'actively seeks to displace both radical feminism and ... a commitment to the abortion struggle.' For Noonan, West gives priority to the connection of motherhood over disparate conditions of women's reproduction. The result is that motherhood and cultural feminism 'thereby become the sanctioned and sanitized version of feminist legal theory, and abortion and radical feminism its exiled dark side.' Abortion, in Noonan's scheme, becomes a contested area in feminist debates. She explores the relation between the official and unofficial in these differences. For Noonan, West effaces radical feminist and lesbian accounts of pregnancy and motherhood that are not portraits of despair. Nor does West take into account differences in language, economics, race, and marital status in the lives of women. According to Noonan, West differs from Catharine MacKinnon because she sees that heterosexual intercourse is a power relation. In Noonan's view, West neglects to make evident the nature of her evidence. That is, her descriptions of unwanted pregnancy come from a legal brief for a trial, which can distort women's experiences. Although West acknowledges that the focus of radical feminism on intrusion and invasion helps to illuminate women's reproduction, she is too close to the liberal legal order and neglects the critique and scepticism that radical feminism brings to feminist jurisprudence. Noonan warns against official stories like West's, and prefers a complex, multi-textured feminist jurisprudence that is opposed to humanist revision.

Richard Devlin's essay also examines conflict over difference. He looks back on the Irish hunger strike of 1981 in terms of a clash between Irish and English law. This parallels Claude Denis's analysis of the striking discord between Canadian and aboriginal justice. Devlin aims to decentre the hegemony of British legal discourse. In a variation on the theme of torture and truth, the proposition that duBois puts forward and which Norris discusses, Devlin claims 'that legal knowledge is itself a terrain of political struggle, and that dominant legal interpretations are only so because of their superior force, not because of their superior truth.' He finds postmodernism and deconstruction useful in their critique of power, knowledge, history, truth, language, and self, but thinks that a study of politics and ethics needs to supplement them. Like Denis, Devlin seeks a middle way. He usefully summarizes several key ideas of postmodernism and deconstruction, including postmodernism's scepticism about Truth and the relational and comparative, but not essential or intrinsic, nature of Derrida's *différance.* Devlin recounts the hunger strike and, in an interesting twist, reframes the activity of fasting as a jural claim. He sees 'law' and 'criminal' as contested terms. Like Denis, Devlin reconstructs a case in a story. He is wary of Derrida's claim that deconstruction is justice. Devlin also contends that discourse is not the only manifestation of power. When Devlin calls for a historicized and relational theory of subject and agency, he is advocating a mediation that has affinities with Julia Kristeva's abject and Ross Chambers's mediation. He shares with Norris, Sypnowich, and Denis an admiration for, but apprehension about, postmodernism. Devlin finds fault with what he calls the political quietism of the post-structural and postmodern projects. In his view, agency and discourse are mutually constitutive: he fears that those in power will use aesthetization of politics, simulation, and hyper-reality. Devlin looks to authenticity in the deaths that occurred in the hunger strike and, like Norris, appeals to Habermas for the establishment of truth. For Devlin, there is truth in the defiance of torture. He hopes for a liberation in identity politics, a view contrary to Chambers's, and asserts 'that difference and identity, are constitutively interlocking.' In group identity, he observes the possibility of empowerment and solidarity, something different from the postmodern devaluation of community (again in opposition to Chambers, and also worth comparing to Sypnowich's critique of strategic essentialism). As Derrida has done previously, Devlin deconstructs the law, but he also manages to deconstruct Derrida's law. Devlin calls for resistance of a different and problematic kind.

Using the 1991 case of *Thomas* v. *Norris* as a useful point of reference, Claude Denis also detects divisions, this time in the political landscape of Canada. He concentrates particularly on how English Canada creates an official narrative in which the marginal narratives of Quebec and the aboriginal peoples are pitted one against the other. English Canada maintains its power through the old technique of divide and conquer, through maintaining its right as well as differences. Denis's central question is the extent to which cultures can communicate between themselves. He sees English law as hegemonic in Canada and examines a civil lawsuit in which there is an illustrative conflict between the narratives of the dominant and aboriginal cultures. The plaintiff's autonomy of the self becomes one of the central issues in the case, a practical instance of the nature of identity, which is a problem that informs all the essays in this collection. Denis retells this case about 'spirit dancing' from three contrasting points of view: the court's reasons for judgment, a newspaper account, and Denis's interviews. In an echo of Chambers's primary concern, Denis focuses on the nature of scapegoating. Denis argues that in significant ways both the *Globe and Mail* and the presiding judge failed to take the claims of the natives seriously. Both relied upon and reproduced the dominant legal culture. In his account, Denis goes on to describe the Coast Salish view of law. He agrees with writers such as Mary Ellen Turpel, who have contended that Canadian courts are incompetent to judge aboriginal cases. Denis constructs a hypothetical narrative to reconstruct the motivation among the Coast Salish in the events of this case. He seeks common ground between the Coast Salish and occidental descriptions of the world, and finds that both allow for a suspension of individual rights in legitimate circumstances. But the one seeks healing while the other metes out punishment. In this case, Denis argues that, despite the judgment of the common law court, due process was followed according to the Coast Salish. He complicates his argument by then collapsing oppositions. He disputes the value of seeing *Thomas* v. *Norris* as involving questions of individual versus collective rights. Native women, he says, are victims. In this case, two women write themselves out of the story. Denis infers from the case that aboriginal women can, in the long run, seek redress for their victimization in the framework of aboriginal values, and that the Canadian state typically has set up a false opposition between women's individual rights and aboriginal collective rights. The main conflict, in Denis's understanding of *Thomas* v. *Norris*, 'stems from the assertion by the Canadian state of cultural authority over aboriginal ways.' Denis presents another version of the Canadian mosaic. As an adjustment to his own 'postmodern sensibilities,' Denis modifies his 'belief in radical incommensurability,' not with 'a renewed universalism of unbiased communication *à la* Habermas,' but with a middle way, with the view that difficult communication is possible. (Here Denis appeals to the philosophy of weak thought from Italian post-structuralism.) Like Chambers, he argues for recognition between cultures and, like Christopher Norris, he seems to find reason in deconstruction. Denis thinks that native self-government is based on precedence and not on difference, but he admits the difference between aboriginal culture and his own, that is Québécois and Canadian.

As her essay shows, Pamela McCallum has less faith than Christopher Norris shows in the emancipatory politics of the Enlightenment. She is interested in what happens to the Enlightenment and to the ideals of the French Revolution when they are transported to the New World, particularly in regard to Alejo Carpentier's novel *El Siglo de las luces*, which literally translates as 'a century of Enlightenment.' McCallum points out Carpentier's awareness of the ironic gap between Paris and the New World. For instance, in the Latin American trade, the Social Contract becomes a slave ship owned by an admirer of Jean-Jacques Rousseau. Carpentier creates the Plenipotentiary, 'whose Janus-faced emblematic persona comes to embody all the insoluble contradictions of the century of Enlightenment.' Victor Hugues represents a figure from baroque allegory, who, in McCallum's view, stands for 'the antimonies of the French Revolution and Enlightenment thought.' The French Revolution was marked by emancipatory potential and systematic repression. At the climax of the novel, Sofia and Esteban, who along with Carlos lose their father in eighteenth-century colonial Cuba, join the people. According to McCallum, their active political commitment opposes subjectivism, and Carpentier's emphasis in the final pages on the Caribbean subplot over the French main plot 'opens up a space for the new collective energies mobilized by the Spanish and Latin American wars of independence, and ushers in a different revolution.' Here, history leads to a new emancipatory project.

The divisions created through, and the ambivalence over, postmodernism, which we characterized at the outset as exemplified in the debates between Habermas and Lyotard and their followers, pervade the essays in this collection. Perhaps more precisely, the contributors both celebrate and lament postmodernism, often in the same essay. In theory and in practice, the essays expound a politics of postmodernism or different postmodernisms while questioning the foundations of that politics. This self-reflexivity itself arises from postmodernism and invigorates the debate on postmodern difference and identity. In exploring differences, whether they arise from race, class, or gender, or whether they are legal, literary, historical, social, economic, or political, it may be that interpretation, to extend Mary Ellen Turpel's view of judging, becomes a problem and not just an accepted function of our institutions.[35] If differences in perspective and context lead to differences in interpretation, can there be a common ground? If there can be a common ground, can it be effective, a means of enabling fulfilment through difference, or will it be another way of imposing a partial or false unity in the name of freedom and equality? The level of language and action, of production and interpretation, of how products and gestures include interpretation, must be opened up to further scrutiny. This book itself embodies differences on difference. The collection is intended to be heuristic, an exploration that is part of a body of texts and colloquia on difference and that will enable further explorations of the differences that define, enrich, and divide communities in Canada and across the world.

NOTES

1 For general accounts of the rise and development of postmodern theories across various fields, in addition to sources cited below, see Andreas Huyssen, *After the Great Divide: Modernism, Mass Culture, Postmodernism* (Bloomington: Indiana University Press, 1986); David Harvey, *The Condition of Postmodernity: An Enquiry into the Origins of Cultural Change* (Oxford: Basil Blackwell, 1989); and Linda Hutcheon, *A Poetics of Postmodernism: History, Theory, Fiction* (New York: Routledge, 1988).

2 A substantial collection of literature in this mode is the symposium entitled 'Deconstruction and the Possibility of Justice' (1990) 11 *Cardozo L. Rev.* 919. For other contributions, see Jack M. Balkin, 'Deconstructive Practice and Legal Theory' (1987) 96 *Yale L. J.* 743; Alan Hunt, 'The Big Fear: Law Confronts Postmodernism' (1990) 35 *McGill L. J.* 507; Anthony Carty, ed., *Post-Modern Law: Enlightenment, Revolution and the Death of Man* (Edinburgh: Edinburgh University Press, 1990); Martha Minow, *Making All the Difference: Inclusion, Exclusion, and American Law* (Ithaca, N.Y.: Cornell University Press, 1991); James Boyle, 'Is Subjectivity Possible? The Post-Modern Subject in Legal Theory' (1991) 62 *U. Colo. L. Rev.* 489; Drucilla Cornell, *Beyond Accommodation: Ethical Feminism, Deconstruction, and the Law* (New York: Routledge, 1991); Mary Joe Frug, *Postmodern Legal Feminism* (New York: Routledge, 1992); Allan Hutchinson, 'Identity Crisis: The Politics of Interpretation' (1992) 26 *New Eng. L. Rev.* 1173; and Peter C. Schanck, 'Understanding Postmodern Thought and Its Implications for Statutory Interpretation' (1992) 65 *S. Cal. L. Rev.* 2505.

3 Linda Hutcheon, *The Politics of Postmodernism* (London: Routledge, 1989), 10. See also Gerald Graff, *Literature against Itself: Literary Ideas in Modern Society* (Chicago: University of Chicago Press, 1979).

4 See Hutcheon, supra n. 3 at 10; and Terry Eagleton, *The Ideology of the Aesthetic* (Oxford: Basil Blackwell, 1990), 366–417. See also John McGowan, *Postmodernism and Its Critics* (Ithaca, N.Y.: Cornell University Press, 1991), who thinks that postmodernism is pessimistic; and Jonathan Arac, ed., *Postmodernism and Politics* (Minneapolis: University of Minnesota Press, 1986).

5 Deconstructionist feminists, such as Barbara Johnson, have increasingly been concerned about the relation of gender and difference to postmodernism. In

her opening remarks to *The Critical Difference: Essays in the Contemporary Rhetoric of Reading* (Baltimore: Johns Hopkins University Press, 1980), Johnson observes that a culture that finds differences with other cultures implies that it has differences within (ibid. at x). In a recent article, 'The Postmodern in Feminism' (1992) 105 *Harv. L. Rev.* 1075, she makes two points in response to meditations by Drucilla Cornell and Mary Joe Frug. In both attempts to confront dilemmas in the relation between feminism and postmodernism, Johnson finds gaps. With respect to Cornell, Johnson finds a 'both longing' that leads to no 'and,' only the white space of desire itself. In Frug, Johnson observes what she calls the lesbian gap, that is, women facing women instead of men, the literal silence of Frug's last sentence, left unfinished before she went out into Brattle Street and was murdered.

Johnson also responds to the 'confrontation with the real differences among women that Mary Joe Frug found both "fascinating" and "terrifying" about the ordinance campaign' (ibid. at 1083). This was the campaign led by Catharine MacKinnon and Andrea Dworkin to enact an ordinance that would give women a civil cause of action for the harm that pornography makes them suffer. Johnson suggests the uncomfortable but necessary task of facing difference among feminists: '... feminists must confront and negotiate differences among women – differences of class, race, culture, age, political affiliation, and sexual practices – if they are to transform such differences into positive rather than negative forces in women's lives' (ibid. at 1983).

For an examination of the conjunction among feminist, aboriginal, and postcolonial issues, see Julia V. Emberley, *Thresholds of Difference: Feminist Critique, Native Women's Writings and Postcolonial Theory* (Toronto: University of Toronto Press, 1993). See also Diana Fuss, *Essentially Speaking: Feminism, Nature and Difference* (New York: Routledge, 1989).

6 Hutcheon, supra n. 3 at 18.

7 See Ihab Hassan, *The Dismemberment of Orpheus: Toward a Postmodern Literature* (New York: Oxford University Press, 1971); and his *The Postmodern Turn: Essays in Postmodern Theory and Culture* (Columbus: Ohio State University Press, 1987).

8 Jean Baudrillard, *Simulations* (New York: Semiotext(e), 1983), 41–3.

9 Jean-François Lyotard, *The Postmodern Condition: A Report on Knowledge*, trans. Geoff Bennington and Brian Massumi (Minneapolis: University of Minnesota Press, 1984). Subsequent page references appear in the text.

10 Compare, in a legal context, the efforts of Critical Legal scholars to challenge traditional categories of doctrinal discourse as not 'descriptive of social life and experience'; see Robert W. Gordon, 'Unfreezing Legal Reality: Critical Approaches to Law' (1987) 15 *Fla. St. U. L. Rev.* 195 at 214.

11 See McGowan, supra n. 4 at 4–5; Eagleton, supra n. 4 at 85–6; Jürgen Haber-

mas, *Legitimation Crisis*, trans. Thomas McCarthy (Boston: Beacon Press, 1973); and Jürgen Habermas, *The Philosophical Discourse of Modernity*, trans. Frederick Lawrence (Cambridge, Mass.: MIT Press, 1987), 68–9.

12 Jürgen Habermas, *The Theory of Communicative Action*, vol. 2, trans. Thomas McCarthy (Boston: Beacon Press, 1987), ch. 6.

13 Jürgen Habermas, 'Modernity versus Postmodernity' (1981) 22 *New German Critique* 3.

14 Ibid. at 11.

15 See Martin Jay, 'Habermas and Modernism,' in Richard J. Bernstein, ed., *Habermas and Modernity* (Cambridge: Polity Press, 1985), 133.

16 See Habermas, *Legitimation Crisis*, supra n. 17 at 1–32; and Fredric Jameson, *Postmodernism, or the Cultural Logic of Late Capitalism* (Durham, N.C.: Duke University Press, 1991), viii.

17 Costas Douzinas, Ronnie Warrington, and Shaun McVeigh, *Postmodern Jurisprudence: The Law of Text in the Texts of Law* (London: Routledge, 1991), 15–16.

18 See supra n. 9 at ix–x; and David M. Rasmussen, *Reading Habermas* (Oxford: Basil Blackwell, 1990), 12.

19 See Jonathan Hart, 'Mythology and Ideology,' in *Northrop Frye: The Theoretical Imagination* (London: Routledge, 1994), 191–242. Also, compare Peter Fitzpatrick, *The Mythology of Modern Law* (London: Routledge, 1992).

20 Supra n. 9 at xii.

21 See Brian McHale, *Constructing Postmodernism* (London: Routledge, 1992), 4–5.

22 Jameson, supra n. 16 at ix.

23 See Simon During, 'Postmodernism or Postcolonialism?' (1985) 39 *Landfall* 366; Simon During, 'Postmodernism or Postcolonialism To-Day' (1987) 1 *Textual Practice* 32; Linda Hutcheon, 'Circling the Downspout of Empire' (1989) 20(4) *Ariel* 149 (reprinted in Ian Adam and Helen Tiffin, eds., *Past the Last Post: Theorizing Post-Colonialism and Post-Modernism* [Calgary: University of Calgary Press, 1990], 167); Arun P. Mukherjee, 'Whose Post-Colonialism and Whose Postmodernism?' (1990) 30 *World Lit. Written in English* 1; Jonathan Hart, 'Traces, Resistances, and Contradictions: Canadian and International Perspectives on Postcolonial Theories' (1994) 1 *Arachné* 68; and Jonathan Hart, 'Response to Shaffer and Brydon' (1994) 1 *Arachné* 113.

24 Raoul Mortley, *Désir et différence dans la tradition platonicienne* (Paris: J. Vrin, 1988), 9 and 80.

25 For an attempt to develop a normative ideal of political life that avoids assimilation of differentiated groups, see Iris Marion Young, *Justice and the Politics of Difference* (Princeton: Princeton University Press, 1990).

26 See Hutcheon, supra n. 3; and Johnson, supra n. 5.

27 [1992] C.N.L.R. 140 (B.C.S.C.).

28 Part I of the *Constitution Act, 1982,* being Schedule B to the *Canada Act 1982* (U.K.), 1982, c. 11.

29 See *Quebec Act, 1774* (U.K.), R.S.C. 1985, Appendix II, No. 2; *Constitutional Act, 1791* (U.K.), R.S.C. 1985, Appendix II, No. 3; *The British North America Act, 1867* (U.K.), R.S.C. 1985, Appendix II, No. 5, renamed the *Constitution Act, 1867* by the *Constitution Act, 1982,* s. 53(2). On the demise of the Meech Lake Accord, see Andrew Cohen, *A Deal Undone: The Making and Breaking of the Meech Lake Accord* (Vancouver: Douglas and McIntyre, 1990); and Patrick J. Monahan, *Meech Lake: The Inside Story* (Toronto: University of Toronto Press, 1991). For an account of the process that gave rise to the Charlottetown Accord and its defeat in a national referendum, see Kenneth McRoberts and Patrick Monahan, eds., *The Charlottetown Accord, the Referendum, and the Future of Canada* (Toronto: University of Toronto Press, 1993).

30 See Michael Ignatieff, *Blood and Belonging: Journeys into the New Nationalism* (New York: Viking, 1993).

31 See Richard W. Bauman, 'Constitutional Reform in South Africa' (1992) 3(4) *Constitutional Forum* 107.

32 Will Kymlicka has noted that, in the United States, for example, the monuments of liberal political theory, such as the work of John Rawls and Ronald Dworkin, are curiously silent about the special status of minority cultures and identities; see Will Kymlicka, *Liberalism, Community and Culture* (Oxford: Clarendon Press, 1989), 136–8. Another example of a Canadian philosopher working out the implications of his political philosophy can be found in Charles Taylor, *The Malaise of Modernity* (Toronto: House of Anansi, 1991); and his *Multiculturalism and 'The Politics of Recognition': An Essay* (Princeton: Princeton University Press, 1992).

33 René Girard, *Le Bouc émissaire* (Paris: Grasset, 1982); and Eve Kosofsky Sedgwick, *Epistemology of the Closet: English Literature and Male Homosexual Desire* (New York: Columbia University Press, 1985).

34 Neil Bartlett, *Who Was That Man? A Present for Mr. Oscar Wilde* (London: Serpent's Tail, 1988).

35 Mary Ellen Turpel, 'Aboriginal Peoples and the Canadian Charter: Interpretive Monopolies, Cultural Differences' (1989–90) *Canadian Human Rights Yearbook* 3 at 25.

THEORETICAL ACCOUNTS

No Montagues without Capulets:
Some Thoughts on 'Cultural Identity'

ROSS CHAMBERS

This is an essay about the othering of mediators – 'mediators' being those people who are held, ideologically, to personify the universal function of mediation, and the othering of such people being, in consequence, an example of what I shall call symbolic scapegoating. We need all the analysis we can produce of discriminatory phenomena, and the contribution of this essay lies perhaps in its attempt to approach cultural analysis through the assumptions of discourse theory.

The reason why we need analyses of this kind is that they can suggest appropriate political tactics to counter the effects of othering. The political proposal to which my analysis will lead is a counter-intuitive one. It will seem incompatible with common-sense (but, then, political common-sense is what has gotten us where we are). I will be suggesting that othered groups might follow the politics of identity by a politics of self-affirmation and by a politics of invitation, seeking gradually to absorb othering communities into their own already diverse group, rather than seeking admission into the affairs of those dominant groups on what can only be terms convenient to those groups.

Such a proposal itself rests on some major propositions, the plausibility of which – nothing in theory can be *proved* – is what the essay seeks to establish. Let me sketch them here for the guidance of the reader in what follows.

(a) Although mediation is an inescapable function, it does not follow that the ideological othering of mediators is inevitable. In the world of social discourse, all differences are ideologically produced, but some are produced as 'differences that make a difference,' and others are 'just differences' – the differences, I will propose, that communities exist to negotiate and without which their existence as communities would have no meaning. It is conceivable therefore that the difference between interlocutors and the mediator, on which othering is based, might be transferred from the category of 'differences that make a difference' to that of the differences that ground communitarian dialogue.

(b) The structure of scapegoating as a practice of rough justice confirms this possibility of transfer, since the scapegoater and the scapegoat are differentiated only by virtue of the fact that the latter is held responsible for that which also characterizes the former (in this case, the function of mediation). Scapegoating has no significance except as the production of difference *within a community*, and its apparently exclusionary logic is in fact that of 'it takes one to know one.' If the membership of the scapegoat in the scapegoating community is therefore a given, so too can a scapegoated community find potential members among the scapegoaters.

(c) The condition of such a reversal of the 'direction' of scapegoating would be that the scapegoated group cease to accept (and affirm) its assigned identity as cultural 'other' (the product of a difference that makes a difference), so as to affirm instead its existence as a community composed of differences, of differences to which the difference of the scapegoating group from the scapegoated group now – no longer being considered a difference that makes a difference – potentially belongs. For such groups to turn from a politics of affirmation to a politics of invitation would not imply the abandonment of their 'difference,' therefore, but only the transvaluation of that difference from one that makes a difference to one that qualifies as the basis of possible communitarian dialogue. The dynamics of power make it unlikely for such a transvaluating move to originate in scapegoating groups; but emanating from an 'othered' community in the form of a politics of invitation and an active search for alliance, it could have considerable tactical success.

My argument is in three main parts. I begin by discussing the backgrounding of mediation as a condition of discourse and its relation to the ideological assignment of cultural 'identity' as a mark of othering. I move in part 2 to a discussion of this phenomenon of othering as a form of symbolic scapegoating and read such scapegoating as a manifestation of the construction of cultures through splitting – that is, through a form of differentiation that cannot be absolute because it is a product of mediation. In the final part, I develop some political implications of cultural split and assess the conditions under which the effect of scapegoating might be reversed and the difference that grounds othering be transvalued so as to become a mark of community.

Cultural Identity, or Othering the Mediator

Whenever Black people are involved in violence in a community we call it 'Black on Black violence' but I didn't hear anybody call the massacre in Texas 'white on white violence.' Of course, there's also Black on white violence as well. But what I'm suggesting is that there's a political and ideological reason for presenting the violence unfolding in South Africa as 'Black on Black violence' as if we as Black people, wherever we are in the world, are supposed to be absolutely united. As if we are not allowed the opportunity to differ with each other.[1]

What does it mean to 'share a culture,' or more technically, to be a 'cultural subject'? It is easy, and consequently habitual, to think of the word *culture* as designating the ways in which groups of people are alike – in some essential sense the 'same' as one another; and I shall be discussing what it means to do that. My own thesis in what follows, however, is that 'culture' names, not so much what makes people alike, as that which permits them to differ. It is culture that permits us to exchange opinions, to argue and negotiate, that is, discursively speaking, to occupy positions that are describable as ideological, if 'ideology' is the sphere in which power differentials are produced, acceded to, or struggled over.

Culture in this sense is the precondition of there being a community, but 'community' must be understood in turn as the precondition of communication – and communication exists and is necessary only to the extent that there are differences to negotiate.[2] (If we were all alike, holding identical views, sharing an identical social identity, and discursively positioned in identical ways, communication would simply have no point.) Communication arises, in short, as a differential matter, dependent as it is on discursive enunciations (not merely verbal ones) which function to produce relationally constructed subject-positions, as addresser and addressee of meaningful discourse, and (in the more specific case of linguistic communication) to produce these positions in turn in relation to a referent (constructed as what the communication is 'about').

My point is that to differ in this way is possible only on the basis of a set of logically prior understandings – for example, about what makes our differences worthwhile or interesting – and that it is these that constitute culture as the set of mediations a given community has in common. But I have a second point, which is that it is in the construction of the 'you and I' of community that an 'us and them' arises that often has something of an 'us v. them' about it because the 'we' of communication is dependent (as I will show) on there being a group of others (the 'them') who can be thought of as 'not-us.' I want to argue that it is to these groups of mediating others – the 'them' without which there would be no 'we' and hence no possibility of communication as the negotiation of differentially constructed subject-positions – that a 'cultural identity' is assigned, an identity that functions as a denial of community membership in the sense I have just outlined. Their members are considered 'all the same' and are thought to occupy communicating positions that are, therefore, not different but interchangeable one with the other, with the result that cultural identity brings with it the twin questions of authenticity and representativeness, both of which depend on the idea of an essential(ized) sameness linking the members of a group. For this reason, so-called 'cultural' identity (a term I retain because it is in current usage) is, I want to argue, an *ideological* construct, that is, a power-laden representation of the phenomenon I will discuss in due course (see part 2) as cultural split.

This ideological understanding of 'culture' as a principle of identity (rather than as the mediating instance that makes difference possible) is very widespread. It activates the figment that it is *others* who are culturally identical, whereas one's own interactions (culturally mediated as they are) are with people with whom one has 'business' to do – business of a political, commercial, emotional, intellectual, sexual, or any other kind. There are, in other words, in this view, those who make history and those who, as Johannes Fabian pointed out in his devastating critique of the grounding assumptions of ethnography,[3] are thought to live outside of historical time, those with whom one visits and who may visit, whose company one may enjoy, but who are marked by a *difference that is disqualifying* with respect to membership in one's own community, such membership being (tautologically enough) exactly what qualifies differences as worth negotiating with.

My proposition is that it is the marker of cultural sameness that has this disqualifying function. It can be clearly seen to operate in all instances of cultural (or 'ethnic') typification or stereotyping, and whenever a function of representativeness is assigned, such that an individual is taken as a token for a type. In the United States, for example, the 'token' woman, or Black, or gay person on some well-meaning committee is a figure often ironically evoked; but the irony does not alter the fact that the person is indeed a token, held to be representative of a group that can therefore be typified. 'Minority' ethnic groups, including the group of women, are supposed to be delighted when one of their number is appointed to a decision-making function, regardless of that person's politics – whereas it is of course *only* the political question that is considered relevant in the case of members of the dominant majority. In academia, Gayatri Spivak amusingly (but angrily) denounces the multiple representative roles that are foisted on her (as a woman, a woman of colour, a Third World person, etc.);[4] and the academy's investment in an ideology of representativeness and cultural authenticity is amply demonstrated in hiring practices that assume that the best person to teach African culture is an African (or, in lieu, an Afro-American), and the best qualified person to do research on Caribbean literature is likely to hail from Jamaica or Puerto Rico. Nobody seems to mind the obvious incoherence of these positions (which would, for instance, disqualify the long tradition of ethnographic research as the study of *other* cultures, and which furthermore seem not to apply when 'harder' forms of knowledge are at issue – say, the study of the Africa economy – as opposed to the 'softer' and more literary realms of mere culture). Indeed, it is frequently the 'natives' themselves who are – from perfectly legitimate political motives but also sometimes with genuine conviction – inclined to give enthusiastic support to such discourses of representativeness and authenticity and hence to the tokenism they legitimate.

It is already a long time since Edward Said published *Orientalism*,[5] a study of the West's production of the category of 'the Orient' and of 'Orientals' as subject to a culture of unchanging sameness; but it seems that some of the lessons of that study have yet to be drawn. As a result, we have the curious situation where 'stereotyping' is universally decried as an oppressive practice while 'cultural identity' is, on occasion, *affirmed* as a source of pride and the basis of an emancipatory politics. Yet the difference between the two is only that between a group identity (based on sameness) that is assigned, in the case of stereotyping, and a group identity (based on sameness) that is claimed, in the case of the politics of cultural identity. The illogic is apparent, but the position is interesting not because it shows a contradiction but because the contradiction is the sign of an *ideological* difference that is being negotiated. As an example of ideological split, it signals that a culturally mediated conversation has begun to take place, along 'you and me' or communitarian lines rather than as an exclusionary, 'us and them' practice. For a discourse of authenticity emanating from a previously denigrated source has an obviously different illocutionary force than the supercilious or patronizing stereotyping to which it responds and with which it dialogues. But it is still important to examine the ideological underpinnings of this collusion in the politics of cultural identity, and to attempt to identify their function in the asymmetrical production of relations of power.

In *The Colonial Harem*[6] Malek Alloula reads a number of postcards stemming from colonial Algeria in which typified representations of (mainly) 'native' women function as figures of a stereotyped 'Orient': indeed, many of these postcards belong to a series that was tellingly entitled 'Scenes and Types.' David Prochaska comments:

The intellectual axes along which this invented world of *scènes* and *types*, this *Algérie imaginaire*, is ordered are types: ethnic types, sexual types, occupational types. Individuals are subsumed in categories, mental boxes – *un caïd*, the *marchand arabe*. In each case, a photograph of a particular person is meant to represent a group, a category of individuals, instead of individuals *qua* individuals. This is synecdoche exercized with a vengeance: a part stands for the whole, an individual is literally type cast.[7]

(No one looking at a family album will exclaim, 'Look at that typical fifties housewife!' But: 'Look! There's Mom!' or 'There's Sis!' or maybe 'Who is that person standing beside Uncle Bob?') Among the 'Scenes and Types' cards reproduced in Alloula's book, one that I find especially memorable represents two *Mauresques d'Alger*, Moorish women from Algiers. The sender of the postcard, presumably a soldier in the colonial army, has written beside (and partially across) the face of one woman: 'La femme à Anatole' (Anatole's woman); and beside the other's face: 'La femme à Raoul' (Raoul's woman).

The de-facing of the women makes the appropriative gesture very visible here. I want to associate it, on the one hand, with the women but also as *typification* of the women, not only as women but also as representatives of a certain cultural identity; and, on the other hand, with the act of *inscription* itself through which the appropriation is realized. For the women are nevertheless *written into* the message that is exchanged, we can safely assume, and using Eve Kosofsky Sedgwick's phrase,[8] 'between men' as well as between Europeans; indeed, they cannot be typified without being written into such a message. And the hypothesis I want to develop is therefore a double one: if (1) to have a cultural identity (in the sense of an 'individual''s being subsumed into a categorized group on the assumption of self-sameness) is tantamount to being appropriated into the position of cultural mediator or mediating other, with respect to a community of differentiated communicating subjects (here 'Anatole,' 'Raoul,' and their friends) – a community whose own cultural status is 'forgotten' by its members while it is in fact constituted by the construction of the cultural other that mediates it – then (2) that other who is inscribed, however facelessly and namelessly, in the community's messages as the object of an appropriating gesture is also, inevitably, *included* in that community's affairs, and forms part of its culture, by virtue of the very gesture that seeks to distance it.

I will come to the implications of this inclusion in due course. For now, let me simply say that the now standard format of the postcard, pictorial representation on one side, verbal message on the other (the older habit of writing on the 'face' of the card being now superseded), authorizes the following formulation of the first part of my hypothesis. It is *on the back* of the typified cultural subject, the cultural other who is represented in terms of cultural identity, that communication occurs between members of a cultural community whose identity, while its construction is enabled by a shared culture, is not thought of as a 'cultural' identity at all, but rather as that of communicating subjects who have personalizing and individualizing names like Anatole and Raoul. The *de*-facement of the cultural other corresponds to this *back*-grounding of the mediating instance. We will need to remember, though, in the context of my second hypothesis, what the older habit of writing on front of a postcard can be taken to emblematize, which is that the distinction between the 'back' (or mediating) position and the 'face' (or communicating) position of any mediated communication is not easy to maintain,[9] so that a message on the back of a 'Scenes and Types' representation *can* become a face with a message of its own. The question that I want particularly to address (see part 3) is how such a (de-faced and back-grounded) face can cease to be typified and appropriated – that is, as I will show in part 2, scapegoated – and achieve instead the status of full community membership. How – to adapt a famous title of Gayatri Spivak's[10] – can the mediator speak?

Michel Serres, however, has influentially described the mediating position as *excluded*: for him, the mediating other is, precisely, the 'excluded third.' Taking as his example the Platonic dialogue, he explains that a dialogue (which includes the possibility of disagreement and dissension) can occur only if there is agreement between the parties about various preconditions. They must agree, for example, to speak Greek; they must share the conventions of a philosophical conversation (knowledge of what constitutes a suitable topic for discussion, of what constitutes a convincing or unconvincing argument, obedience to the rule of turn-taking that distinguishes a dialogue from, say, a lecture), and so on. But each of these agreements implies exclusions: if we are speaking Greek, then Persian or Egyptian speakers cannot participate in our conversation; if the genre is philosophical, trivial concerns are out of place, etc. 'To hold a dialogue is to suppose a third man and to seek to exclude him; a successful communication is the exclusion of the third man.'[11]

Serres stresses exclusion because his main interest is in the way the excluded mediations 'return,' in a given dialogue, in the form of noise. 'We might call this third man the *demon*, the prosopopeia of noise.' The power of the excluded third to make noise (the translation 'third man' for *le tiers* is unfortunate, but its personification of the mediating function is serendipitous in the context of my present argument) is an important consideration, and Serres has expanded on his initial insight in later publications.[12] But my own immediate interest is in the mode of *inclusion* of mediating instances in communicating communities; for, as Serres mentions, the 'third man' must first be *supposed by the speakers* in order for them then to seek, imperfectly, to exclude him. It is certainly true that the noise consequent on exclusion can seriously disrupt a conversation: if I have to remember to speak Greek or remind myself of the conventions of philosophical discourse, it will be an impoverished dialogue. Things like a knowledge of Greek or of the rules of philosophical conversation need, as we say, to be 'internalized' if they are not to return as noise and hamper the dialogue. But it is also true that the jointly or communally 'supposed' third party is not just the 'prior' condition of the messages that pass between the participants in a dialogue. It is an actual constituent of their communication, and arguably its substance, since it is *that which defines and qualifies them* as *the* communicating parties. Who the qualified speakers are is as much the message as what they say.

In other words, the alleged exclusion of the mediating third is better described as a matter of *controlling* the mediator, so that the speakers themselves may figure as the subjects produced by that act of control. The successful dialogue is one in which the mediator is present, and indeed omnipresent, but occupies a backgrounded position, like the 'Scenes and Types' image on the reverse of a postcard. But to control the mediator and maintain it in the purely mediating position, 'in back of' the communication, is therefore to introduce that figure into a specific configuration of power, that is, to assign it a place that is ideologically constructed as disempowered, excluded from the making of history that is going on in the dialogue. And such a construction of place necessarily introduces the mediating figure into the sphere of a shared culture, without which (for lack of a mediating instance) the ideological distribution of power could not occur. Thus, not only the participants in the dialogue (the communicating community) but also, when the mediator is personified by proso-popeia, the mediating third as well (marked by 'cultural identity') are necessarily sharers of a common culture, and what the mediating third is excluded from is not culture but the exercise of discursive power as a participant in dialogue.

It is when the mediator fails to accede to this ideological positioning 'in back of' a community's communications and thus ceases to be fully controlled or controllable – in short, when ideological split occurs – that the likelihood of disruptive noise arises, in the form of a a politics of protest, revolt, or emancipation. But such noise can only arise *within* a given community because the potentially disruptive element was culturally included from the start – culturally included although ideologically excluded, or more accurately still, culturally included *so as to be* ideologically excluded from the making of history. My argument, then, is that the assignment of so-called 'cultural' identity is an ideological phenomenon aimed at controlling cultural mediators, while the claim to a 'cultural identity' (as in the *négritude* movement, for instance) functions as the sign of a certain ideological resistance or revolt on the part of the mediators, who thereby become capable of making noise within the cultural community. (But note that making noise is not *necessarily* the same as participating in the dialogues that make history, a point I shall return to soon.)

In linguistic terms, the paradigmatic controlled mediator is language itself, internalized by its speakers as the back-grounded instance without which acts of communication could not occur and which produces noise in communication only to the extent that it is not fully 'mastered.' In Chomskyan vocabulary, it is the 'competence' on which 'performance' depends. In the way that internalized competence in a given language is the precondition for verbal dialogue, cultural competence is the mediating 'third' of the discursive enunciations (where 'discourse' refers to all the signifying practices of a given community, including but not restricted to language) that can be classified, because they are acts that institute and are governed by relations of power, as ideological. But *one* such act of ideological enunciation at the discursive level (not necessarily the verbal) consists precisely of identifying the function of cultural mediation, without which there is no discursive community, with specific persons and/or groups of persons, whose place is thus *ideologically* produced, and back-grounded, as that of the *cultural* other. This place is marked by the 'cultural identity' that is assigned to such groups, an identity that is held to make their members all the same but which, as members of the culture, they may ideologically accept or question. For, to repeat and emphasize my point, the so-called cultural other is an ideological construct, by means of which specific discursive communities, within culture, are produced.

Thus – to take a pedagogically clear example – in the case of male homosociality as it has been influentially described by Sedgwick,[13] relations of power between men are mediated by women (or by a representative woman) who are excluded from the negotiations of power (in which they serve as tokens) but who are necessarily included in the total cultural configuration precisely because they constitute the indispensable mediating third without which men could not negotiate. Indeed, they are included *because* they figure those cultural mediations that enable men to communicate; but they are constructed ideologically as culturally 'other' than the community of men, and marked by the interchangeability that is assigned to women's 'identity.'[14] In marriage, for instance, a woman passes, as a mere token of exchange, from man to man; yet, interestingly, this institution of marriage which actualizes the dialogue of male power is simultaneously regarded (because it functions to control the 'natural' phenomenon of desire by maintaining the incest taboo) as the very foundation of *human* culture, in which women are necessarily included and have their (mediating) place. The control of women by men is thus perceived as homologous with the control of nature through the institutions of culture, which accounts for the standard identification of women with nature. Yet, without the mediating role of women there could be no culture and hence no discourse between men, and women are just as frequently held to personify the artifice and changeability of the cultural sphere as they are identified with nature and supposedly natural desire. Men's power within culture thus depends in part on identifying women with nature, as that which culture controls, and in part on identifying them as the cultural other whose place is to ground the communications of men – which suggests finally that both 'nature' and 'women' are names given, within culture, to culture's own mediating other.

One can note homologies between the positioning of women as mediators of homosocial culture and, say, that of black people or certain other 'ethnic' minorities in a dominant white culture which, in the United States, continues to regard itself as charged with the responsibility for the making of history; or that of the so-called Third World in the relations of global power; or that of lesbians and gay men in a society that remains officially heterosexual. (In these comparisons, and others to follow, I am not implying that the historical 'experience' of such different groups has been or is the same; it is the structural similarities that I am pointing to.)

Needless to say, the effects of such positioning are not limited, either, to the gross ideological categories of gender, class, race, or (to add the fourth that is often omitted) of the 'abnormal' or 'deviant' with respect to the 'norm,' a fourth that perhaps gives an important key to the positioning of others as 'exceptional' in terms of the first three categories as well. Anyone who has been positioned as, say, a 'theorist' among political activists (and conversely as an 'activist' among 'theorists'), or as a 'liberal' among conservatives (or radicals), or just as the only person who doesn't see a joke or doesn't catch the interest of some exciting piece of gossip, knows the 'feel' of being cast in the role of 'cultural' mediator. For culture is infinitely divisible and at the same time endlessly expandable; it constitutes a non-totalizable 'whole' in which 'cultures' (in the plural) are produced, in a way I will explore further in part 2, through a splitting process. Any given discursive community is thus constituted as a culture in and by the act of producing an other as its mediator – an 'other' group to which are ascribed the characteristics of 'cultural identity' and which is therefore, as I have tried to show, produced as both *part* of the communicating community and *different* from it or exceptional with respect to its 'norms,' that is, in a relation of split with(in) it. Such communities can therefore be as small as a couple of people chatting on a street corner, or as large as a nation or a 'world' (first, second, or third). But none can exist without, as Serres put it, 'supposing' a third instance that functions as the mediator of the communication that culture fosters, and therefore as its other.

To be cast in the role of mediating third or cultural other and to seek nevertheless to join the dialogue as a communicating partner is subjectively an uncomfortable experience, which women know well as that of being a 'nag.' One has discursive competence, but the performance falls short; although one speaks, what one says is not heard; the *énoncé* has structure and sense, but its illocutionary and more particularly its perlocutionary force, as an act of enunciation, approaches zero. It is inconceivable to the hearers that what is said might make a difference, and it falls therefore on deaf ears. It is to them exactly what Serres would describe as 'noise,' that discourse which, in this particular community, is out of its place or has escaped control and which consequently interferes with the community's messages even though it might well be in its place in another community, the community imagined as 'other' (let the women talk among themselves and not bother the men). As noise, it is indeed the sign of another message seeking to interact with the first, but it is received not as a message but as unarticulated sound, words and syllables that are 'all the same': what a woman attempts to say at a gathering of men, what a theorist may try to contribute to a gathering of activists, is heard only as *typical* – 'the sort of thing women say,' or 'more theoretical flim-flam.' It is predictable, informationally impoverished, and therefore discursively irrelevant; it can safely be ignored. And yet, this gathering of men is constituted, as a *men's* gathering, only by its positioning of women as 'other,' just as the gathering of activists achieves its identity as a community only by 'supposing' a theorist, as a non-activist, whose discourse can be heard as a nagging noise, somewhere in the background.

The political problem of the mediating third who wishes to speak from that position is therefore to get the attention of the discursive community, in the sense of ceasing to provide mere (back-grounded) noise that can be ignored as so much nagging, and beginning to furnish the kind of *disruptive* noise that signals, in Serres's formulation, the 'return' of the excluded and, in the perspective I am adopting here, the insistence of a potential message that has not been heard, the message of the mediator who wishes to speak. To assume positively, to lay claim to the 'cultural identity' that is assigned the mediating instance, is one way to get such a result, since such a gesture is received as unexpected and information-rich; it is, surprisingly, an assumption of the power to make history on the part of an instance whose ideological definition has supposedly precluded such power. 'Strategic essentialism' among feminists, the *négritude* and Black power movements, and affirmations of 'la raza' and 'gay pride' are paradoxical moments because, in the first instance, they confirm the assignments of cultural identity that function as markers of the status of mediating third and justify exclusion from the power to participate in the making of history. And yet these discourses are difficult to classify as so much nagging because they reverse the relation of the *énoncé* to enunciation that is characteristic of nagging's cultural situation: where the nagger produces a predictable *énoncé* that can be ignored as enunciation, the *énoncé* of gay pride or Black activism is unexpected and full of information, precisely because it consists of the claim to constitute the speaker as a historical subject, that is, as an enunciating instance as opposed to a mediating one, a participant in the dialogue and not its constitutive cultural other. It claims access to and control of a discourse of identity that has heretofore been the prerogative of the discourse community itself. It thus signals that a failure of ideological hegemony has occurred, but it does not constitute a critique of the identity construction on which the hegemony depends.

An illuminating instance of the power of cultural affirmation as a noisy, attention-getting gesture occurred at a professional meeting I attended in 1991 in Australia. In this gathering of academic, mainly white, lefties and feminists, all practitioners of 'cultural studies' or of the cultural study of literature, a lone aboriginal scholar was scheduled to speak. Muttering at the back of the room while another critic spoke, he forced a negotiation as a result of which he took over the lectern. Announcing that he felt lonely among so many white faces and needed company, and turning on a video-cassette, but without the sound, of a performance by the aboriginal poet who was the subject of his paper, he read a speech against that frustrating background so that neither his own discourse nor the poet's verse was fully available to the audience. This was a prosopopeia of noise with vengeance, and it could be taken to signify: 'We are a community, which no single member can "represent."' The tactic was remarkably successful, not only in disrupting the calm interchange of serene views in which the meeting had previously been engaged, but also in insisting on the need for *another* dialogue, this time between the academic community and those back-grounded others who were so often inscribed in its discourse as an object of concern but whose faces and voices had heretofore been absent.

Needless to say, to get attention in such circumstances, as the hero of this story did, is already to have achieved the position of participant in the dialogue: getting attention is what participation, as opposed to mediation, means, as the Civil Rights movement of the 1960s and the 70s also effectively demonstrated. But I would argue that such participation is still not *full* participation. Although it constitutes disruptive rather than background or controlled noise, the discourse that reverses the assignment of cultural identity into a claim to being heard as the *bearer of such identity* is still noise from the point of view of the participants whose dialogue is being interrupted. *Their* enunciations do not have, as the content of the *énoncé*, a claim to the right to speak and/or to determine their own identity; they consist rather of getting on with the business that their already fully authorized positions as enunciators permit. As qualified participants in the dialogue, they do not have to use their turn-taking to make raucous claims to qualification. Such noisy claims for admission to the status of participant can therefore be met either by being *shut out* (so that 'legitimate' communication can continue), or by *recuperation*.

In the former case, ideological exclusion is reaffirmed, together with the difference (between communicators and the mediator) that grounds it, a difference the noisy other has not challenged but confirmed. In the latter case, the noisy, disruptive message is accepted into the dominant dialogue, but at the price of its being interpreted as non-disruptive (and, of course, at the further price of another 'other''s being identified as the mediating third of the newly constituted discursive community). The excluded other is 'invited' into the dominant community but on terms that are dictated by the dominant group, whose hegemonic control is reaffirmed, although its population changes, because its identity constructions have not been called into question. Thus I learned recently from the newsletter of the association that sponsored the Australian conference that the aboriginal scholar whose claim to speak was so effectively made has been invited to become a member of the association's advisory board, and has accepted the invitation. In that setting, his views are likely to be listened to attentively and sympathetically, and may well be acted upon; and that is not in itself a small achievement. But it is hard to imagine his being positioned there as anything other than a 'representative of his people,' that is, in terms of the very identity construction against which his intervention had seemed to protest.

In practice, recuperation of this kind is rarely complete. It is mainly in the academy that feminist discourse has become institutionalized; and capitalism welcomes as consumers groups, such as gay men, whose political voice continues to go largely unheard. But the device is nevertheless effective in that it blurs the cultural specificity of groups whose initial claim to partnership in the dialogue was made precisely on the grounds of the difference implied by their cultural identity. It was the claimed right to speak from that position of difference that constituted the noise; not much is gained if the noise is abated by eliminating that particular category of difference, in the way that, under apartheid, the government of South Africa invented the category of honorary white person for certain visiting Asians and Africans. This is what is at stake in the 'equality v. difference' debate that periodically surfaces in feminist politics: should women seek equality with men (at the expense of their difference) or maintain their difference (and suffer consequent inequality)? But, as Joan Scott in particular has pointed out,[15] the terms here are not incompatible: it is precisely in the name of difference that equal participation is being claimed.

In part 3, I will propose, not exactly an alternative, but a successor tactic to the politics of cultural identity as the unexpected reversal of an assigned identity (as mediator) into an assumed or claimed identity (as enunciating subject). The real political gains that have been made by identity politics on the part of marginalized groups can now be capitalized on, subject only to a more careful rethinking of what constitutes a community's 'identity' and of what is entailed in pronouncing the strange pronoun 'we.' What I will call a politics of community would challenge the assignment of cultural identity that makes equality and difference look antithetical, and would work, not for the denial of certain differences in the name of equality, but for a transvaluation of those differences, such that they cease to be disqualifying and become qualifying – differences of the kind that a community values because they constitute the differential positions without which there is no communication. I will argue, however, that it is most plausibly in the perspective of disempowered communities that such a policy becomes truly possible, because recuperation is the normal mode of assimilation practised by dominant communities.

On the other hand, a community to which cultural identity is assigned but which becomes aware of the degree to which such a characterization obscures its own constitution *as a community* – that is, not as a matter of sameness but of the differential positioning that grounds communication – is in a position to challenge the forms of othering that are practised by dominant communities, and to do so without abandoning a positive evaluation of its difference. Such a community can then expand, through policies of alliance, by extending the principle of mediated difference that grounds it to a population that is (potentially) all-inclusive. The fact that the mediating instance can be excluded from the power relations of a given community but not from its culture means that this mediating group is potentially includable in the dialogues of that community; but it also means, more dramatically, that the dominant group can (potentially) be absorbed by the 'minority' community formed by the mediators themselves, on the sole condition that that group perceive itself *as* a community in the sense I have sketched. That perception in turn depends on a willingness to accept, rather than deny, that difference is a phenomenon of mediation. For mediation in the form of a policy of bridge-building, networking, and alliance-formation[16] can become a principle of generalized inclusion rather than the object of an attempted (but always failed) exclusion. The mediator is a figure who can *never* be excluded (but only backgrounded) and who can *always* work inclusions, since difference is by definition that which mediation mediates and can be viewed as disqualifying the other from dialogue only when the powers and possibilities of mediation as the *factor* of community are denied. To see how that may be so we need first to look more closely, however, at the practices of exclusion that attempt, precisely, to deny or 'forget' mediation – the mediation by which one's own community is constituted as a community of differences – by projecting it onto a cultural other constructed, in terms of 'cultural identity,' as a function of sameness. My argument will be that this is a form of scapegoating which, because it is culturally mediated, is subject to being reversed (that is, re-mediated) through a politics of community.

Montagues and Capulets, or Scapegoating the Mediating Other

PRINCE ESCALUS:
And I, for winking at your discords too,
Have lost a brace of kinsmen ...

Romeo and Juliet, 5. 5

'What does "we" mean?' asks Jean-Luc Nancy.[17] 'What is the meaning of this pronoun which, in one way or another, must be inscribed in any discourse?' If to say 'we' is tantamount to what in the opening question of part 1 I called sharing a culture, the pronoun must be the site of a split (it might perhaps be written 'w/e'). For it emerges from the foregoing analysis that one cannot *share a culture* in the sense of forming a discourse community ('we' in the sense of 'you and I' or 'you-all and we') without at the same time *partitioning culture* ('we' in the sense of 'us v. them') by 'supposing' a mediating other to whom cultural identity is attributed. This, in Nancy's phrasing, is the problem of 'the partition and the sharing of the in' of 'being-in-common' (10): 'being "is" the *in* that divides and joins at the same time' (8). From my point of view, it involves examining the phenomenon of cultural split whereby 'a' culture acquires identity as a function of there being at least one other culture with which it shares culturality, so that it is both divided from and joined with that other.

Indeed it is a condition not only of there being cultures, but also of there being culture that culture be split. The fact that discourse is mediated culturally would be of no significance if it were not differently mediated on different occasions, at different times, and among different groups. If there were only *one* culture to mediate human discourse, the fact would make no difference – it would be of no interest, and presumably it would not even be perceptible. Instead of 'one' culture, however, we have, as English usage indicates, on the one hand, a *general* phenomenon known as 'culture' (as in French one might say, 'Il y a de la culture'), and, on the other, *particular* manifestations of that general phenomenon, marked by relations of difference, and called in the plural 'cultures' (cf. 'Il y a des cultures'). Cultures arise as a function of difference, but differences between cultures cannot be absolute (one culture cannot be radically distinct from another) since such differences arise only from a splitting of culture in its general sense, with the consequence that all cultures have in common their culturality, in the way that texts have in common their textuality. In other words, the relation between cultures, like that between texts, is a mediated one – mediated, that is, by the general culture or the 'general text' of which they partake. As a result there is no 'outside' of culture, but cultures arise, in the plural, as a consequence of the *production of difference* between them: one can step outside of 'a' culture (into another culture) but not outside of culture itself. It is this production of cultural difference that I want to concentrate on in this section.

Notice, however, that the same analysis will hold true for other cases of the mediated production of difference. As one can say that there is culture and there are cultures, one can say that there is ideology and there are ideologies, there is genre and there are genres, there is family and there are families, there is language and there are languages ... In each of these cases, and various others (my list is not limiting), the relation between the plural entities is produced by a split within the singular entity, and without that split we would have no particular use for the general notion.

The reason I want, in what follows, to explore this circumstance is that, if the difference between cultures is mediated, then to identify another culture as 'the' mediating other that permits one's own culture to function as a communicating community while marking that other with a particularizing attribute such as cultural identity, is to displace onto that mediating culture the responsibility for what is in fact a *general* phenomenon, that of (cultural) mediation. The other is held to be the mediator even though it is in fact the phenomenon of mediation itself that produces, through the splitting effect I have just mentioned, the very otherness of that culture, for cultural difference is always the product of mediation. In notation adapted from Lacan, one could say that the small-*o* other is held responsible for the large-*o* Other, that is, for the process of othering itself through which *all* cultures are produced – not only the culture of the other but also the culture that produces itself as a community by othering the mediator.

Furthermore, and as a result, the othering culture is itself internally split since 'differences between,' as Barbara Johnson observed some time ago,[18] always imply 'differences within.' It has a mixed identity since it harbours traces of the mediating other(s) in the way that in any differential system the terms, none of which is positive, are marked by traces of one another.[19] No cultural community is ever 'pure.' But the othering culture is split, also, by its ignorance of the mediation to which it owes both its identity and the mixedness of that identity: it has, in other words, an 'unconscious.' This ignorance – which would more accurately be described as a denegation – is produced, I will argue here, by means of an act of symbolic scapegoating which excludes the 'mediating other' from the affairs of community, and stamps that other culture (which is in fact another community) with the mark of sameness as the site of a cultural identity. Sameness (this is going to be a bit confusing) thus functions to convert a mediated split between cultures into an absolute difference (along the lines of '*we* are each different but *they* are all the same'), at the same time as it functions both to deny the characteristics of community (the 'we are each different') to the cultural other and to authorize the exclusion of cultural subjects so marked (marked as being 'all the same') from participation in the historical affairs of the other community.

The function of words like 'culture,' 'ideology,' 'genre,' and 'family' when they are used in the plural is to categorize. On the one hand, they *sort* items into two or more differentially constructed groups, and, on the other, they *collect* those items that are held to 'belong together' in a given group by virtue of the fact that they 'do not belong' in the other(s). Such items may and do differ among themselves in countless ways; their identity as a group derives *solely* from the negative feature of their not presenting the defining characteristics of the other group, which itself includes items that may differ among themselves in all but one or more crucial feature. When I sort my papers for taxation purposes at the end of the year, they go into two different piles, one of documents that are 'relevant' for IRS purposes, and one of documents that, for the same purposes, are 'not relevant' – but each pile contains a wildly heterogeneous set of items, from receipts, letters, and old cheques to miscellaneous scraps of paper and notations on the back of envelopes. A different sorting principle (or mediator of difference) – say, by size of paper – would redistribute the items between different piles, but the composition of each pile would remain heterogeneous in every other respect.[20]

Just so (but with concomitant power differentials) does cultural sorting split cultures into groups that are, like the contents of my shoebox, in other respects heterogeneous, the effect of power being visible in the fact that heterogeneity is valued in the case of the dominant community and made to disappear into sameness in the case of the back-grounded group. This effect arises whether the group constituting a community is as small as a couple of friends (to whom the anonymous mass of non-friends are the cultural other) or as large as a tribe, a national, or a supranational entity. The more obviously ideological construction of groups such as those of gender, race, and class depends on a similar mechanism: a given gender, race, or class owes its identity *only* to the existence of at least one other gender, race, or class, *each* of which is sorted into categories that necessarily have many internal differences, both by virtue of 'mixture' – the fact that other principles of categorization would produce quite other differences as relevant – and by virtue of 'split' – the axiom that 'differences between' imply 'differences within.' Each of these constructed groups therefore qualifies as a *community*, in the sense of a set of different possible subject-positions mediated by a common context that is productive both of what defines them as belonging together and of what they regard as their other. But the dominant community has the power to produce *its* other as non-community (not a community, and not part of the dominant discursive community) by virtue of attributing to it cultural identity.

To understand how this comes about, we can begin by noting that categorizing words appear themselves to fall into two paradigms although – since 'paradigm' is itself a categorizing word – it is precisely the relation of split that accounts for the complexity of concepts like 'culture' and 'community,' which seem to belong undecidably to each paradigm. There is a paradigm of 'family' and a paradigm of 'context.' Words like 'culture,' 'ideology,' and 'genre' belong most clearly to the paradigm of context: like 'context' itself, they designate the mediating instances without which enunciations would not be meaningful, the 'excluded third' of which Serres demonstrates the inevitable 'presence' in every dialogue. ('Language,' as the verbal mediating factor without which there can be no speech, might seem a natural head-word for this paradigm, but 'context' has the advantage of referring to the mediating element present in discursive enunciations in general, that is, to cultural 'practice,' as well as to linguistic ones in particular. Furthermore, the problematics of context, as a 'local' phenomenon (one context, among others) that nevertheless cannot be localized, because no context can be dissociated from its others, has oddly enough been more fully explored, in the branch of linguistics known as pragmatics, than the very similar problematics of language itself.)

As for the paradigm of family, it includes most obviously (as well as 'family' itself) words like 'gender,' race,' and 'class,' which can be thought to group individuals by virtue of some supposed 'natural' kinship or affinity, with little reference to the mediating context that makes of them a community. We have here the germ of the idea that permits a cultural group to be marked with a cultural 'identity,' by virtue of which its members are perceived as essentially the same as one another. The metaphor is that of family-likeness, derived genetically from a so-called 'pool' (note the delimiting concept); and the underlying idea is therefore the perception that families form distinct groups. In short, there are in this view Montagues, on the one hand, and, on the other, Capulets; similarly there are 'blacks' and 'whites,' or 'men' and 'women,' or 'first-worlders' and 'third-worlders,' and the like; and, as Kipling put it, 'never the twain shall meet.'

It takes only a moment's thought, however, to realize that families are *not*, and cannot be, absolutely distinct one from another but are, to the contrary, the product of differential splitting, such that 'differences between' imply 'differences within.' The practice of exogamic marriage, already mentioned as the device by which culture is instituted in the control of desire and the exchange of women, clearly enacts the interdependence of families one upon the other for their identity, the fact that it is a *condition* of there being Montagues that there also be Capulets and vice versa. It is unsurprising, therefore, that in the person of Romeo, a Montague should show up at the Capulets' feast, or that the love between Romeo and Juliet should figure the exogamic link on which differences between families depend, including those that are hostile to one another. The control of desire in the interest of maintaining intrafamilial difference (by enforcing the incest taboo) makes it impossible to enforce *absolute* difference between any family and its other; and indeed, at the end of Shakespeare's play, we suddenly learn that the warring families have been, in fact, closely interrelated. Tybalt is 'cousin' to Romeo, old Montague 'brother' to old Capulet, and the Prince has lost, in the deceased (which include Paris, who is neither Montague nor Capulet), a 'brace of kinsmen' – Juliet being subsumed also, I take it, under these kinsmen. The general principle (no Montagues without Capulets) is the same when Trinh T. Minh-ha points out that there is a First World in every Third World and a Third World in every First World;[21] and the principle could obviously be extended without difficulty to the supposed 'family'-groups of race, class, and gender, to which – as always – should be added those constituted by the constructed difference between the 'normal' and their allegedly 'deviant' others.

More significant, though, in the context of my present argument, is the degree of contamination between the two paradigms of categorizing words, the ease with which certain 'family' words function as 'context' words and vice versa. 'Gender' is a case in point: although it belongs clearly enough to the family paradigm, there are some who regard gender as constituting a context, of such a kind that it determines differences in the way women and men communicate with one another and hampers cross-gender communication. Gender in this sense is, like culture, the mediator of discourse communities: men and women bring different pre-suppositions to a conversation, and these presuppositions function as a mediating culture or ideology, fostering communication among group-members and hindering it across groups.[22] On the other hand, 'culture' and 'ideology,' which are perhaps predominantly thought of as mediating context, are commonly used also as markers of family affinity, and as ways of designating the differential features of groups thought to form 'natural' communities (as in 'middle-class ideology' or 'lesbian culture'). Perhaps the Greek word *ethos*, as the 'spirit of a city,' went closest to incor-porating the dual sense of mediating instance (i.e., the 'spirit' that binds the citizens into a community) and family grouping (i.e., the 'city' as the natural group formed by people who are 'fellow' citizens of one another). But the word 'community' itself is haunted by similar indeterminacy, just as 'culture' is. Does 'culture' refer to a group of people (as when one speaks of the Berbers or the Mountain Arapesh as 'a culture'), or to what mediates their affairs (as when one says that the Berbers or the Arapesh 'have' or 'share a culture')? Is 'community' the mediator of communica-tion, as I have been proposing here, or is it a family of people having something essential in common, as fascistic discourse historically claimed and as much common usage – to my mind, unfortunately – seems to accept?

The answer must be that 'community,' like 'culture,' 'ideology,' or 'gender,' sometimes means one thing and sometimes the other. This point is important, and I am stressing it because it indicates why it is so easy to make ideological distinctions between 'our' community and 'their' culture: *we* are a group of communicating subjects; *they* are a group of people characterized by family likeness. For, as I have already pointed out, there are two factors that determine the scapegoating of the mediat-ing other through the stereotyping characteristic of the concept of 'cul-tural identity.' One is the mechanism of mediation I have discussed, whereby 'context' (as culture, ideology, genre, etc.) is the inescapable condition of communication, a condition that inevitably produces other-ness as the fate of the mediating third: without mediating others, and hence the othering of the mediator, there is no communicating community. But the other is the factor that gives this condition of alterity its *ideological* significance, so that it becomes, as Gregory Bateson might have put it, a 'difference that makes a difference.'[23] And it is here that the easy translatability that is characteristic of the category of categorizing words in general and of concepts like 'culture' and 'community' in particular between the paradigm of context and the paradigm of family, that is, between recognition of a purely discursive phenomenon (that of mediation) and the social construction of humans as belonging to different groups or families, intervenes so as to permit the scapegoating of the cultural mediator. In brief, what happens is that the stereotyping of cultural identity translates the figure of the mediating third out of the discursive language of 'context' and into the social language of 'family' and designates that figure as alien – as 'not of *our* (supposedly natural) family' – with respect to the community of those who are engaged in actual discursive enunciations. It is not, then, that the culturally stereotyped figure of the other necessarily mediates, in a literal sense, specific or local discursive exchanges; it is rather that the cultural other is stereotyped as a figure of the cultural mediation, productive of community, that is the condition for such exchanges.

'Symbolic' scapegoating of this kind, underlying as it does the ideology of 'us v. them,' is not a bad model for understanding the working of ideology in general, as the naturalization of mediated (i.e., historical) situations that involve an uneven distribution of power. Unlike the 'actual' scapegoat, a symbolic scapegoat is not physically excluded from a community that is defined, a priori, by topographical limits – not driven out of a city into the desert, for example. The 'exclusion' of a symbolic scapegoat (which can be an individual or a group) is what *produces* a community that is discursively defined; and the symbolic scapegoat is not physically excluded from the cultural group so much as he or she is the object of ideological practices through which is constructed, within a cultural context, an asymmetry of power. The important point here is that it is this *cultural inclusion* of the *ideologically disempowered* that eventually provides the latter with an opportunity to 'return,' as Serres might say, within the discursive community that represents the sphere of power. But once these distinctions between 'symbolic' and 'actual' scapegoating are made, the general laws of scapegoating, as they emerge from a lifetime's work by René Girard,[24] can be seen to apply without modification to symbolic scapegoating of the kind I am discussing, that is, to the ideological construction, within culture, of a difference that makes a difference. In all scapegoating, the 'sins' of a community are heaped on a figure who must

(a) be a member of that community but (b) be marked by a specific difference that can come to make a difference. As a result, the scapegoat is
always guilty as charged – but so too is the scapegoating community itself,
which absolves itself of that charge, however, through the very operation
of scapegoating the 'other.'

Thus, as I have pointed out elsewhere,[25] to scapegoat a mediator is to
absolve oneself of the 'crime' of mediation and to naturalize a powerful
discursive community, but to do so through what is itself an act of
mediation (the act of producing a difference between oneself and the
mediating other). This description of scapegoating as the mediated
incrimination of the mediator is not Girard's, but it is entirely consonant
with Girard's understanding of the archetypal sin of the scapegoating
community as the sin of sameness or indistinction, manifested in a crisis
of social indifferentiation. One need only recall that mediation necessarily implies a certain 'sameness' within difference (since mediated differences cannot be absolute) and that it is therefore through mediation that
differences are reduced as well as produced. By projecting such 'sameness,' the product of mediation, onto the scapegoated other, for example
in the form of cultural identity, the scapegoating group simultaneously
absolves itself of that sameness and actually recreates difference within
itself (in the first instance, by singling out a scapegoat from its own undifferentiated mass). In this way, it reconstitutes itself as a *community* – the
community of those whose difference from the scapegoated individual or
group lies in the fact that they are not 'all the same.'

In short, to create through scapegoating a 'difference between' where
none existed before also produces 'difference within,' the only price to
be paid lying in having to accommodate the contradictory status of
the scapegoat. This is the status, clearly articulated in the situation of the
'symbolic' scapegoat, of one who must simultaneously be a *member* of the
'group' and *different* from the 'community.' In the case of the symbolic
scapegoat, it is the split between culture and ideology that authorizes this
contradiction, the 'other' being ideologically excluded (i.e., from power)
but culturally included in the group, if only as the object of an ideological
exclusion. This ideology/culture split, however, as we have seen, in fact
enacts the same difference as that between a discursive community and its
scapegoated (mediating) other, since culture is itself defined as the mediating other of ideology, something like the 'language' that enables the
enunciations of discursive power. And furthermore, culture itself is a site
of split (there is culture and there are different cultures), so that the relation between a cultural community and its own (cultural) mediating

other is exactly homologous with that, within a culture, between an ideological community and its own (ideological) mediating other. That, I think, is why it is so easy to attribute *cultural* 'identity' to a group whose identity is in fact *ideologically* produced. The so-called cultural other is always an ideological object, that is, the product of 'symbolic' scapegoating, if only because in the last analysis there is no outside of culture.

By now it must be evident, not only that the whole system of scapegoating I have outlined hinges on the phenomenon of split, but that it does so because split authorizes two different ways of understanding, or valuing, difference. Split produces an alterity, but one that cannot be absolutely distinguished from identity, so that it can be held to be a difference, or a difference that makes a difference, according to (historical) circumstance. *Certain* differentially produced relations can be positively valorized (they do not constitute a disqualifying difference): such is the case of the 'I'/'you' difference that constitutes the 'we' of a communicating community. These positions, being discursively mediated, cannot be absolutely distinct, but the degree of 'sameness' that arises from shared mediations serves only, in this case, to ground a sense of the commonality on which community, as a site where difference flourishes, rests. On the other hand, a split such as that between discursive enunciations (the enactment of positively valorized difference) and the mediating other can be valorized negatively, so that the mediator is scapegoated by being disqualified from participation in the very dialogue that mediation makes possible. Thus the mediating instance that is culture and the sharing it implies among members of a group is understood, in the first case, as the factor of positively valorized differences between people and, in the second, as the factor of sameness that negatively distinguishes the class of people to whom cultural identity, as opposed to membership in the cultural community, is attributed.

Qualifying and disqualifying differences are not, therefore, 'in themselves' ('prior' to their ideological valorization), qualitatively different or different in kind. In other historical circumstances, they might readily switch roles. But in the case of certain differences, those that are positively valorized, it is as if there is an agreement to disregard or 'forget' the element of cultural 'sameness' that arises from their mediated character, whereas in the case of others, those that are negatively valorized, the agreement is to 'remember' and to foreground that sameness so as to attribute it, as their defining characteristic, to the members of groups whose difference is regarded as disqualifying. And the back-grounding of culture in one instance – its effacement through the ideological construc-

tion of community as a 'naturally' occurring group of individualized subjects – is a function of its foregrounding in the other, that is, in the
production of culture as the defining trait of a group, in the form of cultural identity, with its consequent de-facement of individuals. Remember-
ing culture as mediating instance produces the kind of difference that,
ideologically speaking, makes a difference; and cultural membership is
perceived, in this case, as something like a factor of 'family' resemblance.
Forgetting culture produces the kinds of difference that are either taken
for granted or are positively valued as markers of individuality and the
sign of membership in a discursive community, whose culture can be
back-grounded – banned from ideological consciousness – as merely the
'context' in which a group of people get on with their business.

In *Epistemology of the Closet*,[26] Eve Sedgwick does not lay stress on the
scapegoating model as the principle of the closet, but she does point to
what is the fundamental law of scapegoating, in the form of the saying 'it
takes one to know one.' All of her work, in fact, rests on the insight that
homophobia is a form of scapegoating that permits a homosocial community of men to 'forget' the homosexual desire that is itself the principal
sign of that community's mediated status. For the homosocial community
is mediated by the women whose exchange between men founds culture
but who are ideologically excluded from male power; and it is the disturbing 'return' of this mediating third as noise, that is, in the transformed
guise of male homosexuality, that constitutes an unwelcome reminder of
the mediated character of the homosocial community and must therefore
be scapegoated by the construction of 'gay' men as fundamentally other
than 'real' men. If *they* are the bearers of homosexual desire, then *we* cannot be tainted with it, such is the reasoning. 'It takes one to know one,'
however, reverses the direction of the scapegoating process, whose dynamic is that of finger-pointing; it does so by turning the finger-pointing
around and recalling the incontrovertible fact that what the scapegoat
stands for is something that is characteristic of the scapegoating community itself – that is, in the final analysis, cultural mediation, which the act
of scapegoating serves to naturalize into the back-ground of the scapegoating community by projecting it onto the scapegoat.

In part 3 I want to return to the possibility of reversal that is inherent in
the structure of symbolic scapegoating as the mediated exclusion of mediation from the sphere of power. There being nothing fundamentally disqualifying in the differences that make an ideological difference as
opposed to the qualifying differences that constitute a discursive community, it follows that what the scapegoating community and the scape-

goated figure or group have, culturally speaking, in common *could* furnish the basis of a new community that would be constituted, not by the exclusion/inclusion of the mediating third, marked by cultural identity, but by *the inclusion of the dominant (scapegoating) community within that formed by the marginalized (scapegoated) group.* Instead of 'returning' to haunt the scapegoating community with more or less insistent requests for (re)admission to that group, the scapegoats might, in other words, adopt the policy of *inviting the scapegoaters* to join their own community, to which they potentially belong by virtue of the axiom 'it takes one to know one.'

For such a development to occur – and I fully recognize that it is a utopian proposal I am making, one whose implementation can only be limited, local, and sporadic, at least for a very long time – two conditions would be necessary. One, it would be necessary for there to be general acknowledgment, in the first instance within the scapegoated group itself, that the group is not characterized by cultural identity but is itself a community, that is, that it is not only a site of differences but of differences that are positively valorized (and not played down, for instance, as a sign of political disunity). Two, the differences that currently make a difference and produce the split between dominant discursive communities and their mediating other would have to cease to make a difference in that sense, and become instead the kind of positively valorized differences that are the mark of a shared community; and this would have to happen on both sides of the split. We are talking therefore of a double transvaluation of difference: those differences that currently do not make a difference (those that are ideologically ignored, so that the scapegoated group can be assigned, or can claim, cultural identity) must *begin* to make a difference, but in a positive sense, so that the group can be perceived as constituting a community; simultaneously, the differences that produce the difference between the dominant community and its mediating other(s) must *cease* to make a difference, in the ideologically negative sense, and become recognized instead as constituting differentially marked discursive positions within a now expanded community.

Such a new community would inevitably have its own mediating thirds; it would necessarily be constituted by the phenomenon of cultural split whereby a culture can achieve the identity of a community only by virtue of there being an other(ed) group whose difference from the first is construed as making a difference. The mechanisms of the mediated construction of discursive communities, and hence of the back-grounding of the mediator, are, as I have stressed (following Serres), inescapable: they are the very condition of communication. What can be worked for, though, is a form of consciousness-raising, that is, of ideological critique. The goal would be recognition that a community – any community – is best understood *as a discursive phenomenon*, that is, as the product of a mediating instance and as subject, in consequence, to the mechanisms of mediation, including the phenomenon of back-grounding. Words like *culture* and *community* can be shifted out of the 'family' paradigm of categorizing words, which so readily gives rise to hostile forms of othering of the Montagues v. Capulets variety, and into the 'context' paradigm, in which the phenomenon of othering can be recognized as a phenomenon of back-grounding but *without the back-grounding's necessarily implying the ideological de-facement of the other* through the attribution of cultural identity. Under these conditions, the othering of the mediator could conceivably be deprived, partially or wholly, of its unpleasant ideological signification, with its unfortunate political consequences; and the difference between a discursive community and its mediating other(s) would cease to be a difference that makes a difference, although it would always remain a difference.

In such a dispensation, the other(ed) group, different and back-grounded but not de-faced, would always be potentially includable (by virtue of the axiom 'it takes one to know one') in the othering group – includable, that is, other than by recuperative assimilation; and the recognition of this potential, on the part of the members of the othering community, would be essential since it would be the grounds of the non-de-facement of the other. But in the first instance, and given the circumstances of the present, when symbolic scapegoating is widespread, the first anti-scapegoating move will inevitably have to be made, as a matter of realism, by the scapegoated groups themselves; and the movement of inclusion will have to go from them in the direction of the scapegoating community rather than vice versa. That is why it is important to see that such an anti-scapegoating move is itself crucially dependent, as I have suggested, on the othered group's willingness to abandon the claims of cultural identity, which are the grounds of its othering, and to explore its own constitution as a community, since it is by an extension of positively valorized differences 'within' that 'differences between' can in turn be positively valorized and cease to make an ideological difference. That crucial step, I think, is what can be seen to have been happening in recent years in the women's movement, which – as so often the vanguard group in oppositional politics – has begun the process of acknowledging that 'woman' does not name a gendered *identity* so much as it refers to a community of historically constituted differences (to which, it is true, unfortunate 'othering' labels like 'women of colour' or 'Third world women' are still attached).[27] Such a development is entirely positive; indeed, it is one of the most encouraging signs on the scene of contemporary cultural politics. And the trend, fortunately, is not an isolated one.

Special Interests and the Politics of Community

Difference ... is that which undermines the very idea of identity.

Trinh T. Minh-ha, *Woman, Native, Other*, 96.

Scapegoating the mediating other was a particular talent of the Reagan administration, among whose most notable inventions must be counted the 'evil Empire,' on the one hand, and, on the other, 'special interests.' Describing as 'special' (that is, different and not equal) the interests of such people as women, Blacks, ethnic minorities, lesbians, and gay men made it possible for another set of special interests, those favoured by the administration, to pass as *general*, as the interests of the community as a whole, referred to therefore as the 'general community.' What community was this? By definition the community of non-women, non-Blacks, non-ethnics, and non-gays; in short, the non-'special.' (In an exactly similar sense, it is feared that AIDS, a disease repeatedly associated with gay men and drug-users, may spread to the 'general community.')

As a result of this powerful move, those whose interests were declared to be special were forced either to acquiesce in this proposition or to allow their legitimate political interests to be dissolved into a spurious generality that in fact denied them, an alternative corresponding to that between affirmation of a cultural identity and recuperative assimilation that I sketched in part 1. It was no longer possible to argue that attention to 'special' interests might be in the general good, the privilege of representing that general good having been appropriated on behalf of the community of the 'non-special.' It is from this Reaganite scapegoating of 'special interests,' with its implication that the general interest is that of the dominant community, that the currently popular conservative (or reactionary) argument that 'equal rights' ought to be blind to differences (of gender, of race and ethnicity, and presumably of class and sexual orientation, which mostly aren't even mentioned) derives its plausibility. To argue otherwise is to be seen to be in favour of 'special interest' groups.

Oddly enough, it is in the recent history of Reagan's 'evil Empire' – this essay is being written in the winter of 1991–2 – that we can see an illustration of the counter-tactic that might be adopted by those whose positioning as the mediating other of a dominant community has taken the form of their being scapegoated as a 'special interest.' It is the tactic of the double transvaluation of difference. Internally, Gorbachev's glasnost policy quickly displayed the 'disunity' of the Soviet Union, that is, the fact that, far from being a monolithic society whose members were all the same, it harboured many competing interests, political, religious, ethnic, regional, and so on – the interests whose interplay seems now to have dissolved the USSR into a loose commonwealth, or community, of allied but autonomous republics. At the same time, Gorbachev's foreign policy strove, unfortunately with less success, to demonstrate that matters like arms control and latterly economic aid to the Soviet Union were not matters of 'special' interest but rather of general concern for the countries of the world; that, in other words, the political differences between the United States and the USSR should not be permitted to 'make a difference' to the extent of keeping the two countries, like the Montagues and Capulets, on a permanent war footing, but that the two nations and their allies ought rather to form a community for the sake of discussing these differences and if possible negotiating a solution.

That these policies have brought about the actual dissolution of the Soviet Union as a political entity is certainly ironic, and Gorbachev's actions may be said to have failed to the extent that they were aimed at preserving a strongly centralized union of soviet republics. But by the same token, the West may be said, in the words of an atypically acute *Detroit Free Press* headline (27 December 1991), to have lost 'the enemy that defined it' and hence its own 'identity.' The outcome actually represents, therefore, a rather dramatic confirmation of the difference between a politics of cultural identity (represented in this case by the aggressive and unified image presented to the world by previous Soviet regimes) and a politics of alliance and negotiation that does not deny differences or essentialize identity and which, consequently, is devoted to the making of community. What Gorbachev's defeat makes clear, however, is that there *is* a price to be paid for the success of a politics of community. Alliance, networking, and negotiation imply the sacrifice, not of difference, but of concepts like cultural identity, with the essentialistic policies of affirmation but also the absolute differences and the equally absolute sameness (of interests and concerns, desires and ambitions) that such policies imply.

Successful and valuable as such policies have been on the part of culturally marginalized groups, in making noise and attracting attention, and
thus in claiming for the mediating other a part in the dialogue of the
community itself and in the making of history, these groups' assumption
of the characterization of sameness continues to mark them for scapegoating and exclusion, for example under the alibi of 'special interests';
that is why I think it is time to find a successor to such policies. What it is
important to understand in this context, however, is that to abandon policies of cultural identity is not necessarily to renounce the particular interests that identity stands for; it is rather to permit, or to seek to permit,
those interests to enter the affairs of a community as one of the various
differential positions that that community takes into account in its
dialogues. In other words, they would cease to be the object, real or
potential, of symbolic scapegoating and become instead legitimate and
acknowledged positions in the general pattern of differences that the
community recognizes as forming its substance *as* a community.

The first move in the tactic of double transvaluation of difference is, as
I have suggested and as glasnost demonstrated, the one in which a group
supposedly characterized (even in its own eyes) by cultural identity discovers instead its reality as a community composed of differences. It is impossible in this regard to overlook the significance of the recent history of the
women's movement, to which I've already alluded; but one of the ways in
which this history is significant is that it took the form of a discovery made
by middle-class white women in the United States, under urgent prompt-
ing by women of colour, that they had in effect been scapegoating, as
'special' and therefore negligible, the interests of non-white, non–middle-
class, non–First World women. They had in other words been replicating
internally the structure of the masculinist scapegoating of the set of *all*
women as mediating others to whom the sameness of cultural identity was
attributed. The dialogue of middle-class white women was predicated on
the back-grounding of 'other' women as the mediators of the community
formed by those women; the recognition of that fact simultaneously shattered the cosiness of that community's dialogue and its claim to speak
from the perspective of sameness implied by gender as a cultural identity.
From this example, we can learn, perhaps, that *internal* scapegoating is
inevitably the practice of scapegoated groups that pursue a policy of
affirming their cultural identity, the identity in question being defined, in
fact, in the dialogue of a relatively powerful community within the scapegoated group, a community that excludes its own mediating others.
Internal de-scapegoating is therefore the necessary first step towards

countering external scapegoating; or, to put it in slogan form, de-scape-goating is the condition of anti-scapegoating.

The second step, for (say) the women's movement – and it is a difficult one – would have to consist of a recognition that there is no essential or absolute distinction between the 'differences within' the community of women and the 'differences between' women and men. Since this is the very difference on which the women's movement, as a movement of women, depends for its self-definition, there is no question of denying its importance. The question, as I've suggested, is not to deny the importance of this difference but to transvalue it. It has been historically constructed, in the context of the scapegoating of women, as one of the differences that make a major ideological difference: is it possible to learn to treat it as a difference that is like the multiple differences that make 'women' not an identity but a community – differences that themselves made a similar difference until they were de-scapegoated (or, to be more accurate, until the work of de-scapegoating them was begun)? If those internal differences can become community-differences rather than back-grounding or scapegoating differences, then the women-men difference might in its turn become the basis of a politics of alliance, a community-difference, within an *extended* women's community.

The debate around 'men in feminism'[28] turns, of course, on this point – are men the hereditary enemy or are at least some men potential or actual allies? – and it is clear that there is considerable historical distance to be traversed before such a utopian concept as a women's community that includes men might become thinkable, let alone realizable, on anything like a grand scale.[29] But since the group of men is itself a community (not an identity) and so is marked by diversity and difference, there is no reason why a move in that general direction might not start with specific alliances, permanent or more likely temporary, between particular men or groups of men and certain women or groups of women, when their political interests happen to coincide or merely to be compatible. These men and women would not have to become identical to one another but would occupy differential positions in the dialogue of a contextually defined communicating community, whose existence, however, would demonstrate the viability of the model and the possibility of its extension. Indeed, my conditional tense is inappropriate since such communities manifestly already exist, whether as political alliances ('men in feminism,' for instance, or the often uneasy working relationship between some lesbians and some gay men) or simply in everyday circumstances (say, the complicities of wife and husband with respect to mediating

others like 'the neighbours' or 'the children'). (The political importance
of the everyday, as the sphere of cultural reproduction – and hence
potentially of cultural change – should not be underestimated.)

I like to think of party-giving as a good model for the kind of politics I
have in mind (provided party-giving is itself defined, not as a way of
affirming closed grounds but as a matter of issuing open invitations). In
Sydney (Australia) there is annually a lesbian and gay Mardi Gras that
takes over a large segment of the city and draws huge numbers of revellers
from the whole resident and tourist population of the city, many of whom
(perhaps most?) are nominally straight. In 1988 in the same city, an
embarrassing political dilemma arose when it was time to celebrate the
bicentenary of the arrival in Sydney Cove of the 'First Fleet,' the tawdry
group of soldiers and convicts who established a British colony there.
How to celebrate two hundred years of 'settlement' that had been pre-
ceded by at least forty thousand years of continuous habitation by the
aboriginal population of what is now Australia? I imagine aboriginal 'leaders' were invited to represent their people at official events on the harbour foreshores. But what the community actually did was – not to disrupt
those occasions – but to organize alternative celebrations, on (border)
land roughly equidistant from the ghetto and the harbour, and to issue a
general invitation for all who wanted to attend. After the first few occasions, dutifully frequented, I suppose, by a few non-aboriginals politically
committed to such gestures, word began to spread that these events were
actually fun, and before long they had become so popular and so successful with such a wide segment of the population that they began to be
announced in the press right alongside of the official celebrations. In the
way that 'everyone' in New York becomes Irish on St Patrick's day and
'everyone' in Sydney becomes gay at Mardi Gras, 'everyone' in 1988 was a
Koori. It did not last, of course – but it is surprising how many Sydneysid-
ers and other Australians have contracted the permanent habit of referring to the events of 1788 – whether earnestly, off-handedly, or ironically –
as 'the invasion.'

It is, of course, Sedgwick's law (if I may call it that) that underlies the
possibility of such anti-scapegoating alliances: 'it takes one to know one.'
As scapegoated groups identify themselves as communities composed of
multiple differences and move to extend the scope of their community by
seeking to transform the scapegoater-scapegoat difference into a community difference, they necessarily rely on the commonality of scapegoater
and scapegoat that this principle enunciates. In slightly more technical
terms, they take advantage of cultural inclusion in order to overcome

ideological exclusion, and it is obviously at the ideological 'borders' between dominant and marginalized groups (where the dominant contains members whose make-up may be quite strongly 'mixed') that the process has the greatest chance of success. But borders, notoriously, can 'creep,' as a formerly ambiguous borderland on both sides of a frontier is incorporated into a community, so that a new border is formed and the process can begin again.

One may think, as the example of party-giving suggests, that desire can be a powerful force in this process of border-jumping and border-shifting. What Sedgwick memorably describes as 'homosexual panic,' for instance,[30] – the fear on the part of homosocial and therefore officially heterosexual men that they may be subjects of homosexual desire – is something like a misfire in the workings of an 'us v. them' ideology, displaying the vulnerability of ideologically constructed differences to disturbance derived from the fact that they are all culturally mediated. Homophobia, as the enforcement of a gay-straight borderline of difference through the scapegoating of homosexual desire among males, thus reveals the potential all such constructed differences harbour for the discovery that they may not make such a difference after all, and 'homosexual panic' names an uneasy recognition, on the part of officially straight men, of their potential membership in the community of homosexual men, the mediating other – or one of the mediating others – of homosocial dialogue. (One may wonder whether there is such a thing as 'feminist panic' corresponding to a parallel misfire in the ideological functioning of misogyny; and if not, why not? Certainly racists are subject to panic fears that their own lineage may be 'impure.') But if straight men, or a certain number of straight men, are capable of recognizing in themselves this potential otherness, it may not be beyond the powers of the imagination for the othered community of gay men to acknowledge their own complementary connectedness to the allegedly straight world – a connectedness of which they are sometimes, too often, forcibly reminded – and to devise policies that would be posited on the possibility of including within their own group, for political purposes, some at least of the men who officially regard themselves as straight. It is only the doctrine of cultural identity as a marker of *absolute* difference that stands in the way of such an extension of the principle of difference to a community in which 'straight' might be perceived as a variant form of 'gay.'

For a hint of how such a policy might be conceived in the gay male community, a brief glance at Neil Bartlett's extraordinary book *Who Was That Man?*[31] might be instructive. Without deploying the rebarbative

vocabulary of critical theory in which I have been indulging, Bartlett analyses the trial of Oscar Wilde as a scapegoating move, and the counter-
moves his book enacts resonate strongly with what I have been proposing
and tend to confirm the structure of my own argument. Bartlett describes
the enforced 'outing' of Wilde as a gesture which, in making Wilde the
representative figure of the male homosexual, functioned to deny the
existence of what was already, in late nineteenth-century Britain, a community of gay men. (An earlier trial – that of Bolton and Parks, a.k.a.
Fanny and Stella – had had the even more remarkable effect of denying
homosexuality itself, on the grounds that if it existed it would certainly
not advertise itself as these men had done.) All homosexuals, that is, were
declared the same (the same as Wilde), and the sentencing of one of
their number thus served logically (in the logic of scapegoating) to
silence their discourse, that is, to exclude it from the historically dominant cultural dialogue. For it was not, of course, literally silence, and as
Bartlett says, 'only ignorance could assert that in a period of threat our
life stops' (220). His book is the record of his passionate 'hunt' for the
surviving historical evidence of the existence of the 'silenced' community
(much of it, as it happens, conveniently preserved in the records of the
trial itself), so as to be able to reassert the continuity of that community
with the contemporary community of gay men. That is, it seeks to reassert
the communitarian character of what was othered into a scapegoated
identity.

His metaphor for community is one that reminds us of the de-faced
women on the 'Scenes and Types' postcard (see part 1) and simultaneously recalls Gloria Anzaldúa's emphasis on 'making faces.'[32] 'We never
get to see the faces and of course it is the faces that I want to see' (29).
Faces signify that a community is not a homogeneous mass but a group –
or, in Bartlett's other key metaphor, a collection – of individual figures,
marked by difference. But, in this case, the difference constitutive of community is also a historical one, since it is precisely the suppression of community brought about in 1895 by the trial of Wilde that has introduced
the historical gap, treated by Bartlett as a split, between members of
today's gay community and the community of the 1890s.

Because of the historical discontinuity, the problem of community
becomes, more clearly than in the case of a synchronically constituted
community, one of recognition. How, given the factor of difference, to be
certain that a given nineteenth-century 'face' is, or is not, a member of
the community the historian, as a collector of faces, is attempting to (re-)
construct? The signs have changed and there are breaks in the collective

memory: no one wears a green carnation any more. It is the practice of sexual cruising that becomes Bartlett's analogue of the historical 'hunt' for faces, because cruising is precisely a matter of mutual recognition. But cruising also, on the one hand, situates community – as does *Romeo and Juliet* – as a function of the mutual acknowledgment of desire, or the acknowledgment of mutual desire, and, on the other hand, it demonstrates the uncertainty of the construction of community, in two interrelated senses that arise from the problematics of difference. For difference means that no one can *automatically* be included in a community: 'What if I rounded the corner of Villiers St at midnight, and suddenly found my self walking by gaslight, and the man looking over his shoulder at me as he passed had the same moustache, but different clothes … – would we recognize each other?' (xx). But it means also that everyone is *potentially* includable: *anyone* who responds to the cruiser's signals becomes, by virtue of that response, a member of the community through the acknowledgment of shared desire, and thus can be added to the 'collection of the men I've met,' 'the gallery of faces' (p.61). 'Gay' or 'straight' thus becomes, not an absolute difference but, simply, a matter of shared, or mutually recognized, *context* – and context, it will be remembered from part 2, is the head-word of the paradigm of sorting/collecting or categorizing words when they refer to communities as groups of communicating individuals, and not as opposed 'families.' 'Walking into a bar I look as identifiably gay as if I had made my entrance wearing a Hartnell gown and tiara,' Bartlett writes (63). 'Wearing the same outfit to make a train journey, leaving London for a small town, I simply look like an ordinary man.' It thus becomes thinkable that on some occasion an apparently 'ordinary' man might recontextualize and discover himself to be a member of Bartlett's gay community.

I want to suggest that his book itself is cruising its readership on the off-chance of sparking such recontextualization, that is, in the hope of encountering signs of recognition in unexpected quarters as well as in the more predictable ones. In particular, Bartlett's casual, confident, and canny use of the pronoun 'we' as the marker of community functions, on the one hand, to indicate the speaker's belonging to the gay community, what he calls his 'solidarity with my gay peers'; but, on the other, it is addressed rhetorically, as a potential sign of recognition, as a 'you' to which *any* reader, however he or she may be self-identified, might respond. Bartlett explicitly commends, as 'moving,' the 'we' in a poem by Marc-André Raffalovich, which, he says, corresponds to an 'us' of gay community v. 'them' (48); but his own deployment of the first-person-

plural pronoun demonstrates that the 'we' of 'us v. them' cannot be absolutely distinguished from the 'we' of 'us and you.' In the Raffalovich
poem as in Bartlett's book, the 'we' of identity blurs with a 'we' of open
address through the potential for recontextualization that open publication actualizes, but to which all writing – it is Derrida's 'iteration' – is subject. The split structure of the pronoun 'we,' which arises from the fact
that sharing *a* culture also implies partitioning culture, is also what
enables the reversal of the direction of scapegoating's finger-pointing, so
that it becomes an invitation to community.

In such a practice of address, difference is not denied – indeed, it is
fully acknowledged – but neither is community limited by the definitions
of 'cultural identity.' Bartlett's 'we' as an anti-scapegoating move could
become a model, I want to suggest, for political practices of 'inclusive
address' that just might prove, for scapegoated groups, to be an appropriate successor to the affirmations of cultural identity. The dynamics of
power are such that it is difficult for members of dominant groups to
address members of scapegoated groups with an inclusive 'we' (as when a
man says, 'we feminists,' or a white says, 'we Black folks'), without sound-
ing patronizing, appropriative, or worse; and I have been painfully conscious, in writing this essay, of the difficulty of speaking 'for' groups to
which I do not, at least manifestly, belong as well as those to which I do.[33]
But in reverse, when a member of a scapegoated community says 'we' to a
figure identified with a dominant group, the tactic sounds as confident
and is certainly as attention-getting, as the tactic of identity affirmation
that consists in the positive assumption of 'cultural identity.' However, the
claim it makes to participation in a dialogue is made on *other* terms. The
reversal of direction in the scapegoater-scapegoat relation amounts to a
denial of that relation, which is converted into an assumption of community. As a result, the dominant group is no longer positioned as being able
to *offer* (or refuse) participation to the noise-making other (a positioning
that effectively retains the structure of dominance and subordination,
and with it, since the offer is inevitably made on the terms of the dominant group, the likelihood of assimilation). Instead, it is the dominant
group that is *invited* to participate in a community of which the other is
already a fully participating member.

It is in this way that so-called 'special interests' could present themselves as the matters of general concern that they are without falling into
either of the traps opened up by the false dichotomy of 'equality' and 'difference.' That is, they would retain and even foreground their difference,
while indicating with utmost clarity that it is not the kind of difference

that makes a difference in the sense of marking out certain people for scapegoating, but the kind of difference that characterizes 'equal' partners in a discourse community.

Obviously, the invitation in Bartlett's 'we' is unlikely to be immediately, universally, or readily accepted. It will be heard most strongly at the border. But an invitation is a performative that is difficult to ignore; and the point would be to issue the invitation and to see who does respond to it and what kinds of recognitions it attracts; for *there* would be at least the beginnings of a political alliance that could be profited from for as long as it would hold and as far as it would go. Alliance politics, as the politics of community, need not and indeed cannot be an all-or-nothing affair; as the negotiation of differences, it is not a zero-sum game in which one either wins or loses. It is inevitably a politics of communication in which history is made, not by victories and defeats, but by the diplomacy of confrontation and accommodation, that is, by the simple recognition that differences are not absolute, and that others are therefore potential partners just as partners are potential others.

Such negotiations and confrontations, as I have stressed, themselves imply othering and the back-grounding of a mediator, according to the logic of the excluded third identified by Serres. But whereas the politics of 'cultural identity' is a scapegoating politics that functions to background the mediator and to *forget* the mediation that constitutes the scapegoating community *as* a community, the politics of community as an anti-scapegoating tactic has to be one that everywhere and at all times *remembers* that communities are made by mediation, that differences are therefore crucial to the constitution of communities, and that no differences can be so absolute as to constitute the grounds of a complete exclusion from the practices of discursive communication. Even the differences that make a difference according to an ideology of 'us v. them,' if they are recognized as mediated differences, can be *re-mediated* and become those differences the negotiation of which constitutes community as a function of 'I and you' or 'us and you.'

It is knowledge of that fact that makes possible the kind of politics of community I have advocated here, and the practitioners of such a politics have no interest in themselves becoming scapegoaters. For to scapegoat the mediator of an alliance that is being constructed today is to construct a difference that makes a difference out of what can be thought of, instead, as a difference that is purely instrumental; and to do that is to alienate the other and to risk depriving oneself, therefore, of a potential ally whose partnership one might need at some time in a future coalition.

The evidence is that today's cultural other is tomorrow's companion in dialogue, communication, and community, and it is only ideological blindness ('only' ideological blindness!) that leads us to think, and to act, otherwise.[34]

NOTES

1 Angela Davis, speaking at the University of Michigan, 17 October 1991, as reported in (Jan. 1992) 65 *Agenda* [Ann Arbor].

2 I share Georges Van Den Abbeele's reservations about the word *community* and its peculiarly seductive force (see his 'Introduction' to the Miami Theory Collective's volume *Community at Loose Ends* [Minneapolis: University of Minnesota Press, 1991], ix). I employ it here without pretending to engage recent philosophical discussions, but in a sense that resonates, I believe, with the aim of the Miami group to think community as a function of difference. My framework is that of discourse theory, that is, of an understanding of communication, not as the transmission of sense but as the distribution of positions – positions of power, positions of knowledge, desiring positions – through which significance is constructed as a function of those differentially related positions, and hence, not as a matter of consensus but of – at best (when people think they agree) – what I call 'misrecognized miscommunication' and, frequently, of conflict, dissension, disagreement, negotiation, persuasion, or acquiescence.

3 Johannes Fabian, *Time and the Other* (New York: Columbia University Press, 1983).

4 See Gayatri Chakravorty Spivak, *The Postcolonial Critic: Interviews, Strategies, Dialogues*, ed. Sarah Harasym (New York: Routledge, 1990), passim.

5 Edward Said, *Orientalism* (New York: Pantheon, 1978).

6 Malek Alloula, *Le Harem colonial: Images d'un sous-érotisme* (Genève: Slatkine, 1979), translated by Myrna Godzich and Wlad Godzich as *The Colonial Harem* (Minneapolis: University of Minnesota Press, 1986).

7 David Prochaska, 'The Archive of Algérie Imaginaire,' (1990) 4 *History and Anthropology* 373 at 408. Thanks to Ali Behdad for drawing my attention to this article.

8 Eve Kosofsky Sedgwick, *Between Men: English Literature and Male Homosocial Desire* (New York: Columbia University Press, 1985).

9 In Choderlos de Laclos's novel *Les Liaisons dangereuses*, a famous letter (XXXI) is written by the rake Valmont on the back of a prostitute, Emilie, as a declaration of love to the respectable Mme de Tourvel. The message is readable, according to context, either as the description of a night of sexual turmoil

(with Emilie) or as an account of the mental and emotional agitations of love (for Mme de Tourvel). Given this indeterminacy, the novel asks which message is the true one (i.e., which context should prevail), and what is the relation between the two (i.e., in what sense and by what means they can be distinguished).

10 Gayatri Chakravorty Spivak, 'Can the Subaltern Speak?' in Lawrence Grossberg and Cary Nelson, eds., *Marxism and the Interpretation of Culture* (Urbana: University of Illinois Press, 1988), 271.

11 Michel Serres, 'Le Dialogue platonicien et la genèse intersubjective de l'abstraction,' in *Hermès, I: La Communication* (Paris: Ed. de Minuit, 1968), translated by David F. Bell as 'Platonic Dialogue,' in *Hermes: Literature, Science, Philosophy* (Baltimore: Johns Hopkins University Press, 1982), 67.

12 See, in particular, Michel Serres, *Le Parasite* (Paris: Grasset, 1980), translated by Lawrence R. Schehr as *The Parasite* (Baltimore: Johns Hopkins University Press, 1982).

13 See *Between Men*, supra n. 8.

14 See R. Howard Bloch, *Medieval Misogyny and the Invention of Western Romantic Love* (Chicago: University of Chicago Press, 1991). Bloch argues, in a way that resonates strongly with my argument here, that misogyny's 'purpose – to remove individual women from the realm of events – depends upon the transformation of women into a general category, which, internally at least, appears never to change' (50) and concludes logically that 'negative and positive fetishizations of the feminine work to identical effect' (11), that effect being to exclude women from the sphere of history.

15 Joan Wallach Scott, 'The Sears Case,' in *Gender and the Politics of History* (New York: Columbia University Press, 1988), 167–77. 'Demands for equality have rested on implicit and usually unrecognized arguments from difference; if individuals or groups were identical or the same there would be no need to ask for equality' (173).

16 Among recent eloquent appeals for a politics of alliance are Gloria Anzaldúa, *Borderlands / La Frontera: The New Mestiza* (San Francisco: Aunt Lute, 1987); and Donna Haraway, 'A Cyborg Manifesto,' in *Simians, Cyborgs and Women* (New York: Routledge, 1991), 149–81 (see esp. 173–81). From another quarter but of related interest, in spite of its rather literary focus, comes Jean Bernabé, Patrick Chamoiseau, and Raphaël Confiant, *Eloge de la créolité* (Paris: Gallimard, 1989). 'If we advise our creative artists to explore our particularity, it is because that will bring us back [from 'colonial madness'] to what is natural in the world, outside of *Sameness* and *Oneness*, and because against Universality it sets the chance for a world diffracted and recomposed, and the conscious harmonization of preserved diversities: DIVERSALITY' (54–5; my translation).

17 Jean-Luc Nancy, 'Of Being-in-Common,' in Miami Theory Collective, ed., *Community at Loose Ends*, supra n. 2 at 6. Subsequent page references appear in the text.

18 See Barbara Johnson, 'Opening Remarks,' in *The Critical Difference: Essays in the Contemporary Rhetoric of Reading* (Baltimore: Johns Hopkins University Press, 1980), x.

19 See Jacques Derrida, 'Semiology and Grammatology,' in *Positions*, translated by Alan Bass (Chicago: University of Chicago Press, 1981), 26: 'Whether in the order of spoken or written discourse, no element can function as a sign without referring to another element which itself is not simply present. This interweaving results in each 'element' – phoneme or grapheme – being constituted on the basis of the trace within it of the other elements of the chain or system ... There are only, everywhere, differences and traces of traces.'

20 My thinking in this paragraph and in my discussion of categorization in general is deeply indebted to work on genre by Anne Freadman. See initially her 'Le Genre humain (a classification)' (1986) 23 *Australian Journal of French Studies* 309; and 'Anyone for Tennis?' in Ian Reid, ed., *The Place of Genre in Learning: Current Debates* (Geelong: Deakin University, Centre for Studies in Literary Education, 1987), 91–124.

21 Trinh T. Minh-ha, 'Difference: A Special Third-World Issue,' in *Woman, Native, Other: Writing, Postcoloniality and Feminism* (Bloomington: Indiana University Press, 1989), 98: 'The West is painfully made to realize the existence of a Third World in the First World, and vice versa.'

22 I am thinking of Deborah Tannen, *You Just Don't Understand: Women and Men in Conversation* (New York: Ballantine, 1990), 17–18: 'The sociolinguistic approach frictions arise because boys and girls grow up in what are essentially different cultures, so talk between women and men is cross-cultural communication.'

23 Gregory Bateson, 'Form, Substance and Difference,' in *Steps to an Ecology of Mind* (London: Paladin, 1973), 428: 'In fact, what we mean by information – the elementary unit of information – is a difference which makes a difference ...' (I am adapting Bateson's formulation for my own purposes here.)

24 See especially René Girard, *La Violence et le sacré* (Paris: Grasset, 1972), translated by Patrick Gregory as *Violence and the Sacred* (Baltimore: Johns Hopkins University Press, 1977); and *Le Bouc émissaire* (Paris: Grasset, 1982), translated by Yvonne Freccero as *The Scapegoat* (Baltimore: Johns Hopkins University Press, 1986).

25 See Ross Chambers, 'Fables of the Go-Between,' to appear in the Proceedings of the ASPACLS Conference held in July, 1991, at Monash University, Melbourne (Australia).

26 See Eve Kosofsky Sedgwick, *Epistemology of the Closet* (Berkeley: University of California Press, 1990), esp. 145–54. 'Snobbism, as René Girard points out, can be discussed and attributed only by snobs, who are always right about it except in their own disclaimers to it. The same is true of the phenomenon of "the sentimental" as a whole and of its other manifestations such as prurience and morbidity. *Honi soit qui mal y pense* is both the watchword and the structural principle of sentimentality-attribution' (152). (The reference is to René Girard, *Deceit, Desire and the Novel* [Baltimore: Johns Hopkins University Press, 1966], 72–3.)

27 Theoretically speaking, the work of Trinh T. Minh-ha, and particularly her concept of the 'inappropriate(d),' has been seminal in this respect, although the initial critique was made by a number of women of colour. See Cherríe Moraga and Gloria Anzaldúa, eds., *This Bridge to Break My Back: Writings by Radical Women of Color*, 2d ed. (New York: Kitchen Table, 1983); and Gloria Anzaldúa, ed., *Making Face, Making Soul. Haciendo Caras: Creative and Critical Perspectives by Women of Color* (San Francisco: Aunt Lute Foundation, 1990).

28 See Alice Jardine and Paul Smith, eds., *Men in Feminism* (New York: Methuen, 1987).

29 Evidence that it is imaginable is in Samuel R. Delaney's novel, *Stars in My Pocket like Grains of Sand* (New York: Bantam, 1984). In the universe of the future, only the pronoun 'she' is used, regardless of gender. 'He' is used, also regardless of gender, only when there is sexual desire for the person referred to.

30 See especially 'The Beast in the Closet: Henry James and the Writing of Homosexual Panic,' in *Epistemology of the Closet*, supra n. 26, 182–212.

31 Neil Bartlett, *Who Was That Man? A Present for Mr. Oscar Wilde* (London: Serpent's Tail, 1988). Subsequent page references appear in the text.

32 See Gloria Anzaldúa, ed., *Making Face, Making Soul*, supra n. 27, xv–xvi. Anzaldúa stresses also the oppositional connotations of the expression 'making faces,' 'haciendo caras.'

33 In a way that exactly replicates the mechanisms of assignment of identity that I am trying to unsettle in this essay, the question of the *positioning of discourse* has tended to become confused, in many areas of contemporary critical practice, with the issue of the *identity of the author* (in terms, most particularly, of gender, class, race, ethnicity, and orientation), an identity that has become associated in turn with an *effect of rhetoric*, the style – 'personal' or 'impersonal' – of the discourse. 'Remember,' writes Trinh T. Minh-ha with irony, 'the *minor*-ity's voice is always personal, that of the *major*-ity always impersonal' (*Woman, Native, Other*, supra n. 21, 29). The concepts of writing (as opposed to voice or style) and of subjectivity (as opposed to personal identity) might as well never have been invented. But the consequence, for an essay such as this, is an insol-

uble dilemma: it cannot rhetorically indicate its political affinities by 'getting personal' without confirming the structure of power that reifies 'minority' identity as 'personal'; it cannot remain 'impersonal,' however, without producing its voice as that of the dominant discourse of which the essay's primary audience is understandably inclined to be suspicious. ('Getting personal' refers to Nancy K. Miller, *Getting Personal: Feminist Occasions and Other Autobiographical Acts* [New York and London: Routledge, 1991].) Possibly the positioning of discourse is best approached as a function of intertext (which prior discourses does it appropriate or contest?), of address (how does it define an appropriate audience?), and – determining the first two – of reception and uptake (how is it read and to what further discourse does it give rise?). If so, it is in its address that this essay strikes me as being most deficient: an essay promoting a politics of invitation ought itself to be less explanatory and more invitational – reminiscent more of party-giving than of lecturing.

34 The idea of this essay emerged in dinner-table conversations with Ali Behdad and Laura Pérez, and it has benefited from their criticisms, of which, however, I have unfortunately not been able to take full account here (they will show their effects in later work). Each in different ways and for different reasons is reserved about my general argument and sceptical about the thesis of part 3. But I realize in retrospect that what the essay is most deeply about is the cordiality of the discussions in which Ali, Laura, and I confront our different positions. It is an attempt to begin the task of understanding both the conditions of possibility of that cordiality and the way in which our tiny cultural group – only *some* of the differences of which can be deduced from our names – might be thought paradigmatic of larger communities. I cannot thank them warmly enough for their friendship.

Reconceiving Rights as Relationship[1]

JENNIFER NEDELSKY

In adopting the *Charter of Rights and Freedoms*, Canada chose to make 'rights' a central and permanent part of its political discourse just when the meaning and legitimacy of judicial review and, more generally, of 'rights talk' was increasingly contested among legal scholars. Of course, one might see these contests as an arcane scholarly preoccupation, since the invocation of rights can be heard in North America in every sphere from self-help groups to environmentalists and is a growing practice worldwide. But I think there are problems with rights that we ought to take seriously. In this essay, I identify a set of problems with how we are to understand the meaning of 'rights' and to institutionalize those understandings. The problems fall into two broad categories: justifying the constitutionalization of rights; and the critiques of 'rights talk' in general. In response to each problem, I will suggest how a central tenet of feminist theory, its focus on relationship, directs us towards solutions. My primary focus is on the constitutional sphere, for which I propose a conception of constitutionalism as a 'dialogue of democratic accountability' that provides a better model than rights as 'trumps.'[2] I will not enter the debate about whether it was a good idea to adopt a charter at all, but I will suggest that the structure of the Canadian *Charter* lends itself to a constructive approach to rights as relationship. In closing, I will try to show how this framework helps us to better understand a set of specific constitutional problems.

Justifying Constitutional Rights

Rights as Collective Choices

Let us begin with the powerful American conception of constitutional rights, so that we can see the need for an alternative paradigm. The notion that there are certain basic rights that no government, no matter how democratic, should be able to violate is a basic idea behind the U.S. Constitution and its institution of judicial review.[3] But the simple, compelling clarity of this idea is difficult to sustain in modern times. The framers of the U.S. Constitution did not worry much about whether there were such basic rights and what they were. The framers were even sure that although there was no consensus on what constituted the violation of rights such as property, *they* knew what property rights really were and what kind of legislation would violate them. Their confidence was the foundation for their vision of constitutionalism. Today, however, we have before us two hundred years of the vicissitudes of rights jurisprudence in the United States: for example, neither property nor equality looks today like it did in 1787. It is hard to believe in timeless values with immutable content. We have disputes about rights at every level: whether natural rights are the source of our legal rights; what would count as basic among a list of rights; and whether there is any value in using the term 'rights' at all. My own view is that it is useful to use the term, and in any case we are institutionally committed to doing so. But if we are to invoke rights to constrain democratic outcomes, we must do so in a way that is true to the essentially contested and shifting meaning of rights.

We need to confront the history of rights and acknowledge the changes that have taken place in both popular and legal understandings of rights. Consider, for example, our understanding of equality. It was not so long ago that great restrictions on both the legal rights and the actual opportunities for women were widely (though I am sure not unanimously) believed to be consistent with a basic commitment to equality for all. And the changes do not exist only at the level of big general terms like 'equality.' Consider the changes in common law conceptions of contract between the mid-nineteenth century and today. At the popular level, we have come to expect constraints on individual contracts such as minimum wage legislation, and in the courts we continue to work out concepts of unjustifiable enrichment and unconscionability in ways that would have been hard to imagine at the turn of the century. These shifts are not just a matter of the past history of conflicts, now long since settled. A workable conception of rights needs to take account of the depth of the ongoing disagreement in Canadian society about, for example, the meaning of equality and how it is to fit with our contemporary – and contested – understanding of the market economy and its legal foundations, property and contract.

Once we acknowledge the mutability of basic values, the problem of protecting them from democratic abuse is transformed. We do not have to abandon the basic insight that democracy can threaten individual rights, but we need to reconsider all of those terms: democracy, individual rights, and the nature of the tension between them. First we must see that the problem of defending individual rights is inseparable from the problem of defining them. Even if there are deep, immutable truths underlying the shifting perceptions of the terms that capture those truths, the ongoing problem of defining the terms remains. And then the relation to democracy becomes more complex, for the definition of rights, as well as the potentially threatening legislation, is the product of shifting collective choice.[4]

We find that the neat characterization of constitutionalism as balancing a tension between democracy and individual rights is not adequate for the actual problem. As a society that gives voice and effect to its collective choices and values through government institutions, both the courts and the legislatures[5] must be seen as expressing those choices and values. Courts have traditionally expressed those shifting collective choices in terms of rights, but we must recognize rights to be just that: terms for capturing and giving effect to what judges perceive to be the values and choices that 'society' has embedded in the 'law.' (Here I am being deliberately vague as to how values come to be seen to be basic to the legal system, and which components of 'society' end up affecting the choice of values.) Consider, for example, the choices between the right to use one's property as one wishes and the competing values of the right to quiet enjoyment. Judges make those choices, whether they think of them as dictated by the basic values of the common law, or as reflecting the choices already made by 'society at large' as expressed through custom and common acceptance, or as guided by the best interest of all. Other examples are judicial decisions about the conflicts that arise over the importance of environmental health, or the 'rights' of tenants to heat and safety.

My first point, then, in seeing the hidden complexity of 'rights v. democracy' is that rights are as much collective choices as laws passed by the legislature. And if rights no longer look so distinct from democratic outcomes, democracy also blurs into rights, for, of course, democracy is not merely a matter of collective choice, but the expression of 'rights' to an equal voice in the determination of those collective choices.

The problem of constitutionalism thus can no longer simply be protecting rights from democracy. The more complex problem can be posed in various ways, with either rights or collective choice on both sides of the 'balance': why should some rights (such as freedom of conscience) limit other rights, namely the rights to have collective choices made democratically? Or, why do we think that some collective choices, that is, those we constitutionalize as rights, should limit other collective choices, that is, the outcomes of ordinary democratic processes?[6] Since the idea of a 'limit' is itself problematic, I think a more helpful way to put it is this: we need a new way of understanding the source and content of the values against which we measure democratic outcomes. Later, I will offer an example of how a conception of rights as relationship helps in this process, by looking at the question of why property should *not* be constitutionalized. First, however, I want to look more closely at some of the prevalent objections to constitutional rights as violations of democratic principles.

Beyond the 'Pure Democracy' Critique

The pure democracy critique is primarily aimed at rights as judicially enforced limits on democratic outcomes (rather than 'rights talk' more generally, which might include common law rights or statutory rights). The argument comes in two forms. One rejects any judicial oversight of democratic bodies. The underlying claim can be that, in principle, there are no rights claims that can legitimately stand against democratic outcomes, or that there is no justifiable way of enforcing such claims, or that, in practice, the best way of ensuring rights in the long run is through democratic procedures, not through efforts to circumvent them. The more common form of the argument acknowledges that even if democracy is accepted as the sole or supreme value of a political system, there may be times when the courts can play a useful role in making sure the procedural conditions of democracy are met. John Hart Ely[7] in the United States and to some extent Patrick Monahan in Canada defend judicial review in these terms, and each claims that the constitution in his country[8] authorizes judicial review primarily or exclusively for democracy-enhancing purposes.

My view is that democracy has never been the sole or even primary value of either the United States or Canada, and it *could* never be the sole basis for a good society. There have been and always will be other values that are not derivative from democracy. Autonomy is one. The development of our spiritual nature is another, captured by notions of freedom of conscience and religion.[9] And, of course, these values can be threatened by democratic majorities wielding the power of the state. If one accepts that there are values we cherish for reasons other than their relevance to the functioning of democracy and that these values may need protection from democratic outcomes, then neither form of the pure democracy critique of rights is persuasive.[10] However, as I have already suggested, the conventional formulations of rights as limits to democracy are not adequate. Fortunately, I think it is possible to do a better job of capturing the multiple values we care about. If we look more deeply at a value like autonomy, we can begin to see that the value itself is best understood in terms of relationship, and once we see that, we can begin to rethink what it means conceptually and institutionally for autonomy to serve as a measure of democratic outcomes.

First let me contrast my conception of autonomy[11] with the kind of vision that I think underlies the American conception of rights as limits. (I also think that this conception has deep roots in Anglo-American liberalism, more broadly.) There the idea is that rights are barriers that protect the individual from intrusion by other individuals or by the state. Rights define boundaries others cannot cross, and it is those boundaries, enforced by the law, that ensure individual freedom and autonomy. This image of rights fits well with the idea that the essence of autonomy is independence, which thus requires protection and separation from others. My argument is that this is a deeply misguided view of autonomy. What makes autonomy possible is not separation, but relationship.

This approach shifts the focus from protection against others to structuring relationships so that they foster autonomy. Some of the most basic presuppositions about autonomy shift: dependence is no longer the antithesis of autonomy but a precondition in the relationships – between parent and child, student and teacher, state and citizen – which provide the security, education, nurturing, and support that make the development of autonomy possible. Further, autonomy is not a static quality that is simply achieved one day. It is a capacity that requires ongoing relationships that help it flourish; it can wither or thrive throughout one's adult life. Interdependence becomes the central fact of political life, not an issue to be shunted to the periphery in the basic question of how to ensure individual autonomy in the inevitable face of collective power. The human interactions to be governed are not seen primarily in terms of the clashing of rights and interests, but in terms of the way patterns of relationship can develop and sustain both an enriching collective life and the scope for genuine individual autonomy. The whole conception of the relation between the individual and the collective shifts: we recognize that the collective is a source of autonomy as well as a threat to it.

The constitutional protection of autonomy is then no longer an effort to carve out a sphere into which the collective cannot intrude, but a means of structuring the relations between individuals and the sources of collective power so that autonomy is fostered rather than undermined.[12] The first thing to note in this reformulation is that it becomes clear that the relation between autonomy and democracy is not simply one of threat and tension – just as the relation between autonomy and the collective is not simply a matter of threat. Autonomy means literally self-governance and thus requires the capacity to participate in collective as well as individual governance. In addition, the long-standing argument in favour of democracy is that it is the best way of organizing collective power so that it will foster the well-being, which must include the autonomy, of all. So autonomy demands democracy, as both component and a means – even though democracy can threaten autonomy. (And, of course, the ideals of democracy require autonomous citizens, so that each expresses her own rather than another's judgments, values, and interests.)

With this relationship-focused starting point, how do we move beyond 'rights as limits to democratic outcomes'? We shift our focus from limits, barriers, and boundaries to a dialogue of democratic accountability – which does not make the mistake of treating democracy as the sole value. We require two things for this dialogue. We need a mechanism, an institutionalized process, of articulating basic values – particularly those that are not derivative from democracy – which is itself consistent with democracy; and we need ways of continually asking whether our institutions of democratic decision-making are generating outcomes consistent with those values, or, to stick with the autonomy example, of asking whether those outcomes foster the structures of social relations that make the development of autonomy possible. This mechanism for holding governments accountable to basic values should take the form of institutional dialogue that reflects and respects the democratic source and shifting content of those values. (Of course, judicial review has for a long time in the United States and recently in Canada been the primary vehicle for the articulation of values against which democratic outcomes can be measured. I will return at the end to a proposal for such a mechanism that is significantly different from judicial review.)

The example of autonomy as relation already helps solve one of the puzzles of justifying rights as limits: how to justify their supremacy over democracy when rights themselves are shifting values. First we no longer have, and thus need no longer justify, simple supremacy, but a more complex structure of democratic accountability to basic values. Second, the shifting quality of those basic values makes more sense when our focus is on the structure of relations that fosters those values. It is not at all surprising that what it takes to foster autonomy, or what is likely to undermine it, in an industrialized corporate economy with an active regulatory-welfare state is quite different from the relationships that would have had those effects in mid-nineteenth-century Canada. These may be different still in Eastern Europe or South Africa. A focus on relationship automatically turns our attention to context, and makes sense of the commonly held beliefs that there are some basic human values *and* that how we articulate and foster those values varies tremendously over time and place.

In this vision, rights do not 'trump' democratic outcomes, and so they and the institutions that protect them do not have to bear a weight of justification that is impossible to muster. Rather, when we begin with a focus on the relationships that constitute and make possible the basic values, which we use rights language to capture, then we have a better understanding not only of rights, but of how they relate to another set of values, for which we use the shorthand 'democracy.' The mechanisms for institutionalizing both sets of values must aim at maintaining an ongoing dialogue that recognizes the ways democracy and autonomy are linked together as values that require each other *and* potentially can be in conflict with one another.

It will probably have already become apparent to many readers that the Canadian *Charter* is much better suited to implementing such a dialogue than the American system of judicial review, for which, at least formally, 'rights as trumps' is an accurate metaphor. The *Charter*'s 'override' provision in s. 33 may be seen as an effort to create a dialogue about the meaning of rights that would take place in public debate, the legislature, and the courts.[13] Section 1 invites a dialogue internal to the courts, or to any body considering the constitutionality of a law, by opening the *Charter* with an assertion that rights are not to be seen as absolute.[14] Legislatures are to be held accountable to the basic rights outlined in the *Charter*, but that accountability must be determined in light of the (implicitly shifting) needs of a free and democratic society.

Perhaps some readers have had occasion to try to explain s. 1 and s. 33 to incredulous Americans – who usually conclude that Canadians simply still do not *really* have constitutional rights. The vision of rights as trump-like limits is so central to their understanding of constitutionalism that American's have a hard time imagining that 'rights' could mean anything else. This is true despite the fact that the increasingly obvious problems with this notion drive American scholars to produce thousands of pages each year in efforts to explain and defend it. Rights as trumps is a catchy phrase and an apparently graspable, even appealing, concept, but it cannot capture the complex relations between the multiple values we actually care about. I think 'dialogue of democratic accountability,' though not quite as pithy, is truer both to the best aspirations of constitutionalism and to the structure of the *Charter.*

Critiques of 'Rights Talk'

Let me turn now to some of the critiques of 'rights talk' in general: (1) 'rights' are undesirably individualistic; (2) rights obfuscate the real political issues; (3) rights serve to alienate and distance people from one another. I will not be trying to present these critiques in detail, but merely to sketch them to show how a focus on relationship helps construct a response.

I will begin with the claim that rights talk is hopelessly individualistic, which my argument above has already begun to address. Of course, I am not going to try here to summarize the ongoing communitarian versus liberal individualism debate – which, in any case, is only one form of the critique of individualism.[15] Let me simply note the core of the critique that I find persuasive (and have participated in myself) and then suggest how rights as relationship helps to meet it. The charge that *Charter* rights express individualistic values will be familiar to many – for example, in arguments about why they should not apply to the collective decisions of First Nations. There are good reasons to believe that the *Charter* draws on a powerful legacy of liberal political thought in which rights are associated with a highly individualistic conception of humanity ('mankind' historically, and there are persuasive arguments that link this gender specificity with individualism[16] – but I cannot go into that here). Indeed, the 'rights bearing individual' may be said to be the basic subject of liberal political thought. Now, to compress many long, complicated, and different arguments into a sentence or two, what is wrong with this individualism is that it fails to account for the ways in which our essential humanity is neither possible nor comprehensible without the network of relationships of which it is a part. It is not just that people live in groups and have to interact with each other – after all, liberal rights theory is all about specifying the entitlements of people when they come in conflict with one another. The anti-individualism theorists claim that we are literally constituted by the relationships of which we are a part.[17] Virtually all these theorists also recognize some significant degree of choice and control over how these relationships shape us. But even our capacity to exercise this choice can and should be understood as shaped by our relationships – hence my argument about the centrality of relationship for autonomy. Most conventional liberal rights theories, by contrast, do not make relationship central to their understanding of the human subject. Mediating conflict is the focus, not mutual self-creation and sustenance. The selves to be protected by rights are seen as essentially separate and not creatures whose interests, needs, and capacities routinely intertwine. Thus one of the reasons women have always fit so poorly into the framework of liberal theory is that it becomes obviously awkward to think of women's relation to their children as *essentially* one of competing interests to be mediated by rights. So, it is not that I think the concerns about the individualism associated with rights are unjustified. Rather, it is my hope that the notion of rights can be rescued from its historical association with individualistic theory and practice. Human beings are *both* essentially individual and essentially social creatures. The liberal tradition has been not so much wrong as seriously and dangerously one-sided in its emphasis.

What I have tried to do elsewhere, and just alluded to here, is to take the concept of autonomy and identify its core elements – which, of course, are connected to our sense of ourselves as distinct individuals – and to see how these elements themselves are best understood as developing in the context of relationship. Here I have used autonomy as an example of a value that is not derivative from democracy and to which democratic decision-making should be held accountable. Now I want to suggest that all rights, and the very concept of rights, are best understood in terms of relationship. Again, I will be quickly condensing a much longer argument, so that we can move on to see how this conception of rights meets the critiques and helps us with concrete problems.

In brief, what rights in fact do and have always done is construct relationships – of power, of responsibility, of trust, of obligation. This is as true of the law of property and contract as it is of areas like family law in which the law obviously structures relationships. For example, as lawyers know, property rights are not primarily about things, but about people's relation to each other as they affect and are affected by things.[18] The rights that the law enforces stipulate limits on what we can do with things depending on how our action affects others (for example, nuisance), when we can withhold access to things from others and how we can use that power to withhold to get them to do what we want (we are now into the realm of contract), and what responsibilities we have with respect to others' well-being (for example, tort law and landlord-tenant law). The law also defines fiduciary relationships. It defines particular relationships of trust and the responsibilities they entail. In the realm of contract, the law takes account of relationships of unequal bargaining power, and it defines certain parameters of employment and of landlord-tenant relationships. In deciding on the importance to give instances of reliance, judges must make choices about the pattern of responsibility and trust the law will foster.

I run through this list only to make it easier to think about my claim that in defining and enforcing rights, the law routinely structures and sometimes self-consciously takes account of relationship. What I propose is that this reality of relationship in rights become the central focus of the concept itself, and thus of all discussion of what should be treated as rights, how they should be enforced, and how they should be interpreted. It is really a matter of bringing to the foreground of our attention what has always been the background reality. My claim is that we will do a better job of making all these difficult decisions involving rights if we focus on the kind of relationships that we actually want to foster and how different concepts and institutions will best contribute to that fostering. I hope my closing examples will give a better sense of this.

My point here is that once rights are conceptualized in terms of the relationships they structure, the problem of individualism is at least radically transformed. There will almost certainly still be people who *want* the kind of relationships of power and limited responsibility that the individualistic liberal rights tradition promotes and justifies. But at least the debate will take place in terms of why we think some patterns of human relationships are better than others and what sort of 'rights' will foster them.

Suppose we have some initial agreement about what we think optimal human autonomy would look like. We could then proceed beyond conclusory claims that autonomy requires individual rights to a close look at what really fosters the human capacity for autonomy and in what ways the relationships involved can be promoted and protected by legally enforced 'rights.' For example, I have looked at how administrative law can be understood as protecting rights in this sense and how we can structure our provision of public services so that they foster autonomy-enhancing relationships.[19] I think all of the traditionally cherished individual rights such as freedom of conscience, of speech, and of 'life, liberty, and security of the person' can most constructively be understood in these terms. It is extremely unlikely that any of them would, under this form of analysis, appear unnecessary. They would thus not disappear. They would not be swamped or overturned by the claims of community. Indeed in constitutional terms their function would still be to stand as an independent measure of the legitimacy of collective decisions (though the determination of that legitimacy would be a process of dialogue, not a one-shot, trumplike decision). However, the specific meaning of each right would probably be transformed as people deliberated on the patterns of relationship that they wanted to characterize their society.

Rights debated in terms of relationship seem to me to overcome most of the problems of individualism without destroying what is valuable in that tradition. Of course, when dealing with such an old and powerful tradition, one has to be ever on guard against the conventional meanings of long-standing terms insinuating themselves back into the conversation. But since I think we do not have the option to simply drop the term 'rights,' and because I think it can be used constructively, that vigilance is the price we will have to pay.

Finally, I will just offer brief suggestions about how this approach can meet the diverse body of criticism (often associated with critical legal studies) that I have lumped into my second category of objection to 'rights talk' as obfuscating. One of the most important parts of this set of critiques is the objection that when 'rights' are central to political debate, they misdirect political energies because they obscure rather than clarify what is at issue, what people are really after. As with the objection of individualism, this critique points to serious problems, but those problems are transformed when we understand rights as structuring relationships.

I think it is in fact the case that many rights claims, such as 'it's *my* property,' have a conclusory quality. They are meant to end, not to open up, debate. As is probably clear by now, I am sympathetic to the idea that, whether the issue is a plant-closing, or an environmentally hazardous development project, or a person who wants to rent a room in her home only to people with whom she feels comfortable, simply invoking property rights does not help, and in some circumstances can hurt – by treating as settled what should be debated. That is only the case, however, if the meaning of property rights is taken as self-evident, or if the right questions are not asked in determining their meaning.

If we approach property rights as one of the most important vehicles for structuring relations of power in our society and as a means of expressing the relations of responsibility we want to encourage, we will start off the debate in a useful way. For example, if we ask whether ownership of a factory should entail some responsibility to those it employs and how to balance that responsibility with the freedom to use one's property as one wishes (a balance analogous to that in traditional nuisance law), then we can intelligently pursue the inevitable process of defining and redefining property. We can ask what relationships of power, responsibility, trust, and commitment we want the terms of ownership of productive property to foster, and we can also ask whether those relationships will foster the autonomy, creativity, or initiative that we value. By contrast, to say that owners can shut down a plant whenever and however they want because it is their property, is either to assert a tautology (property *means* the owner has this power) or a historical claim (property has in the past had this meaning). The historical claim does, of course, have special relevance in law, but it can only be the beginning not the end of the inquiry into what property should mean. The focus on relationship will help to give proper weight and context to the historical claims and to expose the tautological ones.

One common form of the allegation of obfuscation is the objection that rights are 'reified.' They appear as fixed entities, whose meaning is simply taken as a given. This thing-like quality of rights prevents the recognition of the ways in which rights are collective choices which require evaluation. Descriptively, I think this is a valid concern about the dominant traditions of rights. But, as is no doubt already clear, I do not think it is inevitable. I think that if we always remember that what rights do is structure relationships, and if we interpret them in that light, and make decisions about what ought to be called rights in that light, then we will not only loosen up the existing reification, but our new conceptions of rights as relationship are not as likely to once again harden into reified images that dispel rather than invite inquiry.

Finally, there is the important critique that rights are alienating and distancing, that they express and create barriers between people.[20] Rights have this distancing effect in part because, as they function in our current discourse, they help us avoid seeing some of the relationships of which we are in fact a part. For example, when we see homeless people on the street, we do not think about the fact that it is in part our regime of property rights that renders them homeless. We do not bring to consciousness what we in fact take for granted: our sense of our property rights in our homes permits us to exclude the homeless persons. Indeed, our sense that we have not done anything wrong, that we have not violated the homeless persons' rights, helps us to distance ourselves from their plight. The dominant conception of rights helps us to feel that we are not responsible.

If we come to focus on the relationships that our rights structure, we will see the connection between our power to exclude and the homeless persons' plight. We might still decide to maintain that right of exclusion, but the decision would be made in full consciousness of the pattern of relationships it helps to shape. And I think we are likely to experience our responsibilities differently as we recognize that our 'private rights' always have social consequences.[21]

Thus my response to the critique of distancing is that rights conceived as relationship will not foster the same distancing that our current conception does. Rights *could*, however, still serve the protective function that thoughtful advocates of rights-based distance, like Patricia Williams,[22] are concerned about. Not only does my vision of rights as relationship have equal respect at its core, but optimal structures of human relations will always provide both choice about entering relationships and space for the choice to withdraw.[23]

These, then, are the outlines of my responses to the critiques of 'rights-talk' as individualistic, obfuscating, and alienating. Before going on to my constitutional examples, let me reiterate what is and what is not novel about my approach. It is important to my argument to claim that thinking about rights as relationship offers a new and better way of resolving a set of problems about rights. But part of what I think makes the argument compelling is that it is not in fact a radical departure from what is currently entailed in legal decision-making, including judicial decision-making. As my earlier examples were intended to show, the novelty lies only in bringing into focus what has always been in the background.

It is important to recognize the *existing* role of relationship in rights in order to see that what I am proposing can happen immediately, without the radical restructuring of our legal system. It is also important to meet the objection that what I am calling for dangerously expands – or creates – a policy-making role for judges. My argument is that recognizing rights as relationship only brings to consciousness, and thus open to considered reflection and debate, what already exists. Here I join a growing chorus of voices that urge that judges will do a better job if they are self-conscious about what they are doing, even if that new self-consciousness seems very demanding.[24]

Applying 'Rights as Relationship'

I turn now finally to my sketches of how my approach helps with some specific problems. I begin with the question of whether property belongs in the *Charter*. This question has the virtue of making more concrete the abstract question I began with of how we are to understand the idea of constitutionalizing rights. Once we acknowledge that constitutional rights are collective choices, we not only make the simple 'democracy v. rights' formulation untenable, we make it a great deal more difficult (or we make it more obvious why it is difficult) to explain why some things we call rights (like freedom of speech or conscience) should be constitutionalized in my dialogue of democratic accountability and others, like property, should not.

My idea of constitutionalism is to make democracy accountable to basic values, to have mechanisms of ongoing dialogue about whether the collective choices people make through their democratic assemblies are consistent with their deepest values. Now there is a certain irony to this idea of 'deepest values' as what constitutionalism protects. When we choose to constitutionalize a value, to treat it as a constitutional right, we are in effect saying both that there is a deeply shared consensus about the importance of that value and that we think that value is at risk, that the same people who value it are likely to violate it through their ordinary political processes. Now, in fact, I think his ironic duality makes sense. There are lots of values like that. Once we recognize the duality, we know that it is not a sufficient argument *against* constitutionalizing a right either to say that it is contested and so does not belong in a charter of rights and freedoms or to say it is so well accepted that it does not need to be in such a charter. Of course, those are both arguments one might make about property.

I think that in Canada, and probably more generally in constitutional democracies, the fundamental premise of constitutional rights is equality. Constitutional rights define the entitlements that *all* members of society must have, the basic shared terms that will make it possible not just to flourish as individuals, but to relate to each other on equal terms. (Which is not to say that the values we protect constitutionally – autonomy, privacy, liberty, security – are themselves identical to or derivative from equality.) Now this sounds at first perilously close to the basic notion of liberal theory: that people are to be conceived of as rights-bearing individuals, who are equal precisely in their role as rights-bearers, abstracted from any of the concrete particulars, such as gender, age, class, and abilities, which render them unequal. This conception has been devastatingly criticized by feminist scholars such as Iris Young.[25] My notion is subtly, but I think crucially, different. The question of equality (to be captured in constitutional rights) is the meaning of equal moral worth *given* the reality that in almost every conceivable concrete way we are not equal, but vastly different, and vastly unequal in our needs and abilities. The object is not to make these differences disappear when we talk about equal rights, but to ask how we can structure relations of equality among people with many different concrete inequalities.

The law will in large part determine (or give effect to choices about) which differences matter and in what way: which will be the source of advantage, power, and privilege, and which will be the source of disadvantage, powerlessness, and subordination. One might say that whatever the patterns of privilege and disadvantage the ordinary political and legal processes may generate, the purpose of equal constitutional rights is to structure relations so that people treat each other with a basic respect, acknowledge and foster each other's dignity, even as they acknowledge and respect differences. Constitutional rights define indicia of respect and requirements for dignity – including rights of participation. Constitutional rights define basic ways we must treat each other as equals as we make our collective choices.

Property fits very awkwardly here. It is, at least in the sorts of market economies we are familiar with, the primary source of *inequality*. Of course, formally, everyone who *has* property has the same rights with respect to it. Nevertheless, property is the primary vehicle for the allocation of power from state to citizen, and in market economies, the presumption has been that that power must and should be distributed unequally – for purposes of efficiency and prosperity and, on some arguments, merit as well. The result, of course, is an ongoing tension between the inequality of power generated by property through the market and the claims of equal rights. We see this, for example, in debates over free speech and access to the media, in campaign spending debates, and, as I will note shortly, in arguments for a social charter.

All of this suggests to me that debates over the meaning of property, over the kinds of power that should be allocated to individuals and the limits on that power (as in my earlier examples of landlord-tenant law, environmental regulation, and minimum wage law) should be part of the ongoing vigorous debate of the most popularly accessible bodies, the legislative assemblies.

There is another, more straightforward, argument against constitutionalizing property: property is really a second-order value, it is a *means* to the higher values we do treat as constitutional rights – life, liberty, and security of the person. It does not really belong up there, treated as a comparable value. This is one more reason why, in the end, property should be held accountable to equality, not vice versa – as would inevitably happen if property were constitutionalized.

We already have in the *Charter* the values we really care about. So much of ordinary governmental decision-making has an impact on property that it becomes extremely awkward and artificial to determine which of these impacts ought to be described as a violation of property rights.[26]

What we really want to know is when the impact amounts to an infringement of one of the basic values that *is* in the *Charter* – most likely liberty or security. For example, arbitrary or punitive confiscations without compensation would surely be deemed to be an infringement on security of the person not in accordance with fundamental justice. We cannot in fact feel secure or free among our fellow citizens, nor can we feel as though we can count on being treated as an equal, worthy of equal respect, if we feel that we may at any time be capriciously deprived of our material possessions. That kind of insecurity would destroy relations of trust, confidence, and equality necessary for a free and democratic society.

This leads me directly into my second example. If property is not in the *Charter,* how do we determine when impacts on property or economic interests amount to violations of liberty or security of the person. Of course, in the space remaining, I will do no more than indicate the ways I think a focus on relationship will help.

Take, for example, the British Columbia doctors' case, *Wilson* v. *Medical Services Commission.*[27] In an attempt to make sure that all areas of the province were adequately provided with medical care, the province decided to restrict the number of doctors to whom it would provide billing numbers in popular areas like Vancouver. In effect, doctors could not practise wherever they wished. Does this amount to an infringement of liberty? Suppose we begin by looking at the network of relationships in which these doctors are embedded – public funding for medical schools, hospitals, and their salaries (hence the problem in the first place). We should then consider more broadly the interdependencies we already formally recognize in a wide variety of schemes that limit access to jobs ranging from chicken farming to taxi driving. Of course, constraints on one's livelihood are serious constraints and come close to our understanding of liberty. But we cannot view any case, like the doctors, in isolation. The relationships in society will be different depending on how much scope for individual choice we allow, and how much we constrain that choice by notions of mutual responsibility. In any given case, we have to ask whether the alleged infringement is designed to foster or enforce social responsibility in ways consistent with other forms of social responsibility in Canada. Or is the infringement unnecessary, arbitrary, or gratuitous? Of course, consistency with other policies might not itself be sufficient. We could ask if the network of mutual responsibility seems to be drawing such a tight net that we cannot imagine those relationships being conducive to individual autonomy (having recognized, of course, that autonomy is not a matter of *independence*, but of interdependent relationships that foster it). I will not go into any more detail here, beyond saying that I think in this example, as in others, the difference a focus on relationship makes is not stark, but subtle. Many of the questions sound familiar and can be generated by other frameworks, but I think the emphasis will be different. Our attention will be drawn to different matters, and the overall result will be better.

Finally, a brief note on what could easily be the subject of another essay – the *Alternative Social Charter* put forward by a coalition of anti-poverty groups during the recent round of constitutional negotiations.[28] There are two basic connections with my theme. First, the *ASC* is an effort to carry through a vision of what it would take for all members of Canadian society to be full, equal participants, to be truly treated with equal respect and dignity. I think the *ASC* grows out of an awareness of the ways the relations of disadvantage in Canada currently preclude that full equality.[29] Conventional rights theory can blind one to the impact of disadvantage. Rights as relationship brings it to the forefront of our attention.

Perhaps most importantly for my purposes here, the *ASC* comes with an extremely attractive form of my dialogue of democratic accountability: a tribunal that is an alternative to the courts as a mechanism for maintaining this dialogue. The tribunal would hear selected complaints alleging infringements 'that are systemic or that have systemic impact on vulnerable or disadvantaged groups and their members.'[30] It would have wide authority to review federal and provincial legislation, regulation, and policies, and to order the government to take appropriate measures or ask it to report back with measures taken or proposed. However, the order 'shall not come into effect until the House of Commons or the relevant legislature has sat for at least five weeks, during which time the decision may be overridden by a simple majority vote of that legislature or parliament.'[31]

This is an imaginative effort to meet the concerns about courts having the power to enforce rights which would often involve the commitment of public funds. This proposal (unlike the one included in the Beaudoin-Dobbie report from the all-party committee of Parliament)[32] would provide an important enforcement mechanism, while giving the final word to the primary forum for democratic decision-making, the legislatures. It seems a promising mechanism for initiating an ongoing dialogue that would make democratic decision-making accountable to the basic values of equality.

The mechanism itself would be highly democratic. The proposal calls for the tribunal to be appointed by the (reformed) Senate, with one-third of the members from each of the following sectors: the federal government; provincial and territorial governments; and non-governmental organizations representing vulnerable and disadvantaged groups. Moreover, the tribunal was structured to provide an ongoing dialogue with the adjudicators, the government. The *ASC* thus provides an institutional structure that recognizes rights as entailing an ongoing process of definition. It creates a democratic mechanism for that process, without simply giving democracy priority over rights. At the same time, it provides a means of ensuring that democratic decisions are accountable to basic values without treating rights as trumps. In short, the *ASC* provides us with an outline of a workable model of constitutionalism as a dialogue of democratic accountability, wherein the rights to be protected derive from an inquiry into what it would take to create the relationships necessary for a free and democratic society.

Conclusion

When we understand the constitutionalization of rights as a means of setting up a dialogue of democratic accountability, we redefine the kinds of justification necessary for constitutional constraints on democratic decision-making. Perhaps even more importantly for the world outside of academia, we provide a conceptual framework that will help us to design and assess workable mechanisms for constitutionalizing rights in modern democracies. This conception of constitutionalism both requires and fosters a new understanding of rights – rights as structuring relationships. This approach to rights, in turn, helps to overcome the most serious problems with the dominant conceptions of our liberal tradition. When we understand rights as relationships and constitutionalism as a dialogue of democratic accountability, we can not only move beyond long-standing problems, but we can create a conceptual and institutional structure that will facilitate inquiry into the new problems that will inevitably emerge.

NOTES

1 The author would like to thank the audience of the 1992 McDonald Lecture

and the participants in the legal theory workshop at New York University Law School and Columbia University Law School for their helpful questions and comments.

2 Ronald Dworkin coined the now widely used phrase in R. Dworkin, *Taking Rights Seriously* (Cambridge, Mass.: Harvard University Press, 1978).

3 As I have argued elsewhere, the Constitution of 1787 did not focus primarily on rights as limits in the sense we now understand as the purpose and legitimacy of judicial review. The Constitution of 1787 was designed to structure the institutions so as to ensure that the sort of men who knew how to govern, including how to respect rights, would be the ones in office. See J. Nedelsky, *Private Property and the Limits of American Constitutionalism: The Madisonian Framework and Its Legacy* (Chicago: University of Chicago Press, 1990).

4 This paragraph is drawn from ibid., ch. 6.

5 To leave aside the complexities of cabinet and administrative bodies.

6 One workshop participant suggested that this formulation rested on a mistake: confusing the question of limits on democracy with the process of determining or enforcing those limits. To the participant, the content of the rights that should serve as limits is given by the theory of rights, derived, I assume, from human nature or the nature of agency or freedom. My point, however, is that we cannot rely on such theoretically derived conceptions to justify limits on democracy. At the least, as I noted in the text above, the legal meaning of such rights must be determined, and the legitimacy of the process of that determination is inseparable from the legitimacy of treating rights as limits. And, in my terms, that process will inevitably be a collective determination and thus choice. More broadly, the historical shifts in meaning and the diversity of constitutionalized rights in different democracies make it difficult to believe that we can rely on a transcendent, universal, immutable source for the content of rights.

Bruce Ackerman, in *We the People: Foundations* (Cambridge, Mass.: Harvard University Press, 1991), also has a compelling argument that the American Constitution is structured in a way that treats 'the people' as the source of the meaning of rights rather than transcendent meaning. Here he contrasts the American Constitution with the German Constitution. In this regard, the Canadian Constitution is like the American.

7 J.H. Ely, *Democracy and Distrust: A Theory of Judicial Review* (Cambridge, Mass.: Harvard University Press, 1980).

8 Monahan draws on Ely, but thinks Ely is descriptively wrong about the United States. See P. Monahan, *Politics and the Constitution: The Charter, Federalism and the Supreme Court of Canada* (Toronto: Carswell/Methuen, 1987).

9 Of course, it is possible to work back from democracy, asking what all the pre-

conditions are for democratic participation, and from that process generate a very wide range of values, including autonomy. But I think such a process distorts our understanding of the genuine diversity of values that in fact are necessary for an optimal society or for the possibility of pursuing a full and good life. It has always struck me as particularly implausible to believe that the value of freedom of religion could be derived from even the most all-encompassing conception of the conditions for democracy. Here I think the distortion involved in such a derivation is obvious.

10 Unless one wants to make the strong claim that even though in principle it would be legitimate to protect those values, there is no institutional mechanism of doing so that could be legitimate.

11 I have developed this conception in more detail in J. Nedelsky, 'Reconceiving Autonomy: Sources, Thoughts, and Possibilities' (1989) 1 *Yale J. L. & Fem.* 7.

12 Note that the sources of collective power might include large-scale corporations, but here I will just focus on the government.

13 Section 33, the so-called override provision or notwithstanding clause, allows legislatures to expressly state that a piece of legislation shall operate notwithstanding provisions in s. 2 (fundamental freedoms of conscience, expression, assembly, and association) or ss. 7–15 ('legal rights' and 'equality rights'). Such legislation has effect for five years and may then be re-enacted.

14 Section 1 reads: 'The *Canadian Charter of Rights and Freedoms* guarantees the rights and freedoms set out in it subject only to such reasonable limits prescribed by law as can be demonstrably justified in a free and democratic society.'

15 An excellent critique and historical account not widely known among legal and political science academics is C. Keller, *From a Broken Web: Separation, Sexism and Self* (Boston: Beacon Press, 1986).

16 Ibid.

17 For example, C. Taylor, *Philosophy and the Human Sciences* (Cambridge: Cambridge University Press, 1985), particularly ch. 7, 'Atomism'; C. Keller, *From a Broken Web*, supra n. 15; M.J. Sandel, *Liberalism and the Limits of Justice* (Cambridge: Cambridge University Press, 1982); I.M. Young, 'Impartiality and the Civic Public,' and S. Benhabib, 'The Generalized and the Concrete Other,' in S. Benhabib and D. Cornell, eds., *Feminism as Critique* (Minneapolis: University of Minnesota Press, 1987).

18 For a discussion of property rights from a relational perspective, see J. Singer, 'The Reliance Interest in Property' (1987–8) 40 *Stan. L. Rev.* 577. My conversations with Joe Singer were also helpful in the early stages of working on this essay.

19 Supra n. 11.

20 Peter Gabel offers an excellent, thoughtful statement of this perspective in
    P. Gabel, 'The Phenomenology of Right-Consciousness and the Pact of the
    Withdrawn Selves' (1984) 62 *Tex. L. Rev.* 1563.

21 This seems the appropriate place for a note of response to the allegation that a
    theory of 'rights as relationship' is consequentialist, and that I must therefore
    enter into the debate over deontological v. consequentialist theories of rights.
    A series of questions at the Legal Theory Workshop at Columbia helped me to
    see why this debate is peripheral to my concerns here. The division between
    consequentialist and deontological theories is premised on the possibility of a
    useful conception of human beings whose nature can be understood in
    abstraction from any of the relations of which they are a part. Once one rejects
    this premise, the sharp distinction between rights defined on the basis of
    human nature v. rights defined in terms of the desirability of the relationships
    they foster simply dissolves. Since there is no free-standing human nature com-
    prehensible in abstraction from all relationship from which one could derive a
    theory of rights, the focus on relationship does not constitute a failure to
    respect the essential claims of humanness. The focus on relationship *is* a focus
    on the nature of humanness, not a willingness to sacrifice it to the collective.

22 P.J. Williams, *The Alchemy of Race and Rights* (Cambridge, Mass.: Harvard Uni-
    versity Press, 1991).

23 There are still some unresolved problems here. We need to figure out both
    the scope for withdrawal that is optimal and the ways of structuring choice
    about entering relationships. These are complicated problems once one starts
    from a framework that treats relationships as primary and in some ways given
    rather than chosen.

24 See, for example, M. Minow, *Making All the Difference: Inclusion, Exclusion and
    American Law* (Ithaca: Cornell University Press, 1990). The strongest argument
    that I have heard against this position has come from some of my students, in
    particular black students. The argument is that even if judges are always
    engaged in what, if they were conscious of it, they would call policy-making,
    they should remain unconscious because that constrains them more. Contrary
    to my claim that we can move forward in the direction I advocate in the
    absence of radical reform, they say, given the current composition of the judi-
    ciary, they want the judges to feel as constrained as possible about innovation.
    They seem to suggest that we should wait until we have a vastly more represen-
    tative judiciary before we advocate a shift in judges' understanding of their
    job.

25 See I.M. Young, 'Impartiality and the Civic Public,' supra n. 17 at 56.

26 Some of the proponents of adding property to the *Charter* seem to have odd
    ideas about just what that would accomplish. In the debate in the Ontario leg-

islature, a whole series of sad stories were related in which people's property was confiscated, and compensated (sometimes at values thought not to reflect the full cost of relocating a home or small business), for various public works projects (some of which never came to fruition). There was not a single story that I thought would have been prevented by the 'takings' clause in the U.S. Constitution (even under the most recent approach). Surely eminent domain would continue to be treated as a legitimate power of the legislature.

27 (1988), 53 D.L.R. (4th) 171, [1989] 2 W.W.R. 1 (B.C.C.A.) reversing *Wilson* v. *Medical Services Commission of B.C.* (1987), 36 D.L.R. (4th) 31, [1987] 3 W.W.R. 48 (B.C.S.C.), leave to appeal to Supreme Court of Canada, refused, 3 November 1988.

28 See J. Nedelsky and C. Scott, 'Constitutional Dialogue' in J. Bakan and D. Schneiderman, eds., *Social Justice and the Constitution: Perspectives on the Social Charter* (Ottawa: Carleton University Press, 1992). For a copy of the Alternative Social Charter (hereinafter *ASC*), see the Appendix to that volume.

29 One might say that because the rights of health care, food, clothing, and child care are, like property, second-order values, that is means to the end of achieving equality and other basic values outlined in the *Charter*, it is appropriate for the *Social Charter* to be a separate document rather than integrated into the *Charter*. There was some disagreement on this among those proposing this form of the Social Charter. In the proposed form, it was/is, a separate document, with a provision that the *Charter* be interpreted in ways consistent with the *Social Charter*. I think health care and food are primary values, although traditional rights discourse has treated them quite differently from liberty or equality – presumably in part because they are more readily seen as 'positive' rights rather than negative liberties. It might seem that health care and the other social rights of the *ASC* are less susceptible of a relational approach. But the meaning of equality needs to be interpreted in light of such social rights and vice versa, all of which requires relational analysis.

30 Section 10(1) *ASC*.

31 Ibid.

32 The Charlottetown Accord left unspecified the enforcement mechanisms for the 'Social and Economic Union.'

Enlightened Pursuits: Truth-Seeking Discourse and Postmodern Scepticism

CHRISTOPHER NORRIS

I

A number of recent studies have argued that there exists an affinity between truth-seeking discourse and the practice of extracting secrets under bodily duress or bringing hidden knowledge to light through techniques of physical coercion.[1] The most obvious source-text is Foucault's *Discipline and Punish*, in particular its set-piece opening description of the torments visited upon the regicide Damiens as a token of feudal authority inscribed through a graphic reversal and literalization of the King's Body metaphor.[2] Nor should we suppose – in the smugness of 'enlightened' retrospect – that those barbarities have now been left far behind on the path to present-day civilized practices and values. For according to Foucault such Whiggish or progressivist notions are really just a species of self-serving fantasy, a means of ignoring the different kinds of violence – the forms of internalized discipline and constraint – that characterize our current sexual mores, social institutions, psychiatric techniques, ideas of justice, projects of penal reform, etc. What we like to think of as 'progress' in these areas is in fact a history of steadily intensifying pressure, a multiplication of the strategies available for constructing the subject in accordance with societal norms and ensuring compliance with this or that mode of acceptable behaviour and belief. Such is the message everywhere implicit in Foucault's Nietzschean genealogies of power/ knowledge: that truth-claims are always, inescapably bound up with the epistemic drive for mastery and control, even (or especially) where it masks behind a rhetoric of liberal-humanist values or emancipatory critique.[3]

Thus Foucault sees nothing but the history of an error – a typical

'Enlightenment' error – in the idea that we have achieved some measure of civilized change when one compares (say) the feudal spectacle of power as a kingly prerogative exerted upon the body of the hapless criminal with modern, more 'progressive' ways of thinking about crime, rehabilitation, social responsibility, and so forth. What such beliefs serve to conceal, he argues, is the extent to which violence has been sublimated in the form of those internalized – quasi-voluntary – checks and restraints that operate all the more effectively for the absence of any overt, sovereign, or juridical machinery of punitive sanctions. From the Christian confessional to Freudian psychoanalysis, these discourses typically take effect by interpellating the subject into a range of conformable positions with regard to the truth – the inward or revealed truth – of his or her 'authentic' desires.[4] From our own point of view there appears a great difference between secrets extracted under bodily duress or by infliction of physical torment, and those other sorts of truth-claim (religious or secular) which emerge through the dialogue of consenting parties or the process of intersubjective exchange. But Foucault will have none of this comforting belief, convinced as he is that the various latter-day discourses of power/knowledge are merely an alternative, more efficient means of achieving compliance with the requisite norms. Indeed there is more than a hint of nostalgia for an epoch when power took the form of an overt (albeit often gruesome) display of monarchical privilege, and when as yet there existed nothing like the present-day range of subtilized discursive techniques for enforcing obedience on the part of notionally 'free' individuals. On Foucault's reading, the passage from feudal to modern disciplinary regimes reveals nothing more than the exchange of one tyranny for another, the replacement of a violence that took the most public or spectacular forms – and was thus always liable to provoke some kind of localized popular backlash –with a violence that worked through modes of inward subjection or identification, and whose effects could thus penetrate into every aspect of our social, political, ethical, and affective lives.

Hence his rejection of the so-called 'repressive hypothesis,' the idea that progress came about through a lifting of the old discursive taboos and a new-found freedom to discuss topics of a hitherto private or secret character. Far from having thrown off the shackles of 'Victorian' prudery and repression in such matters, we are now – Foucault argues – approaching a point where there is simply no escape from the compulsive need to make everything (our 'innermost' desires included) into a topic for the various expert discourses – psychoanalysis among them – which constitute the modern disciplinary regime of 'enlightened' self-knowledge and truth. If we are seeking a metaphor for this condition, then we should think of Bentham's 'Panopticon' project, his idea for a prison (and, beyond that, an entire social order) that would dispense with the clumsy apparatus of overt surveillance and control by exposing each inmate – each subject or citizen – to the universal 'gaze' of an authority whose centre is everywhere and nowhere, and whose effects are so thoroughly dispersed and internalized that nothing eludes its sovereign command. Or again, Foucault offers the Gulag Archipelago as an analogue for this present-day 'carceral' society where discipline is exerted through constant subjection to the manifold technologies of power/knowledge, and where truth-claims are always already made over into new techniques for ensuring compliance with the ethos of confessional authenticity or the inward, self-monitoring vigil of the subject-presumed-to-know. Any resistance to this order will not come about through the appeal to some notional truth behind appearances, or some enlightened (e.g., Kantian or Marxist) attempt to lay bare the mechanisms of social repression and thus restore suffering humanity to a sense of its real historical vocation, its genuine emancipatory interests, or its capacity to grasp the conditions of its own enslavement and thereby take the first step towards transforming those same oppressive conditions. Such ideas amount to nothing more than a form of grandiose delusion on the part of those old-style 'universal' intellectuals who cling to the belief that truth is an ultimate good, that 'reality' is in some sense there to be grasped, and that the path to enlightenment leads through stages of disciplined reflective self-knowledge.[5]

It was Kant who first set this project under way with his subject-centred doctrine of the faculties (pure reason, theoretical understanding, practical reason, and aesthetic judgment) conceived as existing in a complex order of inter-articulated truth-claims with 'man' as the privileged focus of inquiry for philosophy and the human sciences at large. But according to Foucault this was just another transient episode in the sequence of shifting paradigms, language-games, or orders of discourse which made up the history of Western thinking to date. And its epoch was already drawing to an end, its demise brought about by the advent of a new (post-humanist) dispensation where language – or discourse – would henceforth constitute the horizon of intelligibility, and where the Kantian subject, that curious 'transcendental-empirical doublet,' would soon appear as nothing more than a momentary 'fold' in the fabric of signs, a figure (in Foucault's famous metaphor) engraved in sand at the ocean's edge, soon to be erased by the incoming tide.[6] From this standpoint, it should now be possible to grasp how the truth-claims of enlightened thought had always been shadowed by a discourse of power, a compulsion to yield up those guilty secrets – hidden desires, unacknowledged motives, prejudicial blind spots, remnants of 'false consciousness,' and so forth – which could only be revealed through their constant exposure to the undeceiving rigours of authentic self-knowledge. Any progress achieved in the passage from feudal to present-day juridical regimes was more than outweighed by the growing range of strategies, techniques and disciplinary resources for maintaining this self-imposed vigil.

Thus the story turns out much the same whether one tells it from a Kantian, a Marxist, a Freudian, or any other critical perspective that holds to some notion of truth at the end of inquiry. For on Foucault's account such ideas take hold only at the point where desire becomes subject to a kind of internalized self-thwarting impulse – like the Kantian 'categorical imperative,' the Marxist dialectic of 'genuine' versus 'false' class-consciousness, or Freud's various models of instinctual repression and control – which effectively carries on the work once performed by other, more overt and spectacular forms of institutional power. In short, every so-called 'advance' on the path to enlightenment, truth, and self-knowledge goes along with a marked intensification of the various disciplines, codes, and interdictions by which the subject monitors its own conformity to the ground-rules and values of civilized discourse. And this is nowhere more apparent (so Foucault believes) than in the history of subject-centred epistemic and ethico-political critique which runs down from Kant to the present-day defenders of a kindred philosophical faith. What these thinkers fail to recognize is the deep affinity that exists between the quest for truth in whatever form – religious or secular, inward or objective, vouchsafed through authentic revelation or arrived at (supposedly) through open debate in the 'public sphere' of uncoerced dialogical exchange – and the workings of an ever more devious and resourceful will-to-power that enlists such claims in order to dissimulate its own ubiquitous nature. On this view, it is no great distance from the fire, rack, and pinion of old-style inquisitorial techniques to the Christian confessional, the psychoanalytic couch, or the Marxist mode of interrogative thought that identifies truth with the laying-bare of ideological illusion. And the same would apply to those thinkers – Habermas among them – who seek to carry on the 'unfinished project of modernity' even while acknowledging the force of recent anti-foundationalist or discourse-oriented arguments.[7] For these theories still involve a residual appeal to the truth-seeking subject of enlightenment discourse, a strategy whose upshot (as Foucault sees it) is to render them complicit with that whole bad history of oppressive monological reason.

II

Catherine Belsey raises some pertinent points in an essay that argues for the tactical alliance of interests between feminism, post-structuralism, and a postmodern attitude of sceptical mistrust towards all such oppressive ('liberal-humanist') truth-claims. 'Our present is postmodern,' she writes. That is to say,

it participates in the crisis of epistemology which has informed western culture since the aftermath of the Second World War. Both the Holocaust and Hiroshima produced a crisis of confidence in the Enlightenment version of history as a single narrative of the progressive enfranchisement of reason and truth. Where in these hideous episodes, and where in the subsequent squaring-up of the superpowers, equipped with their apocalyptic arsenals, were reason and truth to be found? Instead, two hundred years after the Enlightenment prevailed in the West, history was seen to be an effect of conflicting interests after all, but interests defined on all sides as absolute certainties.[8]

But the question remains: *from what critical standpoint* can we offer such judgments on the monstrous folly of the arms race, the exterminist 'logic' of deterrence theory, or the war crimes and acts of mass murder committed in the name of some ultimate, all-justifying cause – National Socialism, racial purity, 'keeping the world safe for democracy,' or whatever – whose 'absolute certainty' brooks no kind of reasoned counter-argument? Of course, Belsey is right to regard these doctrines – along with their peremptory claims-to-truth – as among the most perverse and destructive forms of mass-induced psychopathology. She is also quite justified in viewing the record of modern (post-Enlightenment) history to date as in many ways a standing reproof to any version of the Whiggish meta-narrative account – or the facile progressivist creed – which ignores all the evidence and pins its faith to the inevitable triumph of reason, democracy, and truth. But there is something decidedly odd about a case which argues from the manifest fact that such principles have not been carried into practice (or that they have often been perverted beyond recognition in the process) to an attitude of downright contempt for any 'discourse' that keeps those principles in view. And the oddity is compounded by Belsey's implicit appeal to standards of judgment – to factual, argumentative, moral, historical, and socio-political criteria – which would lack all conviction were it not for their reliance on the truth-claims of enlightened critique.

There are two main sources of confusion at work in this desire to have done with reason and truth in whatever philosophical guise. The first is the claim that 'Enlightenment' thinking has somehow been responsible for those various forms of injustice, cruelty, and oppression whose origin should rather be sought in the outright *rejection* of Enlightenment values, most often – as with Heidegger – in favour of a potent irrationalist mystique grounded in notions of revealed truth, of national destiny, or of language (some single, privileged language) as the bearer of 'authentic' wisdom and truth. Insofar as any chapter of intellectual history can be thought of as having pointed the way towards Auschwitz, Hiroshima, and kindred barbarities, it is the line of counter-Enlightenment thinking which runs from Nietzsche to Heidegger and other latter-day apostles of unreason, and not – as postmodernists like Lyotard would have it – the tradition they set out to attack.

The second confusion – closely allied to this – is the notion of 'Enlightenment' as a monolithic creed, a set of doctrines whose rigidly prescriptive and authoritarian character lays them open to the worst, most inhuman forms of socio-political implementation. But this reading is really little more than a travesty, ignoring as it does both the sheer variety of projects and arguments subsumed under that all-purpose label, and the way that these thinkers ceaselessly worked to question, challenge, or problematize their own more taken-for-granted habits of belief.[9] At the furthest point of historical disillusionment, it was even possible for one like Adorno – most rigorous and consequent of modern dialecticians – to impugn what he saw as the fateful complicity between reason in its 'positive' or affirmative aspect and the forces of destruction unleashed upon mind and nature alike by an implacable 'dialectic of enlightenment.'[10] To this extent his case might seem to fall square with the charges mounted against that tradition by postmodernists, neo-pragmatists, Foucauldians, and others. Yet it is clear to any reader of Adorno's work that he is far from rejecting the claims of critical reason, seeking as he does to contest those forms of oppressive monological thought through a mode of 'negative dialectics' that subjects every truth-claim – its own propositions included – to a vigilant process of immanent critique. Nothing could be more alien to Adorno's thinking than the kinds of irrationalist or reflex anti-Enlightenment rhetoric which currently pass for advanced wisdom in many quarters of the postmodern cultural scene.

Hence the idea – almost an article of faith for those who adopt this line – that reason is somehow inextricably bound up with the workings of a malignant power/knowledge whose effects can be resisted only by refusing any part in that whole bad legacy. Thus, in Catherine Belsey's words,

the Enlightenment commitment to truth and reason, we can now recognise, has meant historically a single truth and a single rationality, which have conspired in practice to legitimate the subordination of black people, the non-Western world, women ... None of these groups has any political interest in clinging to the values which have consistently undervalued *them*. The plurality of the postmodern, by contrast, discredits supremacism on the part of any single group. It celebrates difference of all kinds, but divorces difference from power. Postmodernism is in all these senses the ally of feminism.[11]

On the contrary, I would argue: postmodernism can do nothing to challenge these forms of injustice and oppression since it offers no arguments, no critical resources, or validating grounds for perceiving them *as* inherently unjust and oppressive. In the end, all this rhetoric of 'plurality' and 'difference' comes down to just another, more radical-sounding version of Richard Rorty's neo-pragmatist message, that is to say, his advice that we should cultivate the private virtues – maximize the range of aesthetic satisfactions, autonomous lifestyles, modes of individual self-fulfilment, etc. – and cease the vain effort to square those virtues with a sense of our larger (i.e., public, social, ethical, or political) responsibilities. Postmodernism cannot do other than promote this view insofar as it rejects the principle advanced by critical-Enlightenment thinkers from Kant to Habermas: namely, that the exercise of reason in its practical (or ethico-political) aspect is such as to require our willing participation *both* as autonomous, reflective individuals *and* as members of a rational community whose interests transcend the private/public dichotomy. For it is precisely the virtue of this Kantian *sensus communis* to challenge the kinds of dogmatic or prejudicial thinking – in Belsey's words, 'supremacism on the part of any single group' – that rest their authority on a direct appeal to the truth as vouchsafed to some racial, religious, social, or other such dominant interest.

It may indeed be the case, as she argues, that 'Enlightenment' values have often been adopted in the service of some far from enlightened ends, from the pursuit of empire to those various strategies of containment applied to women, racial minorities, or dissident cultures of whatever kind. But it is just as clear – and Belsey's argument implicitly concedes as much – that these are *perversions and betrayals* of the Enlightenment legacy, instances that may involve a specious appeal to the rhetoric of truth, equality, freedom, etc., but which 'in practice' stop far short of applying those standards in a uniform and consistent way. Nor is such consistency the product of a drive to homogenize social, cultural, or gender-role differences through the enforced subjugation to a 'single truth and a single rationality' equated with the norms of Western ethnocentric or patriarchal order. On the contrary: it is only by applying these criteria – of logic, reason, and reflexive auto-critique – that thought can resist the kinds of dogmatic imposition which derive their authority from a mystified appeal to notions of absolute, transcendent truth. Any self-styled 'critical theory' that rejects such principles is in effect harking back to a pre-critical stage of consensus belief when truth was indeed whatever counted as such according to the dictates of this or that interest group with the power to coerce or manipulate public opinion. In this respect – as Habermas convincingly argues – postmodernism is a retrograde cultural phenomenon which unwittingly runs into many of the dead-end antinomies encountered by thinkers in previous phases of anti-Enlightenment reaction.[12] Worst of all, it embraces a thoroughgoing version of the Nietzschean-relativist creed according to which there is *simply no difference* between truth-claims imposed by sheer, self-authorizing fiat and truths arrived at by process of reasoned debate or open argumentative exchange.

For the effect of such thinking is to block any challenge to false or presumptive truth-claims, those which rest on a direct appeal to some ultimate source of wisdom – whether religious or secular – whose authority is placed beyond reach of counter-argument or criticism on social, political, historical, or ethical grounds. Hence the persistent blind spot in Foucault's sceptical genealogies of power/knowledge: namely, his tendency to level any distinction between the various types of social order – despotic, feudal, monarchical, liberal-democratic, or whatever – all of which are treated as manifestations of that same implacable drive.[13] On the one hand, this produces a marked fascination (also to be found in New Historicists like Stephen Greenblatt) with the exercise of power in its most 'spectacular,' public, or physically manifest forms, like the famous set-piece description from *Discipline and Punish* which I cited at the beginning of this essay.[14] Such gruesome evocations at least have the virtue – from Foucault's standpoint – of graphically displaying how power operates through mechanisms of overt subjection, surveillance, and control, as distinct from those other, more 'enlightened' regimes where its workings are diffused through the various modes of sublimated power/knowledge. On the other hand, it leads to an attitude of extreme scepticism with regard to those forms of self-styled progressive or emancipatory thought which assume – in the manner of critical philosophers from Kant to Habermas – that the interests of humanity are best served by exposing false or dogmatic claims-to-truth and allowing reason the maximum liberty to challenge orthodox or consensual habits of belief. For Foucault this amounts to nothing more than a piece of self-serving bourgeois-liberal ideology, a failure to perceive how the repressive apparatus has now become internalized to the point where subjects willingly consent to police their own thoughts, beliefs, and desires in accordance with a new set of self-imposed disciplinary imperatives. Any Kantian notion that things are changing for the better – that, for instance, we have achieved a greater measure of humane insight in matters of sexual, psychiatric, or sociological understanding – is treated by Foucault as the merest of illusions, brought about by our acceptance of the standard left-liberal or 'Enlightenment' line. Quite simply, there is no appeal to reason or truth – least of all in the human or the social sciences – which does not involve the conjoint appeal to a range of authorized 'discourses,' defining both what shall count as veridical utterance and – by the same token – what must be seen as marginal, deviant, or lacking in the requisite kinds of disciplined self-knowledge. In which case (he urges), we should give up thinking in those old, self-deluding ways and take to heart the two main lessons of a Nietzschean-genealogical approach: firstly, that there is no 'truth' outside the force-field of contending discourses or representations; and, secondly, that any kind of truth-talk is sure to perpetuate the in-place structures of authority and power.

III

Such – briefly stated – is the current *doxa*, the background of taken-for-granted belief, which unites the various schools of 'advanced' thinking from Foucauldian genealogy to post-structuralism, New Historicism, and its British ('cultural materialist') counterpart. What is wrong with all this – as I have suggested above – is that it fails to take account of the crucial difference between truths imposed by arbitrary fiat, through presumptive access to *the Truth* as revealed to some body of priests or commissars, and truth-claims advanced in the public sphere of open argumentative debate. By a curious irony, nothing could be more dogmatic – less willing to engage in debate of this kind – than the new ultra-relativist orthodoxy which allows its opponents the unenviable choice of figuring either as dupes or inquisitors, victims or agents of that will-to-power which masquerades as critical reason.

Norman Geras makes this point most effectively in his recent polemical rejoinder to Ernesto Laclau and Chantal Mouffe.[15] Geras has numerous objections to their work and to other such *soi-disant* 'post-Marxist' interventions from theorists of a broadly Foucauldian persuasion. For their aim – as he sees it – is to undermine every last category of socialist thought while claiming to offer a new kind of 'strategy,' a politics of multiple, decentred 'discourses' which allows of no appeal to such old-fashioned notions as experience, class-interest, ideology, forces and relations of production, etc., replacing them with talk of 'subject-positions' constructed in and through the play of various (often conflicting) discursive alignments. Thus Laclau and Mouffe can go as far as to argue that there is *simply no relation* between class or gender as conceived in 'traditional' (i.e., Marxist or feminist) terms and the range of strategies that is now opened up for a 'democratic socialism' happily disabused of such 'essentialist' ideas and willing to take its chance with one or other of the discourses currently on offer. In short, there are as many subject-positions as there are points of conflict or tactical alliance within and between those shifting discursive registers. From which it follows, according to Laclau and Mouffe, that Marxism can keep pace with these developments only if it gives up its old truth-telling illusions – like that of a determinate reality beyond the realm of contending 'ideological' discourses – and accepts those discourses for what they are, the very arena of political action and choice.

Geras sees clearly what is at stake in this attempt to 'update' the categories of Marxist thought in line with the current postmodernist wisdom. More specifically, he sees how it amounts to a new kind of relativist orthodoxy, one that makes much of its 'democratic' or pluralist credentials while working to close off any possibility of reasoned counter-argument. Thus:

Marxism and Marxists, for aspiring to cognitive objectivity, are held to lay claim to certainty, absolute knowledge, transparent access to truth and so on; whereas the theory of discourses, being (what I call) a cognitive relativism, is supposedly undogmatic, open and pluralist ... But, unlike faith and dogma, genuine knowledge is always provisional, subject to revision in the light of new information and evidence, needing periodically to be restructured, fallible; open therefore to 'pluralist' discussion and criticism, yet at the same time, pending possible rebuttal or revision, *knowledge* so far as we have managed to get. This aspiration, and all claims to knowledge in the sense just explained, are democratic by their nature, because they have to satisfy rules of consistency, external reference, evidence, that are accessible in principle to all, *public and accessible* – if sometimes only with difficulty – *as are the realities themselves to be known.*[16]

This seems to me a very cogent defence of objectivity and truth as the requisite criteria for any 'discourse' that seeks to make good its claims through the process of open participant debate, as opposed to the dogmatic imposition of truths known only to a privileged interpretive elite. For without such criteria – minimally those of 'consistency, external reference, evidence,' etc.– 'truth' is purely and simply what counts as such according to the current consensus-view or the authority of those with the power to enforce their own (self-interested) version thereof. The critique of scriptural revelation is perhaps the most telling instance of a progress brought about by the sustained application of exactly those enlightened truth-seeking standards, deployed – over many centuries – against sizeable odds of entrenched belief and coercive institutional constraint.[17] Such thinking involved both the generalized principle that reason (not faith) was the best source of guidance in matters of intellectual conscience, and the specific endeavour to criticize false claims-to-truth in light of scholarly, historical, textual, and documentary evidence.

It is ironic, to say the least, that these critical techniques started out in close alliance to the kinds of philological inquiry which later gave rise to modern hermeneutics and the warring schools of present-day literary theory. For what has now come about is a curious reversal, a process of wholesale re-mystification, whereby the conventional lifting of truth-claims as applied to literary texts is taken as a paradigm instance of the way that 'discourses' circulate beyond all reach of factual or historical accountability. So it is that theorists like Laclau and Mouffe – along with poststructuralists, Foucauldians, New Historicists, and others – can argue that 'reality' is entirely a construct of linguistic, discursive, or textual representation, and do so, moreover, confident in the knowledge that such claims will pass without challenge from thinkers *au courant* with the latest wisdom. It is hardly surprising that Geras waxes indignant, given the way that these ideas have caught on among 'radical' theorists of various persuasion who show little grasp of their disabling political consequences. For at the end of the road these thinkers are travelling there is a choice of just two destinations, the one (after Rorty) marked 'North Atlantic postmodern bourgeois-liberal neo-pragmatist,' or however one prefers to juggle those terms, while the other points back to a pre-modern phase of consensus-belief in which issues of truth and falsehood give way to issues of authority and power. What becomes simply unthinkable, from this point of view, is the idea that reasoned argument or criticism could ever do more than provide handy psychological or rhetorical back-up for beliefs that already carry weight with a large enough proportion of the relevant 'interpretive community.'[18] In which case one might as well grasp, the nettle – as Rorty does, but not (understandably) 'post-Marxists' like Laclau and Mouffe – and proclaim that 'ideology' is henceforth an empty notion, that consensus beliefs go all the way down, and that this is no cause for concern since 'we' postmodern-bourgeois liberals inhabit the best of all currently conceivable worlds.

Geras offers a fair (if scathing) account of what happens when relativism is raised into a high point of doctrine, a fixed idea that all talk of 'truth' has now been played off the field and that any opposition on reasoned argumentative grounds – in point of consistency, analytical rigour, historical, grasp or whatever – signals a retreat to those bad old 'Enlightenment' habits of thought. For these latter-day sophists

'democratically' cut *everybody* off from access to what could meaningfully be called either truth or objectivity – with the single exception, dear to all relativists, of themselves. Overtly denying that there is any being-as-such, any in-itself, in terms of which competing discourses might be adjudicated, they install somewhere out of sight a secret tribunal of truth, mysterious in its ways, which allows *them* to judge here: as 'essentialist,' hence *wrong about the nature of the world*; as economist, thus unable to understand the *reality* of the social; as determinist, therefore misconstruing history's *actual* openness etc.; which allows them to employ a language of external reference, of objectivity, of truth ... which allows them that long, that tireless, that never-ending 'this is how it is' with which the relativist tells you why you cannot say 'this is how it is,' thus sending knowledge and consistency to the devil.[19]

Geras's reference to the 'secret tribunal' – the dogmatic assurance that undergirds these relativist arguments despite their overt rhetoric – is of particular interest in light of what duBois has to say about the deep-laid kinship between 'torture' and 'truth.' This case only holds, I would argue, for those kinds of truth-claim that shun the process of reasoned critical debate, and which stake their authority on a direct appeal to presumptive sources of revealed or self-authenticating truth. In other words, it applies well enough to the tradition which duBois traces down from its origins in ancient oracular or proto-philosophical thought, and whose avatars include not only the proponents of unquestioning religious faith but also those thinkers – Heidegger among them – who trade on a similar species of high-toned verbal mystification. For it is, as she writes, 'this ancient, traditional, religious view of truth – contested by democratic process, by selection according to lot, by mass debate in agora and assembly – that anchors philosophical practice, that of many of the pre-Socratics, that of Plato, that of his modern critic, Martin Heidegger.'[20] But her argument demonstrably misses the mark when duBois extends it, in the postmodern-pragmatist fashion, to cover all varieties of truth-claim save those that acknowledge their own contingent or derivative status, their ultimate reliance – as Rorty would have it – on the currency of in-place consensus belief. For the effect of these ultra-relativist arguments is to throw thinking back to a stage of pre-critical tutelage where the only thing that counts is the trick of commanding assent through a rhetoric adapted to the purposes and interests of those with the *de facto* power to decide such matters.

Such thinking has a number of unfortunate consequences. One is the widespread tendency – manifest in Foucault's writing and in the work of New Historicists like Greenblatt – to treat 'power' and 'knowledge' as wholly interchangeable terms, and thereby to dismiss any index or criterion of civilized progress that involves the appeal to 'Enlightenment' values like reason, autonomy, or freedom of thought and speech. It is in this context that we can best understand the current fascination with the human body – most often, the body in pain or under physical duress – as a site where the various disciplinary practices (or regimes of instituted power/knowledge) are supposedly inscribed in most graphic and legible form. What these 'readings' amount to is a postmodern version of the arguments and the imagery of Hobbes's *Leviathan*, one that takes over his cynical analysis of the state as an instrument of collective self-discipline, his view of the subject as a point of intersection between various conflicting power interests, and his use of bodily metaphors and allegories by way of enforcing this harshly 'realist' message.[21] Our contemporary theorists arrive at the same conclusion by rejecting all ideas of practical agency, knowledge, truth, or critique, and proclaiming that nothing can be thought outside the range of positions imposed by some existing configuration of power/knowledge. All of which tends to bear out Habermas's claim: that in abandoning the 'unfinished project of modernity,' these thinkers have not only renounced all warrant for criticizing false or deluded beliefs, but have also effectively reverted to an outlook predating the emergence of that same project.[22] In short, what they have taken as their operative norm – their bottom-line account of knowledge, truth, and belief formation – is precisely the kind of orthodox consensus-based polity which requires unthinking doctrinal adherence and which works to enforce such an attitude through forms of overt (or highly 'spectacular') physical coercion.

Hence the otherwise strange predilection – in Foucault and the New Historicists alike – for harrowing scenes of judicial torture or public execution which are always recounted in a style of studious drawn-out detachment, as if to emphasize the error of judging such episodes from our own, supposedly more humane or liberal viewpoint. Indeed, despite occasional protests to the contrary, there is often a sense in Foucault's writing that he wishes to reverse – not merely to suspend – those facile progressivist notions. Far from having left such barbarities behind, we have now moved on (so it appears) into a new and yet more repressive disciplinary regime, a social order in which subjects are required to monitor their own desires, dispositions, and beliefs, and the corrective applications of power/knowledge take the form of those various 'expert' discourses – psychoanalysis and the 'human sciences' among them – whose will-to-power is disguised by a rhetoric of good-willed therapeutic intent.[23] All of which follows consistently enough from Foucault's five major premises, namely: (1) the obsolescence of truth-claims in whatever 'enlightened' or quasi-transcendental form; (2) the reduction of all such claims to so many 'discourses' indifferent with regard to veridical warrant; (3) the dispersal of the subject – the Kantian knowing, willing, and judging subject – over a range of heterogeneous 'subject-positions' likewise inscribed within this or that constitutive discourse; (4) the ubiquity of power/knowledge differentials as the locus of social and political struggle; and (5) the primacy of the body – the desiring, suffering, subjugated body – as the site whereon those struggles are enacted in their most direct and tangible form. Hence the tone of derisive, hard-bitten cynicism which marks so many current pronouncements on the legacy of so-called 'Enlightenment' thought. For, given these assumptions, there would seem no alternative to the kind of extreme sceptical or levelling view that perceives little difference between regimes founded on the infliction of brute (albeit 'symbolic') physical violence and regimes which claim to transcend or eliminate such violence through reasoned argument, civilized values, and humane understanding. Any rejoinder that invoked those old-fashioned 'liberal-humanist' criteria would simply be met with a flat restatement of the standard Foucauldian line.

It is the same set of premises that duBois takes over when she treats 'truth' and 'torture' as well-nigh synonymous terms, each of them involved in a violent logic which requires the extraction of some occult knowledge through various disciplinary techniques. Most often, she argues, these techniques are caught up in a specular relationship between self and other where the other is conceived – like the slave or the woman in ancient Greek thought – as somehow giving access (under 'expert' guidance) to a truth beyond reach of his or her inward, authentic, self-knowing grasp. And so it comes about, in duBois' words, that

a hidden truth, one that eludes the subject, must be discovered, uncovered, unveiled, and can always be located in the dark, in the irrational, in the unknown, in the other. And that truth will continue to beckon the torturer, the sexual abuser, who will find in the other – slave, woman, revolutionary – silent or not, secret or not, the receding phantasm of a truth that must be hunted down, extracted, torn out in torture.[24]

It is a powerful indictment, especially when read in light of what duBois has to say about the extent of such practices in our own time, very often by nominally 'Third World' agencies whose schooling – whose acquired expertise in these matters – came by way of U.S. 'counter-insurgency' or psychological warfare units. As she remarks, there is still a tendency on the part of many Western commentators to pretend that these practices only occur elsewhere, in regions of the world as yet unconverted to the values of freedom and (capitalist) liberal democracy. But in so doing, they fall straight back into the old pattern of thought, the need to cast some other in the reassuring role of scapegoat, alien or stigmatized bearer of a dark knowledge whose import can only be assessed from 'our' more humane or enlightened standpoint. Thus:

Torture has become a global spectacle, a comfort to the so-called civilized nations, persuading them of their commitment to humanitarian values, revealing to them the continued barbarism of the other world, a world that continues to need the guidance of Europe and America, a guidance that is offered in the form of a trans-national global economy controlling torture as one of the instruments of world domination.[25]

Anyone who doubts the truth of such claims need only reflect on the record of U.S. *Realpolitik* as manifest in its dealings with various dictatorial regimes in South America, Southeast Asia, the Gulf region, and other parts of the world perceived as crucial to its geo-political or military-strategic interests. Had duBois' book been published a year or so later, she could have pointed to the Gulf War, its background history, and the subsequent course of events as evidence enough of U.S. willingness to switch tactical alliances almost overnight and to back any government – no matter how brutal or repressive – just so long as it served the purpose of maintaining regional hegemony.[26] For there was, to say the least, a certain grim irony about the notion of waging war to 'liberate' a country like Kuwait, one whose subjects – or a large majority of them – can scarcely have relished the liberators' promise of a swift return to the *status quo ante*.

Nothing could more clearly illustrate duBois' point about the massive hypocrisy that often goes along with Western talk of liberal democracy, 'free world' values, and other such well-worn propaganda slogans. For what usually gets exported under cover of this high-sounding rhetoric is yet another opportune shift in the balance of power – along with the requisite weapons technology, military back-up, training in advanced methods of surveillance and control, etc. – whose aim is to secure 'stability' in the region as viewed from the Pentagon or Capitol Hill.[27] And if erstwhile 'tyrants' or 'dictators' can be thus transformed into new-found 'friends' and 'allies' – on condition (of course) that the process also works in reverse elsewhere – then liberal opinion is best assuaged by regarding these turn-arounds as only to be expected when dealing with such volatile regimes and characters. Moreover, it is this same self-exculpating logic – this habit of projecting blame and guilt onto a racial or cultural 'other' conceived as lacking the basic democratic virtues – which in turn permits 'us' more civilized types to enjoy an easy conscience despite all the evidence of Western complicity, connivance, or worse. Such alibis are always available, as duBois says, 'to comfort American liberals who rest contented in their view that these things could never happen here ... They confirm the perspective from the United States and Europe that barbarism resides elsewhere, in the other, that other world, unenlightened, steeped in medievalism and bloody cruelty.'[28] To which one can only respond by acknowledging the justice of this claim as borne out by the recent history of U.S. strategic interventions in various 'trouble-spots' around the world. And, of course, there has been no shortage of well-placed apologists – media commentators, think-tank pundits, 'end-of-ideology' ideologues, and the like – to justify each new shift of tactical alliance and explain how it all contributes to the aim of making the world safe for democracy.

The most prominent of these 'liberal' voices recently has been that of

Francis Fukuyama, a Rand Corporation protegé and inventor of some novel variations on the old (no longer very persuasive) line of Cold War propaganda. Fukuyama achieved instant fame on the U.S. lecture circuit for his thesis that 'history' had effectively come to an end – not to mention 'ideology' and other such obsolete notions – with the advent of a New World Order founded on the principles of liberal democracy and free-market economics.[29] He followed this up with an article on the Gulf War ('Changed Days for Ruritania's Dictator'), whose closing sentences can best be read in conjunction with the passages from duBois cited above:

A large part of the world will be populated by Iraqs and Ruritanias, and will continue to be subject to bloody struggles and revolutions. But with the exception of the Gulf, few regions will have an impact – for good or ill – on the growing part of the world that is democratic and capitalist. And it is in this part of the world that we will ultimately have to make our home.[30]

It never occurs to him to ask how far those 'bloody struggles and revolutions' have been the outcome of Western interests pursued by every available strategic and military means; what a history of betrayals and proxy or delegated violence lies behind this talk of exporting the benefits of liberal democracy; how the 'impact' is more often the reverse of what Fukuyama thinks, being experienced most keenly by those on the receiving end of U.S. foreign policy initiatives; and finally, how the geo-political carve-up between 'them' (the Iraqs and Ruritanias) and 'us' (or that fortunate part of the world that 'we will ultimately have to make our home') is based not so much on the limits assigned to this benevolent sphere of interest as on the need for new enemies – or scapegoat regimes – to bolster a U.S. economy dependent on massive and continued military spending. And so it comes about, in duBois' words, that

the ancient model of truth, and slave torture as the extraction of truth, still defines the first world's relationship to third world torture. While the suffering of victims under the regimes of torturers punishes and controls the citizens of their nations, the citizens of the first world observe and deplore the spectacle of third world primitivism and barbarism. The first world contents itself with other ways of achieving truth – the so-called pluralism of mass consumerism, the 'freedom' capitalism offers to choose among an assortment of putative truths as one chooses among alternate toothpastes. But the truth is that torture still exists, it has not been eliminated in a surge of enlightened globalism, and the third world, in its complexity, multiplicity, multiple sites, has become, besides the site of torture, the spectacle of the other tortured for us.[31]

It is not hard to see what a swath this cuts through the orchestrated plati-tudes currently on offer from Fukuyama and the feel-good ideologues of U.S. 'liberal democracy.'

But one should also notice how duBois abruptly shifts ground, in this last and most eloquent passage of her book, from attacking truth-claims in whatever form to attacking those varieties of 'first world' postmodern scepticism that would relativize issues of truth and falsehood to the point where they resemble free-market options or items of consumer choice. In fact there is a problem in squaring this passage with her earlier praise for those heterodox thinkers – from the ancient sophists to the present-day neo-pragmatists – who have held out against the coercive regimen of truth, and thereby pointed the way towards achieving a genuine, open, fully participant democracy. It seems to me that this unresolved tension in her argument is perhaps best explained by considering the role of such ideas – the way that they have been taken up, exploited, and put to all manner of rhetorical use – by apologists for Bush's 'New World Order' and its various associated myths. For there is, as I have argued, a complicitous relation between fashionable slogans like the 'end of ideol-ogy' or the 'end of history' – slogans whose effect is to disguise and legiti-mate the interests of U.S. *Realpolitik* – and those versions of the postmodern-pragmatist creed which likewise proclaim the obsolescence of values such as truth, reason, and critique, and which offer in their place a consensus-based appeal to what is currently 'good in the way of belief.'[32] This argument may start out from the liberal premise that truth-claims have all too often gone along with a notion of privileged access or superior wisdom on the part of those elect individuals with authority or power to impose their version of the truth. Hence Rorty's genial recommendation that we substitute 'solidarity' for 'objectivity,' or a sense of shared (that is, 'North Atlantic postmodern bourgeois-liberal pragmatist') values for the attempt to get things right from a critical standpoint which challenges the currency of consensus belief. But such arguments take on a less benign aspect if one considers how easily public opinion can be mobilized – or consensus attitudes swung – to support the kinds of thinking that find expression in Fukuyama's Gulf War arti-cle. For if truth is in the end simply what counts as such according to our present interpretive lights, then one might as well push this argument all the way – along with its strategic implications – and endorse whatever line of state-sponsored doublethink happens to suit the current mood of revived interventionist zeal.

Thus (in Fukuyama's words) 'any "New World Order" will not be built upon abstract principles of international law, but upon the common principles of liberal democracy and market economics.'[33] And, by the same token, any local resistance or opposition to those principles will be met with a placid assurance that might is right, just so long as 'right' can be defined for all practical purposes as 'good in the way of free-market doctrine and liberal-democratic belief.' This is not to cast doubt on the good faith and decency of those – Rorty among them – who appeal to such values as the last, best hope in an age that has supposedly witnessed the collapse of 'Enlightenment' values and truth-claims. 'Consider,' Rorty asks us,

the attitude of contemporary American liberals to the unending hopelessness and misery of the lives of the young blacks in American cities. Do we say that these people must be helped because they are our fellow human beings? We may, but it is much more persuasive, morally as well as politically, to describe them as our fellow *Americans* – to insist that it is outrageous that an *American* can live without hope.[34]

Terry Eagleton cites this passage as an epigraph to his recent book *Ideology: An Introduction*, along with another sentence from Rorty which declares simply: 'On the uselessness of the notion of "ideology," see Raymond Geuss, *The Idea of a Critical Theory.*'[35] Aside from Geuss's role as an unsuspecting pawn in this exchange, one can see very well why Eagleton singles out such passages for what they tell us about current neo-pragmatist thinking and its alignment with an updated version of the 'end of ideology' thesis. For the appeal to 'us' Americans as a bottom-line of liberal reformist concern may always turn out to have sharp limits when it comes to imagining how non-Americans – in particular those condemned to inhabit Fukuyama's 'Iraqs and Ruritanias' – can somehow be brought to appreciate the benefits on offer. If their interests are to figure at all, then this requires something more than a good-willed stretch of the terms on which present-day Americans (politicians, military strategists, and think-tank pundits, as well as benign individuals like Rorty) happen to define their preferred cultural self-image. Otherwise the talk of consensus-values can very easily serve, as it did during the Gulf War, to legitimate some far-from-liberal forms of public opinion management. And from this point the way is clearly open for opportunists like George Bush – or cynical ideologues like Fukuyama – to promote their vision of a 'New World Order' exempt from even the most basic standards of historical, moral, and political accountability.

It seems to me that such conclusions are hard to avoid if one assumes, like duBois, that a pragmatist or cultural-relativist outlook is the only defence against what she calls 'the coercive, philosophical, othering, torturing mode of seeking truth.' For according to this drastically polarized view there is no alternative – least of all a 'philosophical' alternative – that would hold out against the various forms of imposed or dogmatic truth while continuing to respect the aims and priorities of enlightened critical thought. Hence her high regard for those genuinely 'democratic' thinkers – from the ancient Greek sophists to their modern neo-pragmatist descendants – who have found no use for any idea of truth that supposedly transcends the localized horizon, the in-place assumptions or consensus values of its own time and place. Even so there are passages in her book which suggest that this cannot be the whole story; that democracy involves something other and more than the appeal to what is currently 'good in the way of belief'; and that any worthwhile advance in this direction will require a criticism of existing institutions which can only come about through enlightened efforts to extend the scope of informed participant exchange. Thus: 'the logic of democracy, the notion of equality and equal power among members of a community, can produce an ever-expanding definition of community.'[36] And again: 'the idea of democracy has its own dynamic, a pressure towards the consideration of all in view as entitled to the privileges of rule by the people.'[37] It is no coincidence that passages like these bring duBois much closer to Habermas's thinking – to his notion of an 'ideal speech-community' as the measure of progressive or emancipatory change – than to anything envisaged on the pragmatist account of knowledge and human interests.[38] For the upshot of any such consensus-based doctrine is to level the difference between beliefs arrived at through the process of open argumentative exchange and beliefs that rest solely on unexamined prejudice, ideological persuasion, or the *force majeure* of propaganda efforts like that mounted during the Gulf War campaign.

IV

It is for this reason – I would argue – that relativist philosophies can offer no defence against arbitrary (and sometimes violent) forms of doctrinal imposition. Postmodernists typically confuse the issue by assimilating all truth-claims to that mystified idea of an inward, secret, self-validating truth which has characterized the discourse of revealed religion and whose resonance persists (as duBois rightly notes) in Heidegger's etymopoeic vagaries, his 'profound' pseudo-arguments and constant resort to an irrationalist jargon of authenticity.[39] No doubt such ideas have been the cause of great confusion, as well as giving rise – all too clearly in Heidegger's case – to some vicious abuses when translated into the sphere of social and political thought. To this extent, duBois is justified in urging that 'torture' and 'truth' should be seen as two aspects of that domineering drive – that will-to-power over bodies and minds – whose genealogy reaches back to the origins of the Western cultural tradition. What she fails to acknowledge, except in those few brief passages, is the fact that such ideas have met resistance only through the kind of enlightened critique that challenges false or presumptive truth-claims by holding them accountable to alternative standards of historical, philosophical, and ethical truth. Insofar as Christianity has been subject to a civilizing influence – induced to give up its persecuting zeal and its demands for unquestioning doctrinal adherence – it is principally owing to these efforts of reasoned counter-argument on the part of thinkers from Erasmus to the present. And the most important factor here has been the growing awareness that truth is best arrived at, not on the basis of inward conviction or self-authorized scriptural warrant, but through a process of open dialogical exchange whose criteria are those of good faith, reason, and valid argumentative grounds.

That literary theorists of a 'radical' bent should now be engaged in a wholesale campaign to denigrate such values is all the more curious given their reliance –however confused or unwitting – on precisely the modes of critical thought which derive from that same tradition. For even when denouncing 'Enlightenment' beliefs as the source of all evil and oppression, these critics (Foucauldians and post-structuralists among them) still lay claim to the kind of demythologizing role which secular intellectuals have typically played over the past two centuries and more. Where they depart from that tradition – and effectively revert to an earlier, proto-theological strain – is in their raising of 'the text' (as of language or 'discourse') to a position of undisputed eminence, and in the conjoint refusal to acknowledge any argument or truth-claim that does not abide by this textualist imperative. No doubt one source of confusion here is a simplified reading of Derrida which latches on to some of his more sweeping pronouncements as regards the Western 'metaphysics of presence,' and takes him to have shown – once and for all – that any talk of truth is inescapably complicit with that age-old logocentric regime.[40] On the contrary, as he puts it in a recent essay:

The value of truth (and all those values associated with it) is never contested or destroyed in my writings, but only reinscribed in more powerful, larger, more stratified contexts ... And within those contexts (that is, within relations of force that are always differential – for example, socio-political-institutional – but even beyond these determinations) that are relatively stable, sometimes apparently almost unshakable, it should be possible to invoke rules of competence, criteria of discussion and of consensus, good faith, lucidity, rigour, criticism, and pedagogy.[41]

One could hardly wish for a plainer declaration of the gulf that separates Derrida's work from the currency of postmodern-pragmatist thought.

Paul de Man makes a similar point – and with the same kinds of misunderstanding in view – when he refutes the idea that deconstruction involves a *tout court* rejection of truth-values, or that it simply suspends all questions of veridical or argumentative warrant. Thus:

Reading is an argument ... because it has to go against the grain of what one would want to happen in the name of what has to happen; this is the same as saying that reading is an epistemological event prior to being an ethical or aesthetic value. This does not mean that there can be a true reading, but that no reading is conceivable in which the question of its truth or falsehood is not primarily involved.[42]

Postmodernism derives much of its suasive appeal from the notion that truth-claims are *always* on the side of some ultimate, transcendent, self-authorized Truth which excludes all meanings save those vouchsafed to the guardians of orthodox thought. It is this supposition that lends plausibility to Foucault's reductive genealogies of power/knowledge, to Rorty's genial postmodern variations on the theme, and also to the link between 'torture' and 'truth' which duBois sees everywhere at work in the history of Western logocentric reason. But such arguments look much less convincing when placed in a wider philosophical and socio-cultural context. For it then becomes clear that without the benefit of those values that Derrida invokes – 'consensus, good faith, lucidity, rigour, criticism' – we should still be labouring against massive odds of doctrinal imposition and entrenched dogmatic belief. Or again – more to the point – we should possess no means by which to criticize such false or unwarranted beliefs and thus attain a better understanding of the forces that had worked to keep them in place.

Of course, it is possible to argue, like Foucault, that 'resistance' comes about solely as a product of power/knowledge differentials; that for every 'discourse' of accredited or authorized knowledge there is a counter-discourse whose social efficacity is directly proportional to the power invested in maintaining the current institutional status quo. But this doctrine really amounts to little more than a metaphor transposed from Newtonian mechanics into the realm of the human and social sciences. That is to say, it trades on a simplified analogy between physical 'forces' and those contests of meaning, motive, authority, and power that involve human agents in distinctive forms of socialized conduct and exchange. The result – as I have argued – is a drastically reductive, quasi-Hobbesian conception of power/knowledge that levels all distinctions between the various orders of state and civil society, and which perceives violence (or some sublimated image of the feudal body-in-pain) as the underlying truth of any such order, whatever its 'enlightened' or progressive self-image.

It seems to me that recent theorists have pressed too far with this oddly seductive equation between 'torture' and 'truth.' To be sure, it has yielded valuable (and cautionary) insights into the way that a certain presumptive, self-authorizing discourse of 'truth' can coexist with forms of social oppression which it serves both to disguise and to legitimate. What duBois has to say on this topic – with examples from Plato to Heidegger – gives evidence enough that such collusions have occurred and that truth-talk *per se* is no guarantee of social or political virtue. But that much should be obvious to anyone who has thought about the varieties of human self-deception and the power of false ideas to pass themselves off as the highest spiritual wisdom. Indeed, it is this supposed link between *inwardness* and truth – the idea of a privileged access vouchsafed to some religious or secular elite – which has done most harm down through the history of violent or persecuting creeds. One need only reflect on the self-righteous rhetoric, the scenes of presidential soul-baring, and the charade of private consciences publicly aired that accompanied an episode like the Gulf War to gain some idea of what might be at stake in Derrida's deconstructive critique of 'logocentrism' and the 'metaphysics of presence.'

However, there is nothing to be gained – and a great deal to be lost – when postmodern theorists take this as their cue for denouncing all the values and truth-claims of Enlightenment reason. For such attitudes amount to a wholesale retreat from one of criticism's primary tasks: that is – in Jonathan Culler's words – its function of 'combating superstition, encouraging sceptical debate about competing religions and their claims or their myths, and fighting religious dogmatism and its political conse- quences.'[43] Moreover, it is the case, as Culler points out, that literary the- ory in its present-day form is very largely a product of those powerful demystifying impulses – historical scholarship, textual hermeneutics, phil- ological inquiry, comparative source-studies, sociology of belief, and so forth – whose most signal achievement was the undermining of revealed or dogmatic religion. 'At the beginning of the eighteenth century,' he writes, '[most] Protestants took the Bible to be the word of God; by the beginning of the twentieth century this belief was untenable in intellec- tual circles.'[44] Nowadays this historical trend has been reversed, at least among the arbiters of lit-crit fashion, to a point where (for instance) deconstruction can be annexed to the discourse of negative theology, and where the values of enlightened or secular critique are routinely dis- missed as an embarrassing throwback to that bad old regime of reason, progress, and truth. And so it has come about that, 'instead of leading the critique of dogmatic theologies, literary criticism is contributing to the legitimation of religious discourse.'[45]

Postmodernism has opened the way to this retreat through its regular confusion between the different orders of truth-claim: on the one hand, those that trade upon notions of inward certainty, privileged access, authentic revelation, and the like; and, on the other hand, those that con- test such ideas – such presumptively self-validating pseudo-truths – by adopting alternative, more rigorous standards of critical accountability. These latter bear not the least resemblance to that composite bugbear image of Truth that postmodernists and neo-pragmatists offer by way of discrediting the whole Enlightenment enterprise. Thus Catherine Belsey again: 'History, in each of its manifestations, was the single, unified, unproblematic, extra-textual, extra-discursive real that guaranteed our readings of the texts which constituted its cultural *expression*.'[46] But such notions of expressive realism – of truth as revealed in the fullness of time through an act of omniscient retrospective grasp – have their place only within a history of thought that runs from Hegel to various forms of latter- day Hegelian *Kulturgeschichte*. Of course, it will be urged on the postmod- ern side that 'Enlightenment' truth-claims always involve this appeal to some deep-laid teleological schema or strong meta-narrative drive; that between Kant and Hegel (or Hegel and Marx) there is little to choose save minor variations on a well-worn historicist theme.[47] To which the only possible response, as I have argued, is that this is a false reading of intellectual history, one that has given rise to some damaging confusions through its will to assimilate every kind of truth to the workings of an undifferentiated power/knowledge.

Kant was clear enough on the main point at issue: on the need to maintain a due sense of the difference between private modes of conviction and belief (e.g., those arrived at through 'authentic,' inward revelation) and the public sphere of openly accountable reasons, arguments, principles, and values.[48] He was likewise much aware of the dangers courted by any interest-group or creed – like the current postmodern-pragmatist trend – that set out to blur the line between these disparate orders of truth-claim, and which thus ended up by effectively endorsing a wholesale reduction of truth to what is presently and contingently 'good in the way of belief.' Hence the importance of respecting those various distinctive criteria – historical, philosophical, ethical, socio-political, and so forth – which alone provide adequate standards for assessing the validity of claims put forward at the level of informed argumentative debate. Hence also Kant's warning (taken up, albeit rather ambivalently, in some of Derrida's recent texts) against the risks attendant on the habit of appealing to private conscience or inward conviction as a substitute for that process of reasoned critical inquiry whereby such claims could properly be tested in point of their truth-telling warrant.[49] Nor can this be seen as just one more manifestation of that inveterate will-to-power – or that sublimated link between torture and truth – which duBois finds responsible for so much misery, oppression, and suffering. On the contrary: insofar as we can register the fact of such evils and seek to understand and to remedy their causes, it is a sign of our having progressed beyond the stage of unthinking doctrinal adherence or passive consensus belief. Postmodernism amounts to a vote of no confidence in this entire tradition of enlightened philosophical, ethical, and social thought. That it is presently enjoying such a widespread vogue among theorists of various political persuasion is reason enough to re-examine its relation to the dominant self-images of the age.

NOTES

1 See particularly, for the purposes of this essay, Page duBois, *Torture and Truth* (New York and London: Routledge, 1991). For other recent work of related interest, see, for instance, Elaine Scarry, *The Body in Pain: The Making and*

Unmaking of the World (New York: Oxford University Press, 1985); Barbara Harlow, *Resistance Literature* (London: Methuen, 1987); and Barbara J. Eckstein, *The Language of Fiction in a World of Pain: Reading Politics as Paradox* (Philadelphia: University of Pennsylvania Press, 1990).

2 Michel Foucault, *Discipline and Punish: The Birth of the Prison*, trans. Alan Sheridan (London: Allen Lane, 1977).

3 See especially Michel Foucault, *Language, Counter-Memory, Practice*, ed. D.F. Bouchard and Sherry Simon (Oxford: Basil Blackwell, 1977).

4 See Michel Foucault, *The History of Sexuality: Vol. 1*, trans. Robert Hurley (New York: Vintage Books, 1980).

5 This argument is pursued at various points in Michel Foucault, *Power/Knowledge: Selected Interviews and Other Writings*, ed. Colin Gordon (Brighton: Harvester, 1980).

6 See Michel Foucault, *The Order of Things: An Archaeology of the Human Sciences*, trans. Alan Sheridan (London: Tavistock, 1970).

7 Jürgen Habermas, *The Philosophical Discourse of Modernity: Twelve Lectures*, trans. Frederick Lawrence (Cambridge: Polity Press, 1988).

8 Catherine Belsey, 'Afterword: A Future for Materialist Feminist Criticism?' in Valerie Wayne, ed., *The Matter of Difference: Materialist Feminist Criticism of Shakespeare* (Hemel Hempstead: Harvester/Wheatsheaf, 1991), 261–2.

9 See, for instance, Peter Gay, *The Enlightenment: An Interpretation*, 2 vols. (London: Routledge and Kegan Paul, 1967 and 1973).

10 T.W. Adorno, *Minima Moralia: Reflections from a Damaged Life*, trans. E.F.N. Jephcott (London: New Left Books, 1974); also T.W. Adorno and Max Horkheimer, *Dialectic of Enlightenment* (London: Verso, 1979).

11 Belsey, supra n. 8 at 262.

12 Habermas, supra n. 7.

13 On this levelling or undifferentiating tendency in Foucault's work, see Michael Walzer, 'The Politics of Michel Foucault,' in David C. Hoy, ed., *Foucault: A Critical Reader* (Oxford: Basil Blackwell, 1986), 51–68.

14 See Foucault, *Discipline and Punish*, supra n. 2; also various passages in Stephen Greenblatt, *Shakespearean Negotiations: The Circulation of Social Energy in Renaissance England* (Oxford: Clarendon Press, 1988); and Stephen Greenblatt, *Learning to Curse: Essays in Early Modern Culture* (London: Routledge, 1990). I should mention that duBois is more alert to this danger – often courted by Foucault and the New Historicists – of coming to regard such scenes of 'spectacular' human agony as further material for set-piece textualist treatment. In this connection, see Scarry, *The Body in Pain*, supra n. 1, especially chapter 1, 'The Structure of Torture: The Conversion of Real Pain into the Fiction of Power,' 27–59.

15 Norman Geras, *Discourses of Extremity: Radical Ethics and Post-Marxist Extravagances* (London: Verso, 1990); Ernesto Laclau and Chantal Mouffe, *Hegemony and Socialist Strategy: Towards a Radical Democratic Politics* (London: Verso, 1985).

16 Geras, *Discourses of Extremity,* supra n. 15 at 162.

17 In this connection, see Christopher Norris, *Spinoza and the Origins of Modern Critical Theory* (Oxford: Basil Blackwell, 1991).

18 See Stanley Fish, *Doing What Comes Naturally: Change, Rhetoric, and the Practice of Theory in Literary and Legal Studies* (Oxford: Oxford University Press, 1989).

19 Geras, supra n. 15 at 163.

20 duBois, supra n. 1 at 137.

21 Thomas Hobbes, *Leviathan* (London: Dent, 1978).

22 Habermas, supra n. 7.

23 See especially Foucault, *The History of Sexuality,* supra n. 4; and *Power/Knowledge,* supra n. 5.

24 duBois, supra n. 1 at 157.

25 Ibid.

26 For some relevant background history, see Christopher Hitchens, '*Realpolitik* in the Gulf' (1991), 186 *New Left Review* 89–101.

27 See, for instance, Edward S. Herman and Noam Chomsky, *Manufacturing Consent: The Political Economy of the Mass Media* (New York: Pantheon Books, 1988).

28 duBois, supra n. 1 at 155.

29 Francis Fukuyama, 'The End of History' (Summer 1989) *The National Interest* [Washington].

30 Francis Fukuyama, 'Changed Days for Ruritania's Dictator' (8 April 1991) *The Guardian* 19.

31 duBois, supra n. 1 at 157.

32 See Richard Rorty, *Contingency, Irony, and Solidarity* (Cambridge: Cambridge University Press, 1989); and Fish, *Doing What Comes Naturally,* supra n. 18.

33 Fukuyama, 'Changed Days for Ruritania's Dictator,' supra n. 30.

34 Rorty, *Contingency, Irony, and Solidarity,* supra n. 32 at 113.

35 Terry Eagleton, *Ideology: An Introduction* (London: Verso, 1991), ix.

36 duBois, supra n. 1 at 124–5.

37 Ibid. at 125.

38 See, for instance, Habermas, *The Theory of Communicative Action,* vol. 1, trans. Thomas McCarthy (London: Heinemann, 1984).

39 This aspect of Heidegger's philosophy is most tellingly criticized by Adorno in *The Jargon of Authenticity,* trans. K. Tarnowski and F. Will (London: Routledge and Kegan Paul, 1973).

40 See Christopher Norris, 'Limited Think: How Not to Read Derrida,' in *What's*

Wrong with Postmodernism: Critical Theory and the Ends of Philosophy (London: Harvester; Baltimore: Johns Hopkins University Press, 1990), 134–63.

41 Jacques Derrida, 'Afterword' to *Limited Inc.*, 2d ed. (Evanston: Northwestern University Press, 1989), 146.

42 Paul de Man, 'Foreword' to *The Dissimulating Harmony*, by Carol Jacobs (Baltimore: Johns Hopkins University Press, 1978), viii.

43 Jonathan Culler, *Framing the Sign: Criticism and Its Institutions* (Oxford: Basil Blackwell, 1988), 78.

44 Ibid. at 79.

45 Ibid.

46 Catherine Belsey, 'Making Histories Then and Now,' in Francis Barker, ed., *Uses of History: Marxism, Postmodernism and the Renaissance* (Manchester: Manchester University Press, 1991), 26.

47 See, for instance, Jean-François Lyotard, *The Postmodern Condition: A Report on Knowledge*, trans. Geoff Bennington and Brian Massumi (Minneapolis: University of Minnesota Press, 1986).

48 See especially Immanuel Kant, *Political Writings*, ed. H. Reiss (Cambridge: Cambridge University Press, 1973); and *On History*, ed. L.W. Beck (New York: Bobbs-Merrill, 1963).

49 Jacques Derrida, 'Of an Apocalyptic Tone Recently Adopted in Philosophy,' trans. John P. Leavey (1984) 6(2) *Oxford Literary Review*.

Some Disquiet about 'Difference'[1]

CHRISTINE SYPNOWICH

Introduction

That human beings, their cultures and identities, are heterogeneous, indeed perhaps as different from each other as they are alike, is not a novel idea. But the idea of 'difference' has recently entered both intellectual and popular culture as a profound challenge to the assumptions and practices of politics. To take some striking contemporary examples, what might have been thought to be two of the most stable and unified political systems, the Soviet Union, bound together by a seemingly impregnable authoritarian system of control, and Canada, united around what seemed a harmonious social-democratic or liberal consensus, are now in the throes of fragmentation. The claims of various ethnic and regional identities have put into question the modern idea of citizenship as membership in a collective, universal entity which subsumes diversity and the particular. Moreover, the liberal and socialist complexions of such modern collectivities as Canada and the former USSR have been targeted in particular as sources of a false universalism. It is perhaps not surprising, then, that the most fragile of universals, the 'international community,' founders in its efforts to halt the tragic ethnic conflict in the former Yugoslavia. Both NATO and the United Nations are hampered by the efforts of some member states to identify the pursuit of national (or, better, ethnic) self-determination on one side or another as worthy of support. These processes of fragmentation in international affairs have been mirrored in philosophical inquiry with the rise to prominence of the idea of difference. Feminist and postmodern critics of liberal and Marxist theories of emancipation have been concerned to expose a myth of homogeneity and universalism in political thought since the Enlightenment.

Instead of 'the citizen,' 'the self,' or even 'the proletariat' or 'Party,' these critics posit human subjects who bear diverse and incommensurable identities which cannot be articulated within the confines of a single discourse. This essay assesses the import of the idea of difference in contemporary political theory and practice. I argue that while an emphasis on difference is a useful antidote to the false universalism of many theories of emancipation, the significance of difference in any large sense is more difficult to make out. In particular, I suggest grounds for disquiet about the role of difference in theories or movements which aspire to equality and justice.

The Metaphysics of Sameness: From the Enlightenment to Marx

While the idea of difference is presented as an attack on the traditions of the Enlightenment, it may be argued that the idea of difference was unleashed by the Enlightenment itself. After all, in both its epistemic project of grounding rational understanding in the deductions or observations of the individual subject, and its political project of assuring the individual agent some measure of liberty, the distinctiveness of individuals was the Enlightenment's starting point. In Descartes's preoccupations with the possibility of knowledge and Hobbes's argument for obligation based on self-interest, we see the emergence of the idea of the uniqueness of the individual perspective, and the impossibility of simply subsuming this perspective under the authority of some community. Difference is inherent in the atomistic subject who doubts the authenticity of others' very existence, on Descartes's view, or who is at war with other self-interested subjects in Hobbes's war of all against all.[2] Difference persists in contemporary liberalism insofar as these considerations have generated a pluralism about values, where moral and political questions must be settled by the natural sympathies or personal choices of disparate selves behind a 'veil of ignorance.'[3] The market economy fits easily into this picture, insofar as it offers the context within which these disparate selves can pursue their diverse material interests.

However, for all its scope for diversity, the Enlightenment project has some obvious homogenizing aspects. First, it assumes that the individual has certain immutable and universal characteristics, such as rationality, autonomy, and self-interest. Indeed, the Cartesian subject is difficult to see as a particular person of any kind. Individuals are thus easily aggregated, however isolated they are from each other. Second, the individual was assumed to have a set of trans-historical concerns; individuals might put their liberty or property to different purposes, but it was supposed that all individuals valued liberty and property. Classical liberalism in particular was thus charged with generalizing from a mode of the person specific to market societies, the possessive individual, to advance arguments about the nature of all human beings.[4] Liberal theories of rights, for example, were criticized for being derived from a false universalism; Marx, in particular, argued that the supposed 'natural rights' proclaimed by the American and French revolutionaries were in fact the rights of 'man as a bourgeois who is considered to be the *essential* and *true* man.'[5]

This brings us to Marxism itself. One might expect that Marxism would not be prey to the false universalism of the liberal tradition since the Enlightenment. Certainly the Marxist critique of capitalism is also a critique of the abstract individualism of liberal thought. According to Marx, the image of the market and state as shaped by the free choices of individuals was an ideological illusion, masking the actual conflicting interests and struggle between classes.[6] Real differences, between historical periods and between different persons, that is, differences in interests and in power, were rendered opaque by the liberal model. For Marxists, true diversity was only possible in a society without the divisions of labour, private property, and class, in which individuals might take on a variety of tasks and form a variety of attachments. Thus the famous description of communism as a society in which one can 'hunt in the morning, fish in the afternoon, rear cattle in the evening, criticise after dinner ... without ever becoming hunter, fisherman, shepherd or critic.'[7]

Nevertheless, Marxism, too, could be said to be imprisoned in a metaphysics of sameness, a universalization of the particular, in three respects. First, in its preoccupation with the contours of capitalist oppression, Marxism excludes other kinds of oppression from its analysis. Social change is guided by 'universal laws,' which refer to economic development alone. If considered at all, other kinds of oppression are simply deduced from the logic of capitalist exploitation; thus Engels explains the subordination of women with reference to private property.[8] Second, this 'economism' prompts Marxism to designate one agent with the task of human emancipation. Thus the working class, whose (real) interests lie in the overthrow of capitalism and its replacement by communism, is the world-historical or universal class who represents the interests of humanity as a whole. The third way in which difference is downplayed in the Marxist account is in the depiction of communism itself. Historically, of course, communist regimes such as that of Stalin or Mao undertook the brutal submergence of the individual into the community, the imposition of consensus by force. But Marxist theory also focuses on the ideal of social unity, considering it, however, as the natural and spontaneous consequence of the abolition of capitalism. The communist individual is a universal being who transcends particular identities or social definitions. Thus communism is a univocal, harmonious community, marking 'the *genuine* resolution of the conflict between man and nature and between man and man.'[9] We thus have the paradox in Marxist theory that the elimination of the division of labour not only makes it possible for the individual to enjoy a life of diversity, but also ensures that unanimity characterizes social relations as a whole.

'Vive la différence'

These images of universal emancipation, be they based on abstract individualism or the exclusivity of class, have come under attack from several quarters. Feminists, in particular, have taken issue with the Enlightenment model of personal identity, although their critiques have implications for issues of race, ethnicity, and a number of other cultural differences. On the face of it, Descartes's rationalism and Hobbes's contractualism look hospitable to a gender-neutral epistemology or politics. But feminists have argued, contra Descartes and Hobbes, that persons are not self-contained atoms, but embodied, intersubjective beings. In this, feminists have invoked, not abstract reason or hypothetical states of nature, but (among other things) empirical studies of early childhood development.[10] Introspective contemplation or the assertion of interests may validate the existence of the self, but relations of attachment with caring others, and attachment to one's own gendered body, bring diverse selves into existence. Post-structuralist feminists take the embodiedness of the subject further, arguing that the female body is the source of an alternative episteme.[11] Thus it is concluded that the Cartesian or Hobbesian self refers, not to an abstract human nature, but to a particular, historically contingent, male nature.

In this, feminists join Marxists in suggesting that the idea of a universal human nature is ideological, camouflaging unequal relations of power. And indeed, feminists have long looked to Marxism for theoretical insights and frameworks to identify inequality between the sexes in liberal capitalist societies. Nonetheless, insofar as Marxism remains attached to a universalist model of philosophical anthropology and political emancipation, it is problematic for feminists. Marxist feminism has thus found itself on the defensive since the analysis of patriarchy as a unique form of oppression emerged in the 1970s. At best, Marxism was blind to the specificities of sex; at worst, it placed women at the rear of the proletariat's march through history. The prospects of a partnership between such different emancipatory agendas looked bleak enough for feminists to decry the union of Marxism and feminism as an 'unhappy marriage.'[12]

However, having liberated itself from the imperialistic designs of liberal and Marxist theory, feminist theory itself has been accused of a homogenous account of oppression. Increasingly, issues of race, ethnicity, and culture have prompted soul-searching among feminists about the extent to which the category 'woman,' introduced as an antidote to the false universalism of 'man,' also abstracts from important distinctions based on diverse identities. Feminists, like their counterparts elsewhere, were urged by black feminists in particular to 'appreciate difference,' to see that 'there was no one strategy or formula for the development of political consciousness.'[13]

The idea of a homogenous female identity was attractive for feminists in part because it seemed to promise an escape from the atomistic conception of the person in liberal political theories since Hobbes.[14] The idea that women acted on an 'ethic of care' in their historical role as caretaker was the basis for this female ontology.[15] Paradoxically, while it insisted on the commonality among women, the ethic of care itself was commended for replacing the universal strictures of rules of justice with a concern for the particular needs of persons in specific contexts. Nonetheless, the emphasis on gender identity produced worries of an unrepresentative feminism focused on the interests of the more privileged of women.[16] Like the liberalism it criticized, such 'cultural feminisms' looked guilty of abstracting from diverse historical reality to fashion a universal model of human agency: here the caring woman, rather than the atomistic individual.

These criticisms, of course, are not new. Activists for other disempowered groups have accused feminism of elitism since the suffrage movement, when the vote for women was often pursued at the expense of alliances with workers or, in the United States, the abolitionist cause. However, what is unique about these criticisms in the current context is their place in a wider disenchantment with the scope and aim of traditional emancipatory political projects, a disenchantment which has crystallized around the idea of difference. Old-style 'grand narratives' of emancipation have been replaced by a plethora of new social movements spanning issues of personal and global politics, from sexual orientation to the right of secession; it would appear that if political coalition is possible, it is only on the terms of a self-conscious 'rainbow coalition.'

These political changes have found a theoretical context within postmodernism, in the writings of thinkers as diverse as Lyotard, Foucault, Rorty, and Irigaray. They can be grouped together as 'postmodern' insofar as they share a critique of fixity, certainty, and unity. This critique undercuts the idea of progress so central to the modern age. Thus a foundation for knowledge, a transparent linguistic medium between world and self, an emancipatory political agent, humanist ideals of freedom or fraternity, the possibility of aesthetic judgment; all have been deconstructed with the idea that the individual subject is imprisoned within language or discourse, so that no Archimedean point from which to perceive, let alone evaluate, the world is possible.

Whether or not the postmodern perspective is compatible with the liberatory projects of the constituents of the 'rainbow coalition' is the subject of considerable debate.[17] But there is reason at least to be guarded on this score. Postmodernism's 'breakdown of the grand narrative,' Heller and Feher note, can take forms as diverse as 'relativistic indifference of respective cultures to one another,' or 'the thoroughly inauthentic ... "third worldism" of first-world intellectuals.'[18] Quietism seems a constant danger in the postmodern enterprise. Lyotard's 'polytheism of values' means that political judgment can only be local and internal to the values themselves, thus suggesting a Burkean reverence for the deliverances of the community.[19] Rorty's critique of foundationalism has generated a self-conscious 'bourgeois liberalism,' which can only muster confidence in the trite injunction not to be cruel.[20] A feminist postmodernism might seem more likely to yield strategies of liberation. But here the critique of androcentrism is sometimes so thorough-going as to suggest a rejection of politics *per se*, and a focus on more amorphous modes of liberation, through poetic expression or dance.[21]

Foucault's preoccupation with power offers the most hope for an insurgent postmodern voice, which rouses 'docile bodies' to challenge the oppression with which they have hitherto colluded. But Foucault suggests that discourse so determines the ground rules for its own unmasking that the prospects for an emancipatory viewpoint threaten to evaporate.[22] At times, Foucault goes so far as to sneer at all previous liberatory projects as 'the forms that made an essentially normalising power acceptable.'[23] While Foucault's scepticism is certainly salutary, it threatens a paralysis that worries the social critic. As Donna Haraway notes, 'for political people' postmodernism or social constructionism 'cannot be allowed to decay into the radiant emanations of cynicism.'[24]

Democracy and Difference

The possibility that the idea of difference might yield apolitical, or worse, conservative conclusions has been countered by some important efforts at uniting the postmodern framework with an emancipatory politics. Thus Iris Marion Young argues in her important and stimulating book, *Justice and the Politics of Difference*, that attention to difference can 'broaden and deepen' traditional socialist commitments to democracy and equality. Focusing on the specific identities which are produced by membership in oppressed groups, Young proposes a new approach to social justice, which eschews liberal ideas of impartiality and distributive fairness, on the one hand, and communitarian ideas of unmediated community and 'the good life,' on the other. For Young, a more ambitious conception of justice is most likely to be realized if we recognize that the plethora of identities and oppressions in contemporary society requires we scale down our ambitions for a single political criterion. Young thus proposes participatory democracy, affirmative action, group representation in political bodies, and indeed, in order to eliminate prejudice and xenophobia, a cultural revolution involving 'politicization' of 'habits, feelings and expressions of fantasy and desire,' 'a kind of social therapy.'[25]

While Young's main target is the liberal-communitarian debates of mainstream political philosophy, a similar argument has been advanced within a 'post-Marxist' terrain by Ernesto Laclau and Chantal Mouffe. In their provocative and penetrating book, *Hegemony and Socialist Strategy*, they criticize the Marxist view of a universal emancipatory subject which emanates from a single set of social relations for being both incoherent in theory and oppressive in practice. They suggest nonetheless that certain Marxist tools, such as Althusser's idea of over-determination and the Gramscian idea of hegemony, can contribute to a politics of diversity and openness which might disrupt the 'logic of equivalence' which has thus far characterized egalitarian thought. On this basis, they urge 'articulatory practices' whereby diverse 'subject-positions' of class, race, occupation, and sexuality can find expression in 'floating signifiers' which do not predetermine or foreclose the political form but might crystallize into 'nodal points' of common resistance. Social antagonisms can thus give rise to coalitions in which the socialist struggle to abolish capitalism is complemented by other struggles in a 'proliferation of radically new and different spaces.'[26]

This vision of an open, democratic politics which includes the disenfranchised on their own terms is a compelling alternative to universalist discourses. One cannot help but be persuaded by the arguments of Young and Laclau and Mouffe that empowering dominated social groups should not mean their assimilation into institutions of domination, but rather, a recognition of their different identities, which would challenge such institutions. How these different identities can come together, however, remains a thorny question. It might be argued that any effort to articulate a theory of social change whereby diverse social groups coalesce around common goals is susceptible to postmodern scepticism. On the postmodern view of difference, political projects can only aspire to the cohabitation of plural identities. Difference is thus bound to defeat the political theories which seek to emphasize and resolve it. With this danger in mind, perhaps political theorists should subject the idea of difference to more careful scrutiny. This is the aim of what follows.

Begging to Differ

Simply from a practical point of view, one might question the confidence of thinkers like Young or Laclau and Mouffe that difference is compatible with egalitarian politics. There seems to be good reason to think that if the distinctiveness of identities is taken seriously, then politics risks being stymied in differences which are ultimately irreconcilable. For example, the demands of gay and lesbian groups are not obviously compatible with those of black, aboriginal, or other ethnic groups which seek the preservation of cultural traditions. The poor find themselves at odds with those who focus on regional autonomy. What is the likely outcome of such impasses?

Fearful of assessing the demands of any group with criteria which lie outside of it, politics may end up performing little more than a brokerage function, as was advocated by liberal theories of pluralism in the 1960s. At best, this produces a politics of compromise rather than one based on principles of justice. Worse, parochialism runs rampant or, as critics of interest-group theory have long argued, the most powerful (best financed) voices will tend to hold sway.[27] As Laclau has recently admitted, 'if universalism does not necessarily lead in a democratic direction, particularism does not do so either.' With the defeat of modernity's confidence in a rational ground of history, 'exclusionary discourses' can develop which lead to intransigency and xenophobia.[28] Not justice or democracy, but paralysis, crisis, or balkanization may thus be the consequence of the idea of difference, so long as external criteria by which to assess the claims of difference are excluded.[29]

It could be argued that the risks of difference are worth taking. After all, the critique of universalism suggested by the idea of difference underscores the extent to which the universal is in fact the particular – the propertied, men, or Caucasians, for example – camouflaged as the general. Xenophobia, it may be retorted, is no less rampant here, insofar as 'the other' is excluded from and oppressed by the pseudo-universalist ontology, metaphysics, or justice.

Nonetheless, there is a not unimportant distinction to be drawn between a universalism which fails to fulfil its promise and a particularism which repudiates the universal. Subjecting the claims of a purportedly inclusive social order to immanent critique to render it truly inclusive is thus important as both strategy and ideal. The contemporary nation-state, for all its bigotry and partiality, has within it the kernel of an emancipatory promise, the aspiration to a unity in diversity, a universal order which, in its general guarantees of citizenship, is open to all. This aspiration should be struggled for and improved rather than rejected. Its full achievement would doubtless require far-reaching social change, so that citizens are equal enough in resources to make good their citizenship. But the aspiration of citizenship is a useful target with which to guide such change. In Canada, it is this aspiration which makes possible welfare programs which constrain the efforts of right-wing regional politicians to cash in the funds devoted to such programs. It made possible the movement for desegregation in the United States. That members of diverse groups might embrace a more general identity as members of a larger society seems all the more important in our times, when conflict between particular identities threatens to destroy any possibility of community in societies as diverse as the former Soviet Union, a post-apartheid South Africa, and contemporary Canada.

Another difficulty with the discussions of difference is the danger of uncritical acceptance of empirically given identities. If differences are born out of oppression, then it is not clear how liberatory the recognition of them can be. This idea has been the basis of criticism of the feminist ethic of care, since it could be argued that this ethic is a result of the stereotypical roles women have played in the home, and thus is unlikely to contribute to equality for women.[30] But it also applies to other group identities; in attending to difference, we should be wary of making a virtue of oppression. The issue is complicated by the different ontological status of different differences, as it were. Some are wholly socially constructed (racism), and some have important physical causes (as in the case of disabled people), some are complex combinations of various factors. This point does not go entirely unrecognized by Young. A significant part of her argument documents the multifarious ways material practices of oppression can construct the identity of the oppressed.[31] But Young's focus on 'cultural imperialism' prompts her to advocate the inclusion of unmediated 'heterogeneous and partial discourses' to combat racism, sexism, and all the other '-isms' that are exclusionary, without considering the ways in which some discourses are more liberatory than others.

Laclau and Mouffe are more cognizant of the dangers of taking given identities as the basis of democratic politics; they therefore chart a progression of articulation from domination, in which the dominated are unaware of their status, to subordination, which is recognized as such, culminating in oppression, which forms the basis of insurgency. However, the process of articulation is itself not much 'articulated' in their theory, so that it looks like little more than a promissory note that, in the absence of the old guarantees of vanguard party, universal agents, etc., the good will win out. On the other hand, this distinction between levels of consciousness is rather difficult to square with Laclau and Mouffe's understandable suspicion of Marxist ideas of false consciousness and their insistence that radical democracy consists simply in a 'polyphony of voices, each of which constructs its own irreducible discursive identity.'[32]

At root the impulse to include difference is driven by a conviction that one's identity as the member of a race, sex, or linguistic culture should not disadvantage one in social life. Giving certain identities a voice may be one way of accomplishing this, but if power resides outside of those identities, and if the identities themselves are the products of oppression, then this strategy has limitations.[33] If we recognize that some differences are the fruits of injustice, then justice may require the elimination of difference, or at least the difference that difference makes.

From a philosophical point of view, it is not clear whether universalism of some kind is avoidable, in any case. After all, the fate that met feminists, who, having rejected the false universalism of androcentric discourse, were then accused of false universalism in the face of race, culture, etc., is a fate that can meet the assertions of identity that come after them; difference unleashes an endless cycle of accusations and inclusions. We are thus left reciting ever longer moralistic shopping lists of identities in a futile attempt to dam up the floods of interminable difference. Ultimately there are as many differences as selves, and thus all our social categories risk essentialism, wherein we reify a certain identity and proclaim its essential nature, without attention to the differences within the identity itself.

In any case, why focus on the politics of difference? So that the different may be part of a 'we' which is a source of social unity. The hope for commonality continues to drive the theories of Young and Laclau and Mouffe, after all, for all their apparent disenchantment with the idea. We cannot do justice to the differences that characterize human beings, not just because of their infinite variations, but because the effort to 'do justice' to them is to somehow mute their salience. The preoccupation with particular local identities emerges as a kind of 'neo-foundationalism' to ward off the vertigo that besets radical thinkers who have been persuaded by the postmodern critique of foundations. In an impulse to restore the security of old forms of collectivism that the postmodern critique destroyed, difference is included in order for it to be tamed.[34]

These considerations suggest that a focus on the inclusion of difference *per se* is problematic; philosophically, the project risks incoherence, and politically, the project risks an impotence in the face of oppression. We thus have grounds for being cautious about the role of difference in political theory. If we are to tackle injustice, which is after all the preoccupation of difference theorists, then we need a broader inquiry than that of difference itself. Is this possible, without being insensitive to difference and returning political philosophy to the false universalism of grand narratives?

Difference's Discontents

It may be suspected that my argument is simply the nostalgic lamentations of a has-been Marxist (I refuse the term post-Marxist!), one who cannot relinquish the ideals of fraternity and unity essential to the socialist project. Such lamentations should be countered by the astute diagnosis of the impulse for community as an impossible 'Rousseauist dream' of a 'unity of subjects with one another,' as Young puts it, or what Laclau and Mouffe indict as the utopia of a transparent society embodied in the 'Ideal City.'[35]

There is no doubt that classical Marxism is shown to be inadequate by these kinds of arguments about the complexity of heterogeneous identities in society. The fate of the Bolshevik project confirms the impossibility of simply incanting old theories in the wake of disturbing new events. As

Eastern Europe abandons Marxism, Western Marxists cannot assume that they have the resources in some unrevised body of theory with which to correct the theoretical disasters that Eastern Europeans have had to live in practice.[36] For Marxists in particular there is much to learn from the insights of the theory of difference about, among other things, the diversity of social injustices and the agents with which to counter them, the reality of micro-oppressions, the importance of a provisional, open approach in theory, and the inevitability of heterogeneity in even the most ideal societies.

However, my misgivings about difference cannot be discounted simply as a communitarian antipathy to the reality of social divisions. These misgivings stem from a concern for how justice is to be achieved in the face of the competing claims of difference, given that no clear political strategies follow from embracing identities as such. I have two, tentative proposals for meeting these concerns, which, by taking us away from the focus on difference, can better remedy the injustice that is the consequence of issues of difference. These proposals are, first, a consideration of how interests are articulated by the discourse of rights and, second, a reassessment of the idea of impartiality.

Rights and Impartiality

Rights are an obvious means of instantiating diversity. Liberal political theories standardly employ rights to defend and resolve individual differences. Moreover, while rights originally referred to abstract liberties such as freedom to own property, the idea of a right has been successively expanded to include political rights such as the right to vote, and social rights such as the right to health care. The achievements of rights discourse have prompted criticisms of the anti-rights thrust of Marxist theory, and the assumption that an ideal society would have no need of legal institutions is one bit of Marxist orthodoxy that must be abandoned once we understand the nature of difference.[37] The fantasy of a univocal, homogenous society which has no need of rights must be countered with a model of rights for articulating the claims of diverse social groups. Insofar as these claims are not merely the claims of abstract individuals, however, they require some revision of liberal theories. Young thus recognizes a role for rights in her theory, suggesting that 'the specificity of each group requires a specific set of rights for each, and for some a more comprehensive system than for others.'[38] For their part, Laclau and Mouffe emphasize that the liberal discourse of individual rights 'permits different forms of articulation and redefinition which accentuate the democratic movement.'[39]

However, it should be recognized that the discourse of rights does not map onto difference in any direct way. Rights cannot take the brute datum of diverse identities at face value. Rights are not the mere effluxes of identities, but politically contested claims that persons make to have their interests protected.[40] We thus must move from the identity of an agent to the interests to which identity gives rise. And having identified the agent's interests, we must then assess their legitimacy. Thus interests must, first, be capable of being formulated in general enough terms to count as rights and, second, be capable of being recognized by others as worthy of the stature of rights. Rights require that difference be mediated by debate and consensus in order to assess competing claims in light of the demands of justice. Thus while difference will give rise to political activity about the terrain of rights, how that terrain is ultimately to be specified requires a reference outside of difference. Questions of human needs, the constituents of human dignity, the prerequisites for self-respect, these are universal ideals to which rights refer.

It must be emphasized, as Benhabib, after Habermas, argues against the abstraction of liberal theory, that rather than a hypothetical thought process, the constitution of rights must come from an 'actual dialogue situation in which moral agents communicate with each other' about their needs.[41] Thus our understanding of justice need not be conceived as an eternal, ahistorical standard, an Archimedean point beyond experience. Rights are inevitably constituted by evolving conceptions of justice, what Haraway calls 'situated knowledges,'[42] which are constructed in the context of struggle and debate. The universalism of rights is thus to be understood in terms of the applicability of their ultimate ideals, rather than the fixity of their content.

The universalism of rights thus makes it possible for diverse groups to unite around a common political ideal. While rights discourse can be used to specify and meet particular needs – parents' rights to childcare, or aboriginal peoples' rights to land – it is by reference to a consensus on a fulfilling or empowered life which is available to all.[43] By protecting different interests, rights give us grounds for a commitment to an entity outside of our disparate identities. In the context of Canada, the *Charter of Rights and Freedoms* has played a significant role, therefore, in debates about national unity. And the specification of a social charter has been commended as another important way of achieving consensus on the integrity of the Canadian polity.[44]

Rights, however, are not typically seen as sources of unity. It must be admitted that rights can pit citizens against each other, as they seek the recognition of opposing interests. How are we to resolve the inevitable disputes that surround claims and counter-claims in terms of both the constitution and enforcement of rights? The idea of impartiality is the usual response in liberal theory. A posture of impartiality is assumed as a political theory establishes rights, and the mechanisms of the rule of law are said to ensure that rights are impartially enforced.

However, the idea of difference has been marshalled to discredit the idea of impartiality. For Young and Laclau and Mouffe, impartiality is both impossible, given the intractability of different identities, and undesirable, since it inevitably imposes one point of view on others.[45] This critique rests, however, on a caricature of the idea. No philosopher or judge can be impartial in the sense of devoid of perspective, interests, or values. But the ideal of impartiality is just that, an ideal to which we should aspire. It would be a mistake to believe that any legal principle could succeed in making social life wholly predictable, but the impartial ideal embodied in the notion of the rule of law, for example, is able to enforce a degree of regularity in political and legal decision-making. Indeed, it is because the weighing of different claims inevitably requires value-judgments and policy decisions that we need some notion of procedural justice in order to prevent these normative processes from becoming wholly discretionary or arbitrary.

This is not to suggest that the status quo is in fact impartial. But our disillusion with the liberal capitalist state should cause us, not to reject impartiality, but to demand it and to point to the ways in which inequality prevents impartiality from being fully operable. The ideal of impartiality can thus figure as part of a struggle for social justice, and our demand for impartial treatment will thus cause us to challenge the unfairness of the advantages of property and social position. The discourses of rights and impartiality therefore – far from being features of a false universalistic discourse – are the means of struggling for that ever-elusive but nonetheless inspiring universalist ideal.

At the same time, essential to these discourses is a tolerance, and indeed protection, of diversity. Rights to privacy and autonomy, together with the rejection of discrimination or bias inherent in the ideal of impartiality, allow us to engage in different ways of living. It should be underlined that rights and impartiality do not make for total freedom and absolute neutrality; but they serve to keep Mill's 'tyranny of the majority' at bay, so that the different are not treated as 'the other.' The challenge of our differences cannot be met by subsuming them within a new, multifarious 'we': rather, the only viable response must be a modest one, that of working towards a culture of openness.

Conclusion

The idea of difference provides an important reminder of the limitations of emancipatory political theory. Emancipation is not a likely prospect unless our political theories and practices stay open to other perspectives, take account of the diverse forms oppression can take, and remain consciously provisional and revisable. In our post-communist age, these are important lessons. However, I have suggested that beyond this injection of caution into our political projects, it is not clear how the idea of difference can shape political theory. Instead of identity itself, we should focus our attention on the interests that accrue from different identities and the extent to which they figure as claims for justice. This enterprise requires a central role for the institutions of rights and procedural fairness. Instead of jettisoning these institutions as the relics of a bygone false universalism, I suggest that we call upon them to express our aspiration for equality and democracy. If we are the bearers of incommensurable, diverse identities, we cannot expect political institutions to recognize and convert these identities into sources of unity and cohesion. What we can demand of our political institutions is that our differences do not give rise to social divisions and unfairness. Thus citizenship provides us with the abstract entitlement to political participation and adequate resources to remedy the inequalities of difference. Postmodernism has underscored the impossibility of bridging differences; but the ideals of liberalism and socialism need not be taken to be the pursuit of such universalist chimeras. Rather, we can live diversely in common only if inequality, not difference, becomes our focus.

NOTES

1 An earlier version of this paper was published in (1993) 13(2) *Praxis International*, 99. I am grateful to David Bakhurst, Don Carmichael, Stephen Andrews, Jerry Bickenbach, and an anonymous referee for University of Toronto Press for helpful comments.

2 René Descartes, *The Meditations*, in *Discourse on Method and the Meditations*, trans. F.E. Sutcliffe (Harmondsworth: Penguin, 1968) and Thomas Hobbes, *Leviathan*, ed. C.B. Macpherson (Harmondsworth: Penguin, 1968).

3 John Rawls, *A Theory of Justice* (Cambridge, Mass.: Harvard University Press, 1972).

4 C.B. Macpherson, *Possessive Individualism* (Oxford: Clarendon, 1962).

5 Karl Marx, 'On the Jewish Question,' in *Marx and Engels: Collected Works* (London: Lawrence and Wishart, 1975–), 3:164.

6 Karl Marx and Friedrich Engels, *German Ideology, Marx and Engels: Selected Works* (Moscow: Progress, 1979), 68–76.

7 Ibid. at 33–5.

8 Friedrich Engels, *The Origin of the Family, Private Property and the State*, introd. and notes Eleanor Burke Leacock (New York: International Publishers, 1972).

9 Karl Marx, 'Economic and Philosophical Manuscripts,' in *Collected Works*, supra n. 5, at 3:298.

10 Nancy Chodorow, *The Reproduction of Mothering* (Berkeley: University of California Press, 1978); and Carol Gilligan, *A Different Voice* (Cambridge, Mass.: Harvard University Press, 1982).

11 Luce Irigaray, *This Sex Which Is Not One*, trans. Catherine Porter and Carolyn Burke (Ithaca: Cornell University Press, 1985). See selections by Irigaray and Julia Kristeva in *New French Feminisms*, ed. and introd. Elaine Marks and Isabelle de Courtivron (New York: Schocken Books, 1988), and Judith Butler, *Gender Trouble* (New York: Routledge, 1990).

12 Heidi Hartmann, 'The Unhappy Marriage of Marxism and Feminism: Toward a More Progressive Union,' in L. Sargent, ed., *Women and Revolution* (Boston: South End Press, 1971).

13 bell hooks, 'Sisterhood: Political Solidarity Between Women,' in ibid.; and M. Lugones and F. Spelman, 'Have We Got a Theory for You! Feminist Theory, Cultural Imperialism and the Demand for "The Woman's Voice"' (1983) 6 *Women's Studies International Forum* 573.

14 I explore this in the context of contemporary debates in political theory in 'Justice, Community and the Antinomies of Feminist Theory' (1993) 21(3) *Political Theory* 484.

15 S. Ruddick, 'Maternal Thinking' (1980) 6(2) *Feminist Studies* 342; E. Feder Kittay and D. Meyers eds., *Women and Moral Theory* (Totowa, N.J.: Rowman and Littlefield, 1986).

16 Gayatri Spivak, 'French Feminism in an International Frame,' in *In Other Worlds* (New York: Routledge, 1988).

17 See, for example, Jürgen Habermas, 'Modernity versus Postmodernity' (1981) 22 *New German Critique* 3; Charles Taylor, 'Foucault on Freedom and Truth,' in *Philosophical Papers*, vol. 2 (Cambridge: Cambridge University Press, 1982); Gad Horowitz, 'The Foucaultian Impasse: No Sex, No Self, No Revolution' (1987) 15(1) *Political Theory* 61; selections by Seyla Benhabib and Nancy Hartsock in

Linda J. Nicholson ed., *Feminism/Postmodernism* (New York: Routledge, 1990); and Donna Haraway, *Simians, Cyborgs and Women* (New York: Routledge, 1991).

18 Agnes Heller and Ferenc Feher, *The Postmodern Political Condition* (Oxford: Polity, 1988), 5.

19 Jean-François Lyotard, *The Postmodern Condition*, trans. G. Bennington and B. Massumi, foreword by F. Jameson (Minneapolis: University of Minnesota Press, 1984).

20 Richard Rorty, 'Postmodern Bourgeois Liberalism' (1983) 80 *Journal of Philosophy* 583; and *Contingency, Irony and Solidarity* (Cambridge: Cambridge University Press, 1989).

21 See selections by Kristeva and Irigaray in *New French Feminisms*, supra n. 11; and Spivak, 'French Feminism in an International Frame,' supra n. 16.

22 So I argue in 'Fear of Death: Mortality and Modernity in Political Philosophy' (1991) 98 *Queen's Quarterly* 618.

23 Michel Foucault, *The History of Sexuality Vol. 1: An Introduction*, trans. R. Hurley (New York: Vintage, 1978), 144; but see also his *Power/Knowledge*, ed. C. Gordon (New York: Pantheon, 1980).

24 Haraway, supra n. 17 at 184.

25 Iris Marion Young, *Justice and the Politics of Difference* (Princeton: Princeton University Press, 1990), 153.

26 Ernesto Laclau and Chantal Mouffe, *Hegemony and Socialist Strategy: Towards a Radical Democratic Politics* (London: Verso, 1985), 176–81.

27 P. Bachrach and M. Baratz, 'The Two Faces of Power' (1962) 56 *American Political Science Review* 947; and S. Lukes, *Power: A Radical View* (London: Macmillan, 1974).

28 'God Only Knows' (December 1991) *Marxism Today* 57.

29 See also Alasdair MacIntyre's critique of liberal individualism in *After Virtue* (London: Duckworth, 1981).

30 See L. Segal, *Is the Future Female?* (London: Virago, 1987); N. Fraser and L. Nicholson, 'Social Criticism without Philosophy,' in Nicholson, ed., *Feminism/ Postmodernism*, 32–3; Susan Moller Okin, *Justice, Gender and the Family* (New York: Basic Books, 1989), 15; Barbara Houston, 'Rescuing Womanly Virtues,' and Marilyn Friedman, 'Beyond Caring,' in M. Hanen and K. Nielsen, eds., *Science, Morality and Feminist Theory* (Calgary: University of Calgary Press, 1987); and my 'Justice, Community and the Antinomies of Feminist Theory,' supra n. 14.

31 Young, supra n. 25, ch. 2.

32 Laclau and Mouffe, supra n. 26 at 191. See the critiques of Norman Geras, 'Post-Marxism?' (1987) 163 *New Left Review* 40; and Peter Osborne, 'Radicalism without Limit,' in Peter Osborne, ed., *Socialism and the Limits of Liberalism* (London: Verso, 1991).

33 Lynne Segal, 'Whose Left? Socialism, Feminism and the Future' (1991) 185 *New Left Review* 81.

34 I am grateful to David Bakhurst for this point.

35 Young, supra n. 25 at 229–32; Laclau and Mouffe, supra n. 26 at 176–93.

36 I make this argument in 'The Future of Socialist Legality' (1992) 193 *New Left Review* 80.

37 This is my argument in *The Concept of Socialist Law* (Oxford: Clarendon, 1990).

38 Young, supra n. 25 at 183.

39 Laclau and Mouffe, supra n. 26 at 176.

40 Thus Ronald Dworkin's idea of rights as 'trumps' in *Taking Rights Seriously* (Cambridge, Mass: Harvard University Press, 1978).

41 Seyla Benhabib, 'The Generalised and the Concrete Other,' in S. Benhabib and D. Cornell, eds., *Feminism as Critique* (Oxford: Basil Blackwell, 1987), 93. See also Jürgen Habermas, *The Theory of Communicative Action*, trans. T. McCarthy (Boston: Beacon Press, 1984).

42 Haraway, supra n. 17 at 191–6.

43 Thus Will Kymlicka advocates aboriginal rights as part of the liberal commitment of treating individuals as equals. See his *Liberalism, Community and Culture* (Oxford: Clarendon, 1989).

44 I develop this argument in 'Rights, Community and the Charter' (1991) 6(1) *British Journal of Canadian Studies* 39.

45 Young, supra n. 25 at 99–107; and Laclau and Mouffe, supra n. 26 at 122–7. This argument has also been made by critical legal theorists such as Duncan Kennedy. See his 'Legal Formality' (1973) 2(1) *Journal of Legal Studies* 351.

INSTANCES

Pertaining to Connection: Abortion and Feminist Legal Theory[1]

SHEILA NOONAN

One of the most persistent debates which besets feminist theory, and in particular feminist legal theory, is the significance to be attached to women's difference. Of course, the phrasing of this question in the first instance is accompanied by a panoply of concomitant disputations: How is one to discern women's difference? What does it consist in? Is it real (i.e., natural) or social? The specifically legal variations address the following dimensions: As a strategy, how might it/they be dealt with in law? Should difference be affirmed or denied, or both?

The legal manifestation of this inquiry has gained new purchase in light of the recent proliferation of visions of justice which stress that group-based oppression might be tackled, at least in part, by affirming rather than devaluing the differences attached to various social groupings.[2] In respect of the various social configurations to which this status might attach, the salient question remains: 'Different from what or whom?'[3] While the question at once suggests the relational quality of difference, it also captures its necessary deviance. As applied to gender, this manner of inquiry operates to foreclose the interrogation of the universality it invokes in the name of revealing women's difference from men.

Of course, in part the task of feminist theory has been to disrupt and expose insidious representations of women generated by and for men. One line of assault against the exclusionary premises and practices of humanism, otherwise known as masculine jurisprudence, has been the valorization of the formerly reviled and degraded. This strategy of challenging male representations of women has countenanced disparate formulations of female essence. In many of the formulations, motherhood, pregnancy, or women's reproductive capacities more broadly defined have become identified as the site of women's difference from men, perhaps because they are so obvious.

The violence which inheres in the creation of simple oppositional narratives or representations should, however, be exposed to the light. Necessarily, such descriptions rely upon reductive and exclusionary practices, which, while allegedly seeking to capture some aspect of self, do so at the expense of expressing another. Such claims not only suppress the contradictory manifestations and trajectories of our multiple selves, but fail to disclose the relational nature of self-definition. These dangers of flattening out the lived disparities between women are particularly acute where these narratives tend to intersect with the universalizing properties of law itself.

The enterprise of legal method as traditionally defined operates on the basis of erasure in the quest to generate coherent content and stable categories. The articulated goals of coherence and stability are facilitated doctrinally through the freezing properties of precedent and *stare decisis*. Moreover, the established canons of reading and relevance permit the exclusionary practices of law itself to play a significant role in maintaining hegemony based on race, class, ability, gender, and sexual orientation. In short, within the legal order erasure and marginalization are violences of the everyday variety.

But it is precisely within the moments of incommensurability that the fundamental incoherence of law is most clearly discerned, and its epistemological bases most baldly exposed. And this, perhaps, is why pregnancy and related reproductive issues are, in fact, direct confrontations with the claims the legal order makes on its own behalf. Within feminist legal theory, then, reproductive struggles represent saturated points of resistance to law's bellicosity.

These challenges to law are often assembled in the name of the female experience of pregnancy, which has no counterpart in male existence. However, seeking to recognize the specificity of women while adhering to aspirations of grand or totalizing accounts risks affirmation of the 'unshakeable hegemony of legal theory.'[4]

Particularly within an oppositional discourse, monolithic accounts of pregnancy, or motherhood, are commonly invoked. Rarely are the premises which accompany these pictures unpacked, and they are, of course, beset with difficulties. At a minimum, they are often generalized in a manner that projects an ethnocentric account of those processes. Reductive descriptions assume an especial significance in law, where singularity best serves the vision of the legal order. Reliance on the notion of the law's web-like consistency often creates results which, while desired in one area, pose insurmountable obstacles in others. Evidence of such tension is in stark relief in the struggle to secure access to abortion services and to render available the various procedures contemplated by the 'new reproductive technologies.' The paradox which ensues from unequivocally embracing 'choice'[5] is heightened by the fact that some 'cultural feminists' have shaped feminist theory around reconceptualizing motherhood. Though it is beyond the scope of this paper to assess the full import of this work, my fear is that certain formulations of cultural feminist theory[6] carry the potential to subvert critique of the varied manifestations of reproductive control.

My concern, though, is more particular, and my agenda more targeted than this initial formulation discloses. It is the tale increasingly told, specifically by Robin West, about radical feminists' relation to 'connection' with which I wish to take issue.[7] I have chosen West both because her work is located within the context of analysing feminist legal theory, and because her account of women's reproductive lives more transparently unfolds as a valorization of selectively presented facets of them. It is the reductionism and essentialism of her descriptions that I find dangerous.

In particular, the phenomenon of pregnancy and the experience of abortion have become the focal points through which very particular accounts of radical feminism are constructed. My primary purpose is essentially twofold: to expose Robin West's construction of radical feminist theory[8] and the implications this carries for the development of feminist legal theory; secondly, to discuss how West's formulation of connection flattens the complexity of women's reproductive lives.

I believe that Robin West's cartography of feminist legal theory, despite claims to the contrary, actively seeks to displace both radical feminism and correspondingly a commitment to the abortion struggle. The picture of radical feminism presented operates to constitute abortion as some women's existential inability to accommodate to the consequences of connection. Largely divorced from the context of the dynamics of institutionalized heterosexuality, and the disparate material composition of women's reproductive lives, radical feminism is abjected in favour of the romantic and logocentric story of connection perfected, namely motherhood. Cultural feminism and motherhood thereby become the sanctioned and sanitized version of feminist legal theory, and abortion and radical feminism, its exiled dark side.

Perhaps this essay assumes its identity primarily as a doleful admonition from the land of the exiled. In an era in which the last vestiges of *Roe* v.

Wade are subject to constant judicial erosion, West's articulation of the connection thesis may result in its hastened demise. But it also seeks to open
a more textured discussion of the disparate narratives that could be told
both about feminist legal theory and reproduction. To this end, the first
reproductive story explores how malestream theory has pitted foetus
against mother. I then wish to turn in the second part to an examination of
West's connection thesis. Story three provides a critique of West's account
of radical feminism and abortion. Finally, I want to explore why abjecting
radical feminism from feminist legal theory is a troubling strategy.

Story One – Separation Thesis: Ad Hominem Homunculus[9]

How did the unborn turn into a billboard image and how did the isolated goblin
get into the limelight? How did the female peritoneum acquire transparency?
What set of circumstances made the skinning of women acceptable and inspired
public concern for what happens in her innards?[10]

In both Canada and the United States, foetal rights have been merged
with and articulated through the rather amorphous concept of state
interest.[11] However, closer examination reveals that legal liberalism for-
mulates the abortion dilemma as requiring the rights of the pregnant
woman to be weighed against the rights of the foetus.

This construction of the abortion issue as the 'clash of absolutes'[12]
which pits mother against foetus (or foetus against mother) operates to
constitute the problem in very particular ways. As Donna Greschner
points out, the exclusion of women in framing the terms and vocabulary
of the abortion debate predetermines its outcome.[13] In her view, it is the
invocation of the discourse of rights which is at the centre of this problematic:

The masculine language and concept that permeates and has especial significance in legal discourse on creation is rights. The traditional, male-stream formulation of rights is that of trumps attaching to separate individuals. A person is
separate from and independent of all others, possessing rights as a means of stop-
ping others from infringing upon his space, his autonomy, his freedom to do what
he wants. Visualizing the foetus as a miniature man fits perfectly and circularly
with the ascription of rights to the foetus: if the foetus is a separate man, he must
have rights, and if a foetus has rights he must be a separate man. Either way, the
foetus has rights that always override, or must at least be balanced against, the
conflicting rights of mothers.[14]

There can be little doubt that efforts to create foetal rights have been mounting, as have the tenacity and virulence of anti-choice demonstrators. Efforts to control women's reproduction through various forms of legal regulation have ranged from deploying child welfare and mental health provisions to direct attacks on clinics and physicians who provide abortion services.[15] None of these incidents can be viewed in isolation, or held in abeyance in weaving our stories related to reproduction. In an age of new technologies when the essence of what defines parenthood is uncertain, constructions of the female body as hostile to the foetus are part of a larger move towards undermining the role of a mother and rendering her contribution to the reproductive process invisible or pernicious. As Hester Lessard suggests, in the abortion context the separation thesis pits rapacious self-interested women against helpless embryos.[16]

The implications for legal doctrine that separation carries must be underscored. The foetus thereby enters legal discourse constructed as a unique entity with a separate legal status.[17] This serves to reinforce its situation within an economy in which the foetus is increasingly displaced and detached from the pregnant woman. That a foetus in fact relies on the body of its mother for survival is thereby obviated and obscured. Mediated in this fashion, the foetus unambiguously achieves centrality as a potential 'victim' bearing interests which warrant protection.

The reification of the foetus central to this paradigm masks the corporeal situatedness of pregnancy. Under this account, the woman is invisible save as womb *qua* entity. Such an abstraction so distorts the condition of pregnancy as to be other-worldly. Moreover, it proceeds from the assumption that the interests of the mother are inimical to those of the foetus. As Shelley Gavigan explains, while the relationship between foetus and mother is not symmetrical, neither is it necessarily antagonistic:

Feminists both acknowledge the fundamental unity of woman and foetus and insist that the relationship is not symmetrical. Indeed, feminist insistence upon pregnancy as a 'relationship' between a pregnant woman and a foetus is as significant as the insight that this relationship is neither symmetrical nor inherently antagonistic. Feminists are thus currently engaged in a concerted struggle to resist the emerging if not yet prevailing image of pregnant women as menacing vessels, an imagery offensive to the integrity and moral agency of pregnant women. But feminists have also had to contend with the new invisibility of pregnant women in this campaign ...[18]

It is only through the endorsement of the premise of abstract 'separation' that an embryo, from the moment of conception, can bear interests which warrant protection and surveillance.[19]

One finds such notions, though, frequently invoked in the arguments in support of foetal rights. When the interests of the foetus are translated into rights talk, the entitlement of the foetus to use a woman's body to ensure its continued life is effectively presumed. The foetal right to life is represented for its own best interest as entirely distinct from the practical meaning and content of women's lives. Given that the right to life is viewed as sacrosanct, interference with women's subjective lives becomes reduced to temporary inconvenience. Christine Overall neatly identifies this process as the covert assumption of foetal rights advocates, namely:

That the fetus has the right to the use of the women's body, that that right should be legally protected, and hence that the pregnant woman has an obligation not to abort and to permit any and all interventions in her body that are medically necessary for the sake of the fetus.[20]

And while these visions of pregnancy have not yet fully manifested themselves in legal doctrine, there is, nonetheless, an increasing tendency for the corporeal locatedness of pregnancy to be masked. Lest this characterization seem insufficiently cognizant of the significant 'gains' women have secured in their legal struggle for abortion, in the recent decision in *Casey* v. *Planned Parenthood of Southeastern Pennsylvania*[21] the United States Supreme Court stated that at viability the 'independent existence of the *second life* can in reason and all fairness be the object of state protection that now overrides the rights of the woman.'[22] While thus far the Supreme Court of Canada has taken a stand which militates against extension of constitutional status to the foetus,[23] it should be stressed that the articulation of state interest in *Morgentaler* appears intended to afford protection to the foetus. As we shall see below, this became the basis in *Casey* for suggesting that cases after *Roe* v. *Wade*[24] had failed to live up *Roe*'s own terms.

If we can identify the separation story as the story of malestream theory, what promise does feminist theory, which begins from the inextricable connectedness of mother and foetus, hold?[25]

Story Two – Stories of Connection

From the publication of Carol Gilligan's celebrated treatise, *In a Different Voice*,[26] much feminist legal theory has sought to locate and give expression to women's unique ontological and epistemological experiences. In any search for 'difference,' pregnancy epitomizes the most striking example of the potentially distinct experiences of men and women.

'Cultural feminist' work takes as its point of departure women's experience of connectedness with, and hence sense of responsibility for, other human beings.[27] While there are a number of variations on work which emerges from women's caretaking, cultural feminism celebrates a 'self that is situated and relational, that views identity and moral choice as a function of particular relationships and changing, contingent responsibilities.'[28] Thus, connectedness and responsibility become a site of difference from men, whose ontological and epistemological experiences are characterized by separation and autonomy.

Gilligan herself was less concerned to construct a theory of female ontology than to account for gender deficiencies in the formulation of Kohlberg's theory of moral development.[29] Essentially, she sought to demonstrate how women render moral decisions from a position which recognizes the 'web' of relatedness of moral agents. Judgments given by women in response to moral dilemmas reflect an ethic of care predicated on concern for the particular context of relationships and responsibilities in which a legal situation arises. Men, on the other hand, render decisions characterized by the abstraction of rights, premised on notions of individual autonomy and separation: 'This is what I mean by two voices, two ways of speaking. One voice speaks about equality, reciprocity, fairness, rights; one voice speaks about connection, not hurting, care, response.'[30]

Connection Revisited

In the work of Robin West, Gilligan's account of the connection thesis is reformulated.[31] Rather than locating the subjective experience of connection in psychology or observable disparities in moral reasoning, West seeks to ground women's subjective experiences in the materiality of pregnancy, or the potential for pregnancy. Her formulation of this materiality is as follows:

Women are not essentially, necessarily, inevitably, invariably, always, and forever separate from other human beings: women, distinctively, are quite clearly 'connected' to another human life when pregnant. In fact, women are in some sense 'connected' to life and to other human beings during at least four recurrent and critical material experiences: the experience of pregnancy itself; the invasive and 'connecting' experience of heterosexual penetration, which may lead to pregnancy; the monthly experience of menstruation, which represents the potential for pregnancy; and the post-pregnancy experience of breast-feeding. Indeed, perhaps the central insight of feminist theory of the last decade has been that women are 'essentially connected,' not 'essentially separate,' from the rest of human life, both materially through pregnancy, intercourse, and breast-feeding, and existentially, through the moral and practical life.[32]

Of these four connecting experiences, it is pregnancy and intercourse which provide a window for current feminist legal theory. In truth, West's project in 'Jurisprudence and Gender' is a somewhat larger mission: she seeks to furnish a guide to the whole of legal theory which explicates the inconsistencies and points of departure between masculine jurisprudence, namely liberalism and critical legal theory, and feminist legal theory symmetrically reduced to cultural feminism and radical feminism. The 'sharp' distinction between these two feminisms, she says, is traditionally expressed as follows: 'According to one group of feminists, sometimes called "cultural feminists," the important difference between men and women is the women raise children and men don't. According to a second group of feminists, now called "radical feminists," the important difference between men and women is that women get fucked and men fuck ...'[33]

In reformulating this distinction, West urges that all feminist theory can be situated in relation to her connection thesis. However, her textual strategies construct disparate hierarchical status in accordance with the type of feminism endorsed. More precisely stated, it is in relation to the stance embraced *vis-à-vis* the connection thesis that one can assess adherence to either official or unofficial feminist story lines:[34]

According to cultural feminism, women's connectedness to the other (whether material or cultural) is the source, the heart, the root, and the cause of women's different morality, different 'ways of knowing,' different genius, different capacity for care, and different ability to nurture. For radical feminists that same potential for connection – experienced materially in intercourse and pregnancy but experienced existentially in all spheres of life – is the source of women's debasement, powerlessness, subjugation and misery. It is the cause of our pain, and the reason for our stunted lives. Invasion and intrusion, rather than intimacy, nurturance and care, is the 'unofficial' story of women's subjective experience of connection.[35]

It is somewhat ironic that in the move which renders radical feminism thoroughly unofficial, and abortion marginal to women's reproductive lives, West fails to disclose why the landscape of feminist legal thought should be reduced to simple binary opposition. And so I feel forced to ask, what purpose does this taxonomy serve?

In fact, the textual strategies West pursues are designed to set a very distinct cast on the visage of feminist legal theory. In this context, it is the abjection of radical feminism, I suggest, that lies at the heart of this enterprise.[36] To this end, the connection thesis propounded by West, rather than furnishing the theoretical basis for a reformulated account of pregnancy, effectively positions abortion as the dark, dank subterranean story of women's reproductive lives.

Story Three – Tales of Abortion (or, Lesbian Trashing and Baby Bashing)

In order to illustrate these claims, it is necessary to outline West's methodology. West provides personal descriptions of women's experience of pregnancy drawn from the amicus brief filed in the *Thornburgh*[37] case by the National Abortion Rights Action League. The following excerpts are among those furnished by West:

'During my Pregnancy,' one women [*sic*] explains, 'I was treated *like a baby machine – an incubator without feelings.*' 'Then I got pregnant again,' another woman writes:

> This one would be only 13 months younger than the third child. I was faced with the unpleasant fact that I could not stop the babies from coming no matter what I did ... *You cannot possibly know what it is like to be the helpless pawn of nature.* I am a 71 year old widow.

'Almost exactly a decade ago,' writes another, 'I learned I was pregnant ... I was sick in my heart and I thought I would kill myself. *It was as if I had been told my body had been invaded with cancer.* It seemed that very wrong.'

One woman speaks directly, without metaphor. 'On the ride home from the clinic, the relief was enormous. I felt happy for the first time in weeks. I had a future again. *I had my body back.*'[38]

My intention is not to contradict the discrete 'moments-of-knowing'[39] furnished by West. Nor to question her assertion that the condition of pregnancy may fundamentally alter many women's sense of themselves. Moreover, there is much to be said for giving expression to subjective experience within a discourse which favours and legitimates objective accounts.

However, the subjective accounts provided disclose little about the speakers or the contexts within which the various subjective understandings of pregnancy were formulated. Clearly, the race and class of the speaking subjects are absent. Patricia Williams stresses that hegemony in theoretical legal understanding is not created solely through the existence of objective voices which express universal truth:

... the supposed existence of such voices is also given power in romanticized notions of 'real people' having 'real' experiences – not because real people have experienced what they really experienced, but because their experiences are somehow *made* legitimate – either because they are viewed as empirically legitimate (directly corroborated by consensus, by a community of outsiders) or, more frequently, because those experiences are corroborated by hidden or unspoken models of legitimacy.[40]

Legitimacy is achieved in West's text in several distinct respects. First, the text by the strategies it deploys furnishes models of pregnancy and motherhood which border on the ecstatic. The heterosexual underpinnings which inform these re-presentations are only rarely exposed or challenged. To the degree to which exposure does occur, it transpires through the invocation of radical feminist discourse, which is systematically undermined and marginalized within the text. In this way, radical feminist and lesbian accounts of motherhood and pregnancy which depart from portraits of despair are effaced. In the end, then, it is perhaps the failure to assimilate comfortably into heterosexuality which appears to be problematic. Secondly, in the constructing of a voice that appears to speak for all women, we must question the unspoken models of legitimacy that may be invoked; namely, the omission of race and class information does not mean that the material presented is race- or class-inclusive. In particular, she ignores in her 'material' analysis the very real material circumstances which effectively undermine the formal legal right to abortion. Nor does West explore the ways in which women of colour, women with disabilities, and poor women have been subjects of eugenic policies that involve the forcible control or elimination of their reproductive capacities. Finally, the significance of pregnancy she attaches to the women's stories of pregnancy upon which she relies is couched in terminology and categories which are more likely to correspond to a lawyer's subjective understanding of that condition.

Radical Feminism, Abortion, and Motherhood

There is little doubt that feminism has not achieved a coherent consensus on the significance of mothering in our lives, nor do I believe this is possible. While radical feminism has always stressed the structural imperatives towards compulsory heterosexuality and the institution of motherhood, it is specious to deliberately construct an image in which motherhood is not part of the landscape of radical feminist or lesbian lives. Such a strategy is frequently employed by anti-choice demonstrators who seek to portray pro-choice activists as baby bashers.

This is substantially the image West creates. For instance, her treatment of radical feminism and pregnancy consists solely of descriptions by women of their experience of unwanted pregnancy. It follows that the exposition of motherhood in radical feminism is thereby characterized as one of absence, dread, and pathology. West is critical of radical feminist work which seeks to assuage the distinction between rape and sexual intercourse.[41] She extends the radical feminist analysis that it is false to speak of consensual and unconsensual sex (in the context of culturally enforced heterosexuality and the sexualization of dominance and submission) to pregnancy. Accordingly, in her account radical feminists valorize abortion and fear motherhood.

West produces a sketch of feminist theory in which abortion and radical feminism are conflated and, in effect, countervailing cultural feminism and motherhood. The narratives of unwanted pregnancy are juxtaposed against the joys of motherhood.

The radical feminist argument that 'pregnancy is a dangerous, consuming, intrusive, invasive assault on the mother's self-identity,' she suggests, 'best captures women's own sense of the injury and danger of pregnancy ...'[42] She draws the view that radical feminism presents pregnancy as something of an existential assault from the writings of Shulamith Firestone. West suggests that 'modern radical feminism is unified among other things by its insistence of the invasive, oppressive, destructive implications of women's material and existential connection to the other.'[43] It begins, 'not with the eighties critique of heterosexuality but in the late sixties, with Shulamith Firestone's angry and eloquent denunciation of the oppressive consequences for women of the physical condition of pregnancy.'[44]

From there West moves into a consideration of radical feminism as demonstrated in the writings of Firestone[45] (pregnancy) and Andrea Dworkin[46] (intercourse). This textual linking of pregnancy and intercourse is of course not counter-intuitive, nor unrepresentative of radical feminist work, but neither in this context is it innocent. First, it begins by privileging as sex, intercourse. It is penetration alone, sexual intercourse, or its (dare I say natural) consequences, which create connection. While West acknowledges that the focus of her discussion is heterosexuality, she ultimately excludes any sexuality which does not take the phallus as its point of reference. As a result, lesbian sexuality or other women-centred sexuality seemingly does not qualify as 'connection.' Nor does any form of women-centred intimacy more broadly defined merit this label. Unsurprisingly, then, lesbian descriptions of pregnancy and motherhood are absent from these accounts.

Less obliquely stated, the problem stems from West's insistence on reading against the grain by substantially isolating discussions of pregnancy and abortion from the radical feminist theoretical framework of culturally enforced heterosexuality. And here I must be clear. Although West includes passages from Dworkin's *Intercourse*[47] which focus upon the physical dimensions of the act of intercourse, she misses entirely the point MacKinnon makes in relation to that which circulates under the sign of sex, namely the power dimension which is expressed in and through heterosexual intercourse:

Sexual violation symbolizes and actualizes women's subordinate social status to men. It is both an indication and a practice of inequality between the sexes, specifically of the low status of women relative to men. Availability for aggressive intimate intrusion and use at will for pleasure by another defines who one is socially taken to be and constitutes an index of social worth. To be a means to the end of the sexual pleasure of one more powerful is, empirically, a degraded status and the female position.[48]

In other words, it is precisely the structural imperatives towards the institution of heterosexuality in the context of women's positionality within the present socio-symbolic order(s) that I believe radical feminism best speaks.[49] West's seeming reluctance to acknowledge this, in the end, makes the choice of abortion appear more like a failure to accommodate to the consequences of 'connection,' or perhaps expressed more starkly, a 'ms.-managed womb.'[50]

Gender Essentialism

The various textual conflations and juxtapositions serve to situate cultural feminism as the pretty and therefore palatable position for feminist legal theory. It is one thing to present an argument in favour of cultural feminist legal theory, but quite another to enlist logocentric support for that position by invoking romantic notions of motherhood. The sentimentality at play in West's work serves to constitute abortion as radical women's existential incapacity to embrace connection. In large measure the success of this strategy rests upon the exclusion of the gross disparities in women's reproductive lives.

While allegedly seeking to capture complexity, the text relies upon monolithically 'phenomenological' accounts of pregnancy which are unperturbed by considerations of sexual orientation, race, or class. Her methodology is beset by 'gender essentialism.'[51] In commenting on 'Jurisprudence and Gender,' Angela Harris remarks:

West's claims are clearly questionable on their face insofar as the experience of some women – 'mothers' – is asserted to stand for the experience of all women ... West argues that the biological and social implications of motherhood shape the selfhood of all, or at least most, women. This claim involves at least two assumptions. First, West assumes (as does the liberal social theory she criticizes) that everyone has a deep, unitary self that is relatively stable and unchanging. Second, West assumes that this 'self' differs significantly between men and women but is the same for all women and for all men despite differences of class, race, and sexual orientation: that is, that this self is deeply and primarily gendered.[52]

Feminists writing out of their experience as women of colour have stressed the relational nature of identity and the inability to separate gender and race.[53] It is problematic that West seeks to ground a theory of women's difference, the material conditions of pregnancy or the potential to become pregnant, without considering the exclusions which produce its coherency.

Although West would acknowledge that not all women essentially, trans-culturally, and trans-historically experience pregnancy in any one way,[54] the voices she chooses to speak do not give expression to the gross disparities in women's economic and social positions. In short, the limited nature of her material analysis does not begin to capture the complexities, nor apprehend the many nuances, of women's reproductive lives. Poverty effectively divests many women and particularly many women of colour and native women from the right to legal abortions. As Angela Davis has stressed:

The renewed offensive against abortion rights that erupted in the latter half of the 1970s has made it absolutely necessary to focus on the needs of the poor and racially oppressed women. By 1977 the passage of the Hyde Amendment in Congress had mandated the withdrawal of federal funding for abortions, causing many state legislatures to follow suit. Black, Puerto Rican, Chicana and Native American Indian women, together with their impoverished white sisters were effectively divested of their right to legal abortions.[55]

Unquestionably in the United States, where access to abortion services for working-class and poor women has been subject to constant judicial erosion, the notion that women live out either pregnancy or abortion in any shared way seems hopelessly inaccurate. The Supreme Court in *Rust*[56] recently affirmed that women receiving service in Title X clinics can receive no information, counselling, or referral with respect to abortion, even when specifically requested.[57] Affirming an earlier pronouncement, Chief Justice Rehnquist declared, 'The financial constraints that restrict an indigent woman's ability to enjoy the full range of constitutionally pro-tected freedom of choice are the product not of governmental restric-tions on access to abortion, but rather of indigency.'[58]

While the so-called 'gag' rule was lifted by the Clinton administration,[59] access to abortion has been dramatically eroded by the refusal of state-funded medicare programs to cover the cost of even medically necessary abortion services.[60] The U.S. Supreme Court has stressed that the state has the authority 'to make a value judgment favoring childbirth over abortion, and to implement that judgment by the allocation of public funds.'[61] Similar disparities in access to abortion services are present in Canada.[62]

The structure of public funding produces the incentive for women to opt for sterilization:

Since surgical sterilizations, funded by the Department of Health, Education and Welfare, remained free on demand, more and more women have been forced to opt for permanent infertility. What is urgently required is a broad campaign to defend the reproductive rights of all women – and especially those women whose economic circumstances often compel them to relinquish the right to reproduc-tion itself.[63]

In point of fact, even framing the terrain of reproduction in terms of motherhood/abortion renders invisible both the historical and contem-porary manifestations of eugenic policies directed against those women with the least power.

Eugenics,[64] the notion that the human species would be improved by selective breeding practices, enjoyed intellectual and legal support beginning in early nineteenth-century America. Indiana passed the first law authorizing the sterilization of 'confirmed criminals, idiots, imbeciles, and rapists' in 1907. Approximately sixty thousand people were sterilized pursuant to programs to remove reproductive ability from those institutionalized. In Canada, Alberta passed legislation in 1928 permitting forced sterilization of the 'feeble-minded.'[65] This law is notorious not only because it remained in force until the 1970s, but also because it inspired Nazi curiosity.[66] In Canada, an early 1970s study reveals that native women were sterilized at a rate five times higher than non-native women.[67]

Representations of black women emerge from the cultural context of slavery in which their bodies were legally constituted as sexually available.[68] Legal regimes continue to rely upon the myths of sexual drives beyond retraint to justify state-imposed reproductive control. Within the discourse of component factors warranting such control, criminality, single parenthood, and poverty are virtually interchangeable categories.[69] Thus for many women who occupy positions of relative social powerlessness, the issue has been and continues to be the removal of reproductive capabilities.

Recent U.S. case law which upholds the involuntary implantation of Norplant as a condition of probation for women convicted of child abuse affords an excellent illustration of the judicial support for eugenic practices. Henley stresses that court-ordered contraception has, in the majority of cases, been deployed against women 'of a marginalized class.'[70]

Eugenic policies are also blatantly at work in IVF processes. Only embryos free of genetic defects are chosen for implantation. Additionally, billions of research dollars have been directed at efforts to map human genomes. Ultimately, the human genome project will permit the detection of 'genetic defects,' despite the fact that the overwhelming majority of disabilities are not genetically inherited.[71]

The agenda of detecting and aborting 'defective' foetuses is difficult to separate from eugenic premises.[72] Nor should we overlook the ways in which access to abortion blurs into eugenics to further contribute to the subordination of women. Internationally, the availability of abortion, where coupled with prescribed limits on family size, has resulted in both female infanticide and the disproportionate abortion of female foetuses.[73] Both abroad and in North America, the increasing availability of post-conceptual sex selection practices has witnessed use of abortion overwhelmingly to favour 'selection' of male foetuses.[74] In short, abortion can be deployed by the state in conformity with economic and social imperatives which do not reflect the objective of eliminating gender oppression.

Coercive family planning strategies have targeted women in India, where incentives have been provided for district collectors to meet sterilization targets.[75] Multinationals operating in Third World countries often prefer employees who have undergone sterilization procedures.[76] For example, in Brazil women are asked for proof of sterilization even though legislation has been adopted granting women four months maternity leave.[77] The private sector in the United States often disguises this by refusing to hire women of child-bearing years.[78]

These scenarios are revealing in terms of whose reproductive 'rights' enjoy social support. They also support Dorothy Roberts's assertion that reducing the terrain of reproduction to abortion rights is problematic.[79] Finally, thinking about abortion in relation to sex selection practices and the creation of 'perfect babies' assists in revealing the limitations of framing reproductive issues strictly within the discourse of 'rights.'

The foregoing suggests that abortion cannot be the only story, or even an unproblematic one, that we tell about reproduction. However, neither should commitment to this struggle be lightly abandoned, particularly at a juncture when the climate for marginalizing abortion is one which finds increasing juridical support.

While the 'essential holding'[80] of *Roe* v. *Wade* was upheld by a slim majority in the latest decision from the U.S. Supreme Court, much of the post-*Roe* jurisprudence was overturned. In fact, the decision in *Casey* v. *Planned Parenthood of Southeastern Pennsylvania* fundamentally alters the state's power to impose limits on abortion. In rejecting the trimester-system approach to regulation adopted in *Roe*, the Court opted in favour of permitting abortion prior to viability. However, only if a law places 'substantial obstacles in the path of a woman' who seeks an abortion prior to viability will the law be unconstitutional. In other words, prior to viability the power to regulate has been vastly increased. The defensive posture of the Court is evident in that the majority in *Casey* expends considerable energy articulating while they are unprepared to overrule *Roe* in its entirety. Yet, many will undoubtedly argue that the core principles have been so eroded by this decision as to effectively remove constitutional protection. On the basis that Court decisions post-*Roe* have failed to protect the state interest in promoting the 'life or potential life' of the unborn, the door is now open for states to take active measures to discourage abortion.

Ultimately, neither concerns about eugenic practices nor the waning of the formal legal right to abortion informs the narratives about reproduction that West presents. Instead, the focus on subjective attitudes obfuscates the material factors which sway moral decisions.[81] The absence of these considerations is especially puzzling given the cultural feminist insistence on contextual analysis. But this is partly the point; the alleged presence of the 'context' is in fact highly selectively constructed.

Additionally we should be dubious of the degree to which West's articulation of women's experience of pregnancy is assigned to legal categories and legal terminology. For example, one might question her claim that women's sense of an unwanted pregnancy is as an 'injury.'[82]

In this respect, it is indeed noteworthy that West's phenomenological descriptions of unwanted pregnancy are drawn from a legal brief prepared for a trial. She neglects to address the potentially distorting impact of the transliteration of women's experiences into legal terminology and categories. The danger of distortion is particularly acute when accounts are drawn from materials generated for trials and subsequently juxtaposed with existing legal categories.

The end result is to render an analysis in which abortion becomes suppressed in favour of the official, and happier, story of motherhood. Once abortion is no longer the project or concern of all women, and radical feminist insights are marginal, this move – intended or not – permits revisitation of the promulgation of liberal contractual discourse in the name of apple pie and ...

Story Four – Motherhood

There is about the invocation of images of birthing and mothering as instances of connection a similar troubling romanticism. Logocentric support is enlisted through reliance on the cultural myths of mother/ body in which women's nurturing functions assume an exaggerated, if not surreal, significance.[83] Fundamentally, there seems no basis for concluding that the category 'mother' is capable of denoting a common identity or experience. Formulations of motherhood, like West's, achieve stability and coherency through reliance not only on 'a traditional heterosexual matrix,'[84] but also through reinstating the constructed female subject of white, middle-class mythology.[85]

Myths of good mothers include that of women devotedly and selflessly dispensing love, warmth, and care to their offspring. As children, these myths serve as a symbol of our loss at both an emotional and psychic level. As mothers, these accounts are internalized and form the standard according to which our failure is judged, by ourselves and others.[86]

Iconography of 'good mothers' almost invariably depicts white women.

However, myths about 'bad mothers' are mapped disproportionately onto the bodies of non-white women.[87] Reliance on idealized accounts of women's caring and nurturing capacities is pernicious in part because perceived deviation from these qualities is so differentially policed in our social order(s). State intervention into either the birthing process or mothering has transpired where appropriate levels of maternal care are seen to be wanting. Intervention of these types has disproportionately affected poor women and women of colour.[88]

In a national survey of U.S. court-ordered obstetrical interventions, twenty-one court-ordered Caesareans were examined. Refusal by the women to submit to the procedure was thought by some to be 'callous or irrational.'[89] It was acknowledged by the authors of the report that the women who were most likely to be subjected to this process were 'women more likely to be subject to various forms of discrimination.'[90] The statistical data on the women who were forced to undergo this procedure were as follows: 'Eighty-one percent were black, Asian or Hispanic. Forty-four percent were unmarried, and 24 percent did not speak English as their primary language.'[91]

Children born in non-white homes still face significantly higher rates of poverty and infant mortality. For many women of colour, the struggle is to retain children once they are born. Disproportionately it is poor women and women of colour who are likely either to face charges for child abuse, or to have their children forcibly removed by child welfare authorities.

Similarly, the social context within which mothering transpires is radically different for women depending on their race and class. Patricia Hill Collins has identified three themes which inform motherwork for racial ethnic women: the struggle for physical survival; the nature of power and powerlessness in structuring motherhood; and the significance of fostering individual and group identity.[92]

In short, the social context(s) within which the law operates on reproductive issues is structured in keeping with the prevailing distribution of power. Romanticized talk about motherhood not only obscures this, it simultaneously locates as 'other' and marks as 'deviant' reproductive lives which unfold outside parameters sanctioned by dominant culture.

Reproduction and Feminist Legal Theory

In the words of Marie Ashe:

Law reaches every silent space. It invades the secrecy of women's wombs. It breaks every silence, uttering itself. Law-language, jurisdiction. It defines. It commands. It forces.

Law as the seamless web we believe and die in. I cannot think of a single case involving legal regulation of motherhood without thinking of all. They constitute an interconnected network of variegated threads. Abortion. 'Surrogacy.' Supervision of women's pregnancies. Exclusion of pregnant women from the workplace. Termination of the parental rights of indigent or battered women. Enforcement of the 'relinquishments' for adoption executed by confused and vulnerable women. Forced Caesarean sections. Policings of home births. Following the thread which is any one, I find it intertwined with each of the others. When I loosen a single thread, it tightens the others. Each knotted and entangled in fabrications of a legal doctrine; each attached to notions of neutrality and generality.[93]

Unquestionably, there is about the legal regulation of women's reproduction a certain seamless monotony. However, striving to preserve the seamlessness of legal doctrine is precisely the pernicious trap that pits abortion against other facets of motherhood, including new reproductive technologies. It is the allure of maintaining consistency against which we must struggle. As many feminists have pointed out, if choice is what women have been demanding in relation to abortion, then the advent of a full panoply of technological devices and procedures merely expands women's access to choice.[94] Simply retaining the standard of the right to choose in relation to all reproductive technologies will merely reinforce existing socio-symbolic disparities.[95]

While West acknowledges that radical feminism's focus on invasion and intrusion has something to tell us about women's reproductive lives, the text is embedded as a subterranean story. Her focus is rather on finding liberating images of intercourse and motherhood to take us beyond critique to a stage of founding a reconstructive enterprise. The seeming ease with which she is willing to transcend extant material conditions in an era in which the right to abortion is clearly under attack is quite simply dangerous.

Central to West's project is restoring the liberating potential of intercourse and motherhood within feminist legal theory. She exhorts us to make 'quantum leaps' outside the realm of patriarchy, where we will find freedom, choice, and equality protected by law through a reconstituted notion of harm:

Feminism must envision a post-patriarchal world, for without such a vision we have little direction ... In a utopian world, all forms of life will be recognized, respected, and honored. A perfect legal system will protect against harms sustained by all forms of life, and will recognize life affirming values generated by all forms of being. Feminist jurisprudence must aim to bring this about, and, to do so, it must aim to transform the images as well as the power. Masculine jurisprudence must become humanist jurisprudence, and humanist jurisprudence must become a jurisprudence unmodified.[96]

This rhetoric, however, is virtually indistinguishable from that generated by the prevailing liberal legal order. It is precisely the critique of and scepticism towards that order which radical feminism lends to feminist jurisprudence. For this reason, radical feminism's contribution to law is of vital importance to the development of sound feminist legal theory. The discourse of liberalism, including choice, may have rhetorical or political purchase, but as an analysis of lived conditions, we sacrifice significantly when we disregard concrete dynamics of power.

There seems little doubt that West's attempt to abject radical feminism is part of a larger attack being waged in the name of sexual and reproductive liberalism. Janice Raymond explains that it has become fashionable to stress female agency and complicity, particularly in relation to sex. Under this new regime, it seems no longer possible to examine the ways in which women's choices are structured, constrained, coerced, or impaired by patriarchy. This sexual liberalism is now being carried to the reproductive realm.[97] Raymond explains:

We all know that because women have been constrained or influenced by a social context that fosters pornography, prostitution, and surrogacy does not mean that women are determined by that social context. But the sexual liberals caricature the antipornography and antisurrogacy feminists as subscribing to a brand of social determinism. The liberals would have it that no one can talk about constraints or influences without lapsing into determinism. This is a convenient reductionism achieved by liberal discourse for the purpose of valorizing both the sexual and reproductive trade and traffic in women's bodies.[98]

It has been suggested that 'in the postmodern condition, women's bodies are the prime afterimage of a strategy of body invasion which occurs in the inverted and excessive language of contractual liberalism.'[99] It is a discourse in relation to sexuality which looks for consensus in rape, which apprehends women's free agreement to participate in the production of pornographic imagery, which can discern only the agreement between abuser and abused to reproduce,[100] and which could witness juridical appropriation of a woman's body in the name of 'surrogacy.'[101] It is a discourse in which abortion is relegated to the domain of nasty radical feminists who live in existential dread of loss of control.

Conclusion

I concede to having provided something of a caricature of West's work, and by extension cultural feminism. I think that I have been unfair in the sense that West wishes to explore paradoxes in feminist theory without simply collapsing them. Her desire to explore the limitations and potential of both cultural feminism and radical feminist theory is ambitious and laudable. However, her textual strategies undercut her stated objectives. In the end, I do not think that feminism can afford an 'official story,' particularly not one that loses sight of power and powerlessness.

At least in principle, power and domination have explanatory force within theorizing around race, class, and gender oppression. This is not to lay claim to the pretence that radical feminism has been free of the exclusions perpetrated by other white feminists or has not relied on its own brand of essentialism.[102] Rather it is to suggest that feminism can no longer afford to project white middle-class heterosexual women's experiences into universalized accounts, even when they are generated in the name of providing *real* women's experiences. This entails resisting efforts to endorse totalizing representations of those experiences. It is exactly such simplicity and reductionism that the law seeks. Therefore, we must be wary of feminist theory which promulgates official stories, for the insights feminism has to offer are not reducible to a hierarchical dichotomy. We would be wiser to continue to pursue the task of formulating a multi-textured, complex, feminist jurisprudence,[103] whatever its attendant conceptual and political difficulties, than yearning for a return to a revamped humanist enterprise.

NOTES

1 The author wishes to thank Diana Majury, Eleanor Macdonald, Martha Bailey, Kathleen Lahey, and Patricia Peppin for their helpful comments on earlier drafts. All errors and omissions remain the responsibility of the author. This paper was presented at the Learneds in Kingston, Ontario, and for the Queen's Critical Theory Seminar. An earlier and different version of this paper appears in (1992) 30 *Alta. L. Rev.* 719.

2 The literature in this area is now extremely extensive and impressive. The fol-

lowing list seeks only to convey a flavour for the distinct contexts within which attending to difference has emerged as a potential legal strategy. On the one hand, it perhaps first arose out of dissatisfaction with the limited legal successes occasioned by the use of 'sameness' arguments. See, for example, M. Fineman, 'Implementing Equality: Ideology, Contradiction and Social Change: A Study of Rhetoric and Results in the Regulation of the Consequences of Divorce' (1983) 4 *Wis. L. Rev.* 789. For an analysis of how s. 15 has assisted men, see G. Brodsky and S. Day, *Canadian Charter Equality Rights for Women: One Step Forward or Two Steps Back?* (Ottawa: Canadian Advisory Council on the Status of Women, 1989).

It also arises within feminist work which seeks to locate the legitimate qualities and characteristics associated with women. See, for example, R. West, 'The Difference in Women's Hedonic Lives: A Phenomenological Critique of Feminist Legal Theory,' in M. Fineman and N. Thomadsen, eds., *At the Boundaries of Law* (New York: Routledge, 1991); and L. Bender, 'From Gender Difference to Feminist Solidarity: Using Carol Gilligan and an Ethic of Care in Law' (1990) 15 *Vt. L. Rev.* 1.

Similarly, feminist work also aims to theorize women's specificities around sexual orientation, disability, and race. See, for example, K. Lahey, 'On Silences, Screams and Scholarship,' in R. Devlin ed., *Canadian Perspectives on Legal Theory* (Toronto: Emond Montgomery, 1991), 319; and R. Robson, 'Resisting the Family: Repositioning Lesbians in Legal Theory' (1994) 19(4) *Signs* 975.

Although the concepts employed by feminist theorists writing out of their experiences of colour cannot and should not be reduced to 'difference' (this terminology is often in fact eschewed because of its hierarchical and linear properties), this work often seeks to expose the violence which inheres in universalism. See, for example, A. Harris, 'Race and Essentialism in Feminist Legal Theory' (1990) 42 *Stan. L. Rev.* 581; M. Matsuda, 'When the First Quail Calls: Multiple Consciousness as Jurisprudential Method' (1989) 11 *Wom. Rts. L. Rep.* 7; P. Williams, *The Alchemy of Race and Rights* (Cambridge, Mass.: Harvard University Press, 1991); and Kimberlè Crenshaw, 'Demarginalizing the Intersection of Race and Sex: A Black Feminist Critique of Anti-discrimination Doctrine, Feminist Theory and Antiracist Politics' (1989) *U. Chi. Legal Forum* 139.

Much of the work of postmodern feminists is informed by efforts to resist essentialism. See, for example, M. J. Frug, *Postmodern Legal Feminism* (New York: Routledge, 1992); and J. Williams, 'Dissolving the Sameness/Difference Debate: A Post-Modern Path beyond Essentialism and Critical Race Theory' (1991) *Duke L. J.* 296.

Some of the work listed above is very attuned to the problems of universalism and reductionism to be discussed below.

3 S. Razack. 'Issues of Difference in Constitutional Reform: Saying Goodbye to the Universal Woman,' in D. Schneiderman, ed., *Conversations* (Edmonton: Centre for Constitutional Studies, 1991), 38. See also N. Iyer, 'Categorical Denials: Equality Rights and the Shaping of Social Identity' (1993) 19 *Queen's L. J.* 179 (Iyer worries especially about how legal categories conflate difference as distinction and difference as hierarchy).

4 See Lahey, supra n. 2.

5 Diana Majury has eloquently explored this paradox in relation to abortion and new reproductive technologies. The use of 'choice' in relation to reproduction generally opens the door to a view which stresses that new reproductive technologies should not be regulated. In other words, expanding access to these services merely expands the range of the reproductive choices available to women (D. Majury, 'At the Feminist Impasse: Choice of Law,' paper delivered at Queen's University, January 1991). See also E. Kingdom, 'Legal Recognition of a Woman's Right to Choose,' in J. Brophy and C. Smart, eds., *Women in Law* (London: Routledge and Kegan Paul, 1985).

6 The material with which I am concerned is principally legal in nature, and particularly that propounded by Robin West. It is imperative to emphasize that this paper focuses on expressions of cultural (or relational) feminism within feminist legal theory. It strikes me that this bears emphasizing for two reasons. First, it has been argued that attacks on cultural feminism are often thinly veiled efforts to assail lesbian feminism (see V. Taylor and L. Rupp, 'Women's Culture and Lesbian Feminist Activism: A Reconsideration of Cultural Feminism' [1933] 19 *Signs* 32). In this respect, it is significant that my concern with cultural feminism within legal theory is precisely its preoccupation with the project of rescuing feminist legal theory from lesbian and radical theory. Secondly, there is, in any event, no consistent meaning assigned to cultural feminism either across or within disciplines. West's articulation of cultural feminism should thus be compared with L. Alcoff, 'Cultural Feminism versus Post-Structuralism: The Identity Crisis in Feminist Legal Theory' (1988) 13 *Signs* 405. There is remarkably little clarity around such classifications, and generally certain feminisms are deliberately constructed in ways which seek to reveal limitations. For a fuller discussion of various definitions of cultural feminism see n. 27 below.

7 R. West, 'Jurisprudence and Gender' (1988) 55 *U. Chi. L. Rev.* 1.

8 As I will argue below, I take the central feature of radical feminism to be an analysis of power. Its virtue, then, is that it concentrates on the structural imperatives operating to uphold phallogocentrism and women's positionality within the present socio-symbolic orders.

9 The *Random House Dictionary of the English Language*, 2d unabridged ed., defines 'homunculus' as:

1. An artificially made dwarf, supposedly produced in a flask by an alchemist.
2. A fully formed, miniature human body believed, according to some medical theories of the 16th and 17th centuries, to be contained in the spermazoon.
3. A diminutive human being.
4. The human fetus.

10 B. Duden, *Disembodying Women: Perspectives on Pregnancy and the Unborn* (Cambridge, Mass.: Harvard University Press, 1993), 7.

11 See S. Noonan, 'What the Court Giveth: Abortion and Bill C-43' (1991) 16 *Queen's L. J.* 321. In *Morgentaler, Daigle, Borowski*, and *Sullivan* the Court has declined to extend *Charter* protection to the foetus. However, I have argued that this does not end the issue, given that the interests of the foetus were articulated through an elision with 'state interests.'

12 L. Tribe, *Abortion: The Clash of Absolutes* (New York: Norton, 1990).

13 D. Greschner, 'Abortion and Democracy for Women: A Critique of *Tremblay* v. *Daigle*' (1990) 35 *McGill L. J.* 633.

14 Ibid. at 652.

15 Five doctors who performed abortions were attacked in the past two years (*Tampa Tribune*, 14 November 1994). Additionally, there have been organized efforts directed against abortion clinics, including arson, stink bombs, and acid attacks (*U.S. News and World Report*, 14 November 1994). For an example of coercive measures employed in birthing practices, see *C.A.S. of Belleville* v. *Linda T. and Gary K.* (1987), 7 R.F.L. (3d) 191 (Ont. Prov. Ct. Fam. Div.) and *Re R.* (1987), 9 R.F.L. (3d) 225 (B.C.S.C.). For a discussion of these cases and this area more generally, see Isabel Grant, 'Forced Obstetrical Intervention: A Charter Analysis' (1989) 39 *U. Toronto L. J.* 217; and Susan Alter Tateishi, 'Apprehending the Fetus En Ventre Sa Mere: A Study in Judicial Sleight of Hand' (1989) 53 *Sask. L. Rev.* 113.

16 H. Lessard, 'Relationship, Particularity and Change: Reflections on *R.* v. *Morgentaler* and Feminist Approaches to Liberty' (1991) *36 McGill L. J.* 263.

17 A disturbing example of this is contained in a Louisiana statute dealing with human embryos which was drawn to my attention by Kathleen Lahey. The statute recognizes in vitro human ovum as juridical persons which can, among other things, sue and be sued (*Status of Human Embryos*, Louisiana Statutes Annotated, Title 9, Book 1, Code Title 1, chapter 3, sections 121–33).

18 S. Gavigan, 'Beyond *Morgentaler*: The Legal Regulation of Reproduction,' in J. Brodie, S. Gavigan, and J. Jenson, eds., *The Politics of Abortion* (Toronto: Oxford University Press, 1992), 130–1.

19 See the discussion by M. McConnell and S. Noonan of the Law Reform Commission of Canada's report *Crimes against the Foetus*, in (1989–90) 3(2) *Can. J. Wom. & L.* 660.

20 C. Overall, 'Mother/Fetus State Conflicts' (1989) 9 *Health Law in Canada* 101.

21 112 S.Ct. 2791 (1992).

22 Ibid.

23 See *Dodds* v. *Daigle*, [1989] 2 S.C.R. 530.

24 410 U.S. 113 (1973).

25 Here I will be examining *legal* theory. It is certainly the case that excellent feminist work on abortion beginning with the premise of connection is available in other disciplines. See, for example, C. Overall, supra n. 20.

26 C. Gilligan, *In a Different Voice* (Cambridge, Mass.: Harvard University Press, 1982).

27 There are many current taxonomies of feminism. Largely there is little consistency among them. I am adopting the term 'cultural feminism' here as it is used by Robin West in 'Jurisprudence and Gender' (supra n. 7) to signal a particular official account of women's experience of connection.

   However, there are many other definitions of cultural feminism. Josephine Donovan suggests that contemporary cultural feminism reflects the view that 'traditional' women's culture can be applied to the public realm to curb 'destructive masculine ideologies.' Stressing the cultural nature of these traditions, it is suggested that men too can absorb these feminine values. See J. Donovan, *Feminist Theory* (New York: Continuum, 1988). On the other hand, A. Echols, in 'The Taming of the Id: Feminist Sexual Politics, 1968–83,' in C. Vance, ed., *Pleasure and Danger: Exploring Female Sexuality* (Boston: Routledge, 1984), 50, seems to identify cultural feminism with sexuality constrained by danger. Interestingly, different accounts of this 'sharp' divide end up employing the same names under different labels. See also supra, n. 6.

28 H. Lessard, supra n. 16.

29 In fairness, Gilligan's own work on abortion reveals a more textured approach to the manner in which abortion decisions are made. Even in this work, though, abortion talk is constituted in ways that speak against abortion rights. See P. Karlan and D. Ortiz, 'In a Different Voice: Relational Feminism, Abortion Rights and the Feminist Legal Agenda' (1993) 87 *Northwestern Univ. L. Rev.* 858.

30 C. Gilligan, in E. Dubois, M. Dunlap, C. Gilligan, C. MacKinnon, and C. Menkel-Meadow, 'Feminist Discourse, Moral Values and the Law – a Conversation' (1985) 34 *Buffalo L. Rev.* 11 at 44.

31 R. West, 'Jurisprudence and Gender,' supra n. 7.

32 Ibid. at 2–3.

33 Ibid. at 13.

34 West argues that as a result of the phenomenal success of Gilligan's book, cultural feminism is most *familiar* (my emphasis) and 'for that reason *alone*' (her emphasis) is called the official story. I think this contention is highly debatable. However, it is the very problematic status of radical feminism within her text that makes it so obviously unofficial and existentially undesirable.

35 R. West, supra n. 7 at 29.

36 Applying Kristeva's concept of abjection seems particularly apposite because it graphically captures both the expulsion and revulsion which the text 'Jurisprudence and Gender' attempts to construct. Loosely speaking, abjection refers to the process of bodily expulsion which constitutes the boundaries, of the subject. In other words, it refers to the process of establishing the clean and proper boundaries of a social body which are necessary in order to assume a position as a speaking subject in the symbolic order. The processes of bodily expulsion attest to the provisional nature of the symbolic's grasp over semiotic drives. The abject thus occupies the space between subject and object. It can never be fully expelled but hovers at the boundaries threatening to disrupt. See J. Kristeva, *Powers of Horror: An Essay on Abjection* (New York: Columbia University Press, 1982).

37 *Thornburgh* v. *McRae*, 476 U.S. 747 (1986).

38 Supra n. 7 at 31.

39 Kathleen Lahey identifies 'moments-of-knowing' as part of the intersubjective process of exchange known as consciousness raising. See K. Lahey, '... Until Women Themselves Have Told All That They Have to Tell ...' (1985) 23 *Osgoode Hall L. J.* 519 at 533.

40 P. Williams, *The Alchemy of Race and Rights*, supra n. 2 at 9.

41 West states:

> Women often, and perhaps increasingly, experience heterosexual intercourse as freely chosen intimacy, not invasive bondage. A radicalism that flatly denies the reality of such a lived experience runs the risk of making itself unintelligible and irrelevant to all people, not to mention the audience that matters most; namely, those women for whom intercourse is not free, not chosen, and anything but intimate, and who have no idea that it either could be or should be both. ('Jurisprudence and Gender,' supra n. 7 at 46)

As Catharine MacKinnon stresses, we should not cling to some false notion of consensual and unconsensual pregnancy:

> Women often do not control the conditions under which they become pregnant; systematically denied meaningful control over the reproductive uses of their bodies through sex it is exceptional when they do. Women

are socially disadvantaged in controlling sexual access to their bodies through socialization to customs that define a woman's body as for sexual use by men. Sexual access is regularly forced or pressured or routinized beyond denial. Laws against sexual assault provide little to no real protection. Contraception is inadequate or unsafe or inaccessible or sadistic or stigmatized. Sex education is often misleading or unavailable or pushes heterosexual motherhood as an exclusive life possibility and as the point of sex. Poverty and enforced economic dependence undermine women's physical integrity and sexual self-determination. (C. MacKinnon, 'Reflections on Sex Equality under Law' [1991] 100 *Yale L. J.* 1281 at 1313)

42 R. West, supra n. 7 at 30.

43 Ibid. at 28.

44 Ibid.

45 S. Firestone, *The Dialectic of Sex* (New York: Morrow, 1970).

46 A. Dworkin, *Intercourse* (New York: Free Press, 1987).

47 Ibid.

48 C. MacKinnon, supra n. 41 at 1302.

49 See, for example, C. MacKinnon, *Toward a Feminist Theory of the State* (Cambridge, Mass.: Harvard University Press, 1989). But radical feminism is also concerned with analysing the structures of male power, more broadly defined. See H. Eisenstein, *Contemporary Feminist Thought* (Boston: G.K. Hall, 1983).

50 E. Manion explains: '... even for feminists of the present generation who accept abortion, to have one is an admission of failure, for we grew up assuming that fertility is manageable and it is our job to manage it' (E. Manion, 'A Ms.-Managed Womb,' in A. Kroker and M. Kroker, eds., *Body Invaders* [Montreal: CultureTexts, 1987], 185).

51 A. Harris, supra n. 2 at 589.

52 Ibid. at 603.

53 Ibid.; K. Crenshaw, supra n. 2; P. Williams, supra n. 2; Audre Lorde, *Sister Outsider* (Freedom: The Crossing Press, 1984).

54 While West acknowledges this point, she does not build it into her theory, which in effect renders this concession invisible and nearly meaningless. Patricia Cain makes the same point when she suggests that 'feminist legal theorists must be careful not to confuse "standpoint critiques" with existential reality' (P. Cain, 'Grounding the Theories' [1989] 3 *Berk. Wom. L. J.* 191).

55 A. Davis, *Women, Race and Class* (New York: Vintage Books, 1983), 206.

56 *Rust* v. *Sullivan*, 111 S.Ct. 1743 (1991).

57 Under Title X of the *Public Health Service Act* 42 U.S.C., s. 300(a), both profit and non-profit organizations can establish and operate voluntary family plan-

ning projects which focus on low-income families. This provides approximately $142.5 million in grants to 4,000 clinics, which serve approximately 4,300,000 poor women (*New York Times*, 31 July 1987, A1, col. 1). State, city, and municipal health departments may receive funds from this source, as well as Planned Parenthood, hospitals, and community health organizations. During the waning years of the Reagan administration, regulations were promulgated which would remove Title X funding from any clinic which included abortion as a method of family planning. Moreover, any project receiving these funds could not refer a pregnant woman to someone who would provide an abortion, even upon request.

58 *Harris* v. *McRae*, 449 U.S. 297 at 316 (1980).

59 See 58 F.R. (Presidential Documents) 7455 (1993).

60 *Harris* v. *McRae*, supra n. 58.

61 *Maher* v. *Roe*, 432 U.S. 464 at 474–5 (1977). See also *Webster* v. *Reproductive Health Services*, 109 S.Ct. 3040 (1989).

62 Access to abortion services remains a significant problem. In its brief before the Parliamentary Legislative Committee on Bill C-43, CARAL addressed the specific inequities in access to abortion:
  - P.E.I. has no access to abortion whatsoever.
  - Newfoundland's regular service is limited to one doctor in St. John's.
  - New Brunswick has no services north of Moncton.
  - One hospital in Halifax performs over 80% of Nova Scotia's abortions.
  - 70–80% of abortions in the province of Quebec are done in Montreal.
  - Access in Ontario is concentrated in the southern cities. Fifty per cent of all abortions in Ontario are performed in Toronto.
  - Women from all over Manitoba travel to Winnipeg to obtain an abortion.
  - Saskatchewan women living outside of Saskatoon have little chance of obtaining an abortion in their own province.
  - Northern Alberta women must wait four to five weeks to obtain an abortion in Edmonton. If a woman is more than 14 weeks pregnant, she cannot find an abortion in the province of Alberta.
  - Access in B.C. is very precarious because of the election of anti-abortion activists to hospital boards of directors. For example, the Nanaimo hospital board voted to halt all abortions as of January 1, 1990. (House of Commons, Legislative Committee on Bill C-43)

63 A. Davis, supra n. 55.

64 The term 'eugenics' was coined by a British social Darwinist, Sir Francis Galton, in 1880; see Lynn Glazier, 'Playing God: Medical Ethics and History's Forgotten Lessons,' in G. Basen, M. Eichler, and A. Lippman eds., *Misconceptions* (Hull: Voyageur Publishing, 1993), 98. The population of criminals, the

disabled, people of colour, Jews, and the poor have all been targeted at various times as the 'unfit' whose numbers must be controlled.

65 Ibid. at 99.

66 For a discussion of the history of eugenics in Canada, see A. McLaren, *Our Own Master Race: Eugenics in Canada, 1885–1945* (Toronto: McClelland and Stewart, 1990).

67 See W. Mitchinson, 'The Medical Treatment of Women,' in S. Burt, L. Code, and L. Dorney, eds., *Changing Patterns: Women in Canada* (Toronto: McClelland and Stewart, 1988).

68 Bordo suggests that black women are constructed as mere body. See S. Bordo, *Unbearable Weight* (Berkeley: University of California Press, 1993), 10–11. See also D. Roberts, 'Punishing Drug Addicts Who Have Babies: Women of Color, Equality and the Rights of Privacy' (1991) 104 *Harv. L. Rev.* 1419.

69 For an excellent discussion of involuntary sterilization, see M. Henley, 'The Creation and Perpetuation of the Mother/Body Myth: Judicial and Legislative Enlistment of Norplant' (1993) 41 *Buffalo L. Rev.* 703.

70 Ibid. at 720, 1149.

71 For a critical discussion of the human genome project, see A. Lippman, 'Worrying and Worrying About – the Geneticization of Reproduction and Health,' in Basen, Eichler, and Lippman, eds., *Misconceptions*, supra n. 64.

72 See S. Goundry, 'The New Reproductive Technologies, Public Policy and the Equality Rights of Women and Men with Disabilities,' in Basen, Eichler, and Lippman, eds., *Misconceptions*, supra n. 64.

73 See N. Menon, 'Abortion and the Law: Questions for Feminism' (1993) 6 *Can. J. Wom. & L.* 103.

74 S. Thobani, 'From Reproduction to Mal(e) Production: Women and Sex Selection Technology,' in Basen, Eichler, and Lippman, eds., *Misconceptions*, supra n. 64 at 140.

75 N. Menon, supra n. 73.

76 See A. Fuentes and B. Ehrenreich, *Women in the Global Factory* (Boston: South End Press, 1983), 13.

77 See P. Williams, supra n. 2 at 32.

78 Ibid.

79 D. Roberts, supra n. 68 at 1424.

80 As articulated by the majority, that consists of three separate parts. The first is that prior to viability a woman has the right to obtain an abortion without undue interference from the state. Secondly, the state is permitted to restrict abortions after viability so long as the legislation provides exceptions when a mother's life or health may be endangered. Thirdly, *from the outset of pregnancy*

the state has legitimate interests in protecting the health of the woman and the *life of the foetus.*

81 R. Petchesky, *Abortion and Women's Choice* (Boston: Northeastern Press, 1990), 373.

82 R. West, supra n. 7 at 30.

83 For an excellent discussion of cultural myths of mother/body, see M. Henley, supra n. 69.

84 A. Schwartz, 'Taking the Nature Out of Mother,' in D. Bassin, M. Honey, and M. Kaplan, eds., *Representations of Motherhood* (New Haven: Yale University Press, 1994), 240.

85 For an excellent discussion of the social contexts of mothering for racial ethnic women, see P. Collins, 'Shifting the Center: Race, Class, and Feminist Theorizing about Motherhood' in Bassin, Honey, and Kaplan, eds., *Representations of Motherhood*, supra n. 84 at 56.

86 See D. Roberts, 'Motherhood and Crime' (1993) 79 *Iowa L. Rev.* 95, where she discusses the implications of race and class on constructions of maternal selflessness.

87 See ibid.; and M. Ashe, 'Bad Mothers, Good Lawyers, and Legal Ethics' (1993) 81 *Geo. L. J.* 2533.

88 D. Roberts, supra n. 86.

89 V. Kolder et al., 'Court-Ordered Obstetrical Interventions' (1987) 316 (19) *New Eng. J. Med.* 1192 at 1194.

90 Ibid. at 1195.

91 Ibid.

92 See P. Collins, supra n. 85.

93 M. Ashe, 'Zig-Zag Stitching and the Seamless Web: Thoughts on "Reproduction" and the Law' (1989) 13 *Nova L. Rev.* 355.

94 See E. Manion, supra n. 50.

95 This argument is supported by a number of women's organizations. The submission from the Canadian Research Institute for the Advancement of Women to the Canadian Royal Commission on New Reproductive Technologies explains the impact of choice on those whose choice is structurally constrained in the following manner:

> The fact the new reproductive technologies enter women's lives within the context of already existing social pressures and prejudices further complicates their impact on women. The easy rhetoric of commercial clinics about 'reproductive alternatives' and the 'increased choice' offered by reproductive technologies rings false when women's 'choices' are often motivated by necessity. Choice means very little when sophisticated proce-

dures are too costly for most women, yet everyday technologies (like ultrasound and amniocentesis) are used whether they are medically indicated or not. While some women are now feeling pressured to undergo experimental procedures, many women may be losing their option to choose not to undergo potentially dangerous 'routine' procedures. In a society in which infertility remains a social stigma, motherhood is often presented as the only acceptable 'choice.' Women may feel compelled to become mothers regardless of the costs to their health.

96 R. West, supra n. 7 at 72.

97 An excellent review and critique of this literature is found in the recent collection, D. Leidholdt and J. Raymond, eds., *Sexual Liberals and the Attack on Feminism* (New York: Pergamon Press, 1990).

98 J. Raymond, 'Sexual and Reproductive Liberalism,' in Leidholdt and Raymond, eds., *Sexual Liberals and the Attack on Feminism*, supra n. 97 at 106. West certainly has now begun to stress complicity in relation to pornography. See R. West, 'The Difference in Women's Hedonic Lives: A Phenomenological Critique of Feminist Legal Theory,' supra n. 2.

99 A. Kroker and M. Kroker, 'Body Probes,' in Kroker and Kroker, eds., *Body Invaders*, supra n. 50 at 97.

100 In the reporting of the Chantal Daigle case, commentators frequently adverted to the fact that she and Tremblay had 'agreed' to have a child. Similarly, a contractual analysis was urged on behalf of a husband who sought to prevent his wife from securing an abortion. For a discussion of this case, see S. Martin, 'Using the Courts to Stop Abortion by Injunction: *Mock* v. *Brandenburg*' (1990) 3 *Can. J. Wom. & L.* 569.

101 In October 1990, Judge R. Parslow of the Orange County Superior Court ruled that the woman who bore a child after having been implanted with a fertilized egg of another couple had absolutely no parental rights to it. The judge asserted that the black birth mother was only 'providing care, protection, and nurture during the period of time the natural mother [sic] ... was unable to care for the child.' The judge stressed that the birth mother is like a 'foster parent,' 'a gestational carrier,' or 'a host in some sense.'

The decision that the birth mother was not the child's natural mother was upheld at two levels of appeal. The majority of the California Supreme Court (Kennard J. dissenting) held that although both consanguinity and giving birth were means of establishing parentage under the Uniform Parentage Act, whereas here, different women claimed this status, the 'natural mother' was she who intended to 'bring about the birth of the child that she intended to raise as her own.' Nor did the birth mother (repeatedly referred to as 'ges-

tational surrogate') have any constitutionally protected interest in her relationship with the child. See *Johnson* v. *Calvert*, 19 Cal. Rptr. 2d 494 (1993).

The Ontario Advisory Council on Women's Issues has recommended that
all reproductive contracts should be null and void. If these proposals were
implemented, where a child is born as a result of an alleged agreement, the
birth mother would be the only legal parent. See 'Presentation to the Royal
Commission on New Reproductive Technologies,' Oct. 1990.

102 See A. Harris, supra n. 2.

103 I think this work is emerging through the scholarship of feminist theorists of
colour which stresses multiple consciousness as jurisprudential method. See
A. Harris, supra n. 2; P. Williams, supra n. 2; and M. Matsuda, supra n. 2.

When Legal Cultures Collide[1]

RICHARD F. DEVLIN

Every society has the tendency to reduce its opponents to caricatures – at least in imagination – and as it were to starve them. Such a caricature is ... our 'criminal.'[2]

Friedrich Nietzsche

The one duty we owe history is to rewrite it.[3]

Oscar Wilde

Introduction

In this essay, I attempt to consider the juridical significance of the Irish hunger strike of 1981. I focus on this almost unreal, but tragically too real, 'event' for two reasons. First, on the basis of the rereading or representation that I offer in this essay, the hunger strike provides an opportunity to reflect upon what is perhaps the most enduring and intractable question of social theory: the relationship between structure and agency. Specifically, it enables us to critically interrogate the aspirations and assumptions of a colonial legal structure and the agentic resistance of the juridically colonized. The second reason for my interest is more personal. As I was a law student in Belfast at the time, the strike has been a key aspect of my formative context and thus a constitutive part of my identity. In particular, by bringing into sharp relief the relationship between law, domination, violence, and death, the hunger strike has turned out to be a (not always conscious but pervasive) backdrop against which I have constructed both my political philosophy and my jurisprudence.[4]

But I want to tell this story with a different voice from that which usually predominates in the dominant discourses of the North Atlantic societies. More precisely, I will filter my interpretation through the insights of both postmodernism and deconstruction. My purpose will be to consider the intersections between postmodernism/deconstruction and nationalism in order to inquire into the utility of such perspectives in helping to de-centre the hegemony of a dominant – read British – legal discourse and thereby to create space for the valorization of a marginalized and subordinated legal discourse. My claim is that legal knowledge is itself a terrain of political struggle, and that dominant legal interpretations are only so because of their superior force, not because of their superior truth.

However, although I will argue that postmodernism and deconstruction enable us to think critically about power, knowledge, truth, history, self, and language, at the same time, this case study will highlight what might be some of the weaknesses of postmodernism and deconstruction in their ability to 'put the dissidents back into history.'[5] In particular, I will argue that the postmodern focus on texts and epistemology, while absolutely necessary, is insufficient, and therefore that it needs to be supplemented by an emphasis on politics and ethics. My suggestion will be that those groups – and, in particular, those theorists – in North American society who espouse the embracement of postmodernism as providing a means for the achievement of difference and inclusion are excessively discursive in their conception of power, and therefore incapable of adequately supporting a sufficiently destabilizing practice. My aim will be to walk the tightrope between those who posit that postmodernism and deconstruction are profoundly liberationist[6] and those who argue that they are dangerously conservative.[7]

My analysis in this essay draws on some key motifs of both postmodernism and deconstruction: alterity, otherness, pluralism, simulation, difference, and incommensurability. The essay is divided into three further sections. In part 2, I apply some of these insights to the events around the 1981 hunger strike by Irish prisoners in British jails in the British-occupied north of Ireland to advance the juridically impertinent proposition that what was at stake was not merely a politically strategic, last ditch act of desperation, but '(an)other' indigenously Irish legal claim based upon a subordinated legal culture, the Brehon Laws. Restated jurisprudentially, I will argue that the hunger strike can be conceived of as a 'jurisgenerative act.'[8] In part 3, on the basis of this story, I develop some reflections as to the utility of postmodernism and deconstruction for others who aspire to the legal recognition of difference. My aim here is to resist the tendency towards disengagement and political quietism which may be engendered by some aspects of postmodernism and deconstruction. Finally, part 4 provides some (in)conclusive thoughts.

The Hunger Strike

A History

In this section, I develop a historical reconstruction and juridical revision of events leading up to and during the hunger strike of 1981. History, as every good postmodernist knows, is contingent upon a choice of starting points and perspectives: it is partial (in both senses of the word) rather than total. Therefore, it seems to me that we can only fully appreciate the interpretation offered in this essay if we begin with the early years of what, colloquially, is called 'this round of the troubles' in Northern Ireland.

In the late 1960s, inspired by the protest movements in both the United States and Europe, a coalition of relatively progressive groups came together in the form of the Northern Ireland Civil Rights Association (NICRA) to protest the discrimination against Catholics in Northern Ireland. Although a few members of NICRA were republicans, the vast majority of those involved were socialists and liberal democrats.[9] In spite of the fact that the demands of NICRA were essentially reformist, the local state response was one of unmediated police repression.[10] Worse still was the collusion between the repressive state apparatuses and segments of the loyalist community whereby the former enabled the latter to embark upon vigilantism and pogroms, which were so widespread that (prior to the current civil war in 'Yugoslavia') they caused the greatest relocation of the civilian population anywhere in Europe since the Second World War.[11]

Thus, I would argue it was the atavistic and repressive activities of the state – both active and passive – which generated the resurgence of the legitimacy of the IRA, because when the pogroms began the only people even partially able to defend the Catholic communities were very small numbers of IRA volunteers who had a few old rifles.[12] With no sign of the pogroms abating, with the Catholics very much under siege, the British government acknowledged that the local security forces were so partisan that they were causing a legitimation crisis for the British state. As a result, the British government decided to dispatch soldiers to carry out what was, in essence, a policing function. For a couple of months, there was a honeymoon period between the British troops and the nationalist community – perhaps bred of dependency – but this began to deteriorate because of the partisan activities of some soldiers in favour of the loyalist communities, a very tentative emergence of military hostility by the IRA against a reintensified British presence on Irish soil, and, eventually, the imposition of a curfew and house-to-house searches in the (predominantly Catholic) Lower Falls area of Belfast in July 1970.

As to the legal system in this period, if people were arrested they were processed under the extremely Draconian *Civil Authorities (Special Powers) Act.* Yet, in spite of this, those processed and incarcerated under the act were treated as 'ordinary decent criminals' or 'odc's.'

Though tension began to rise in 1970 between the IRA and the British Army, mostly in the form of rioting, it was not until February 1971 that the first British soldier was killed in Northern Ireland since the 1920s, and from April forth the IRA began to develop a campaign of bombing.

The response of the British state, at the bidding of unionist politicians,[13] was to introduce internment without trial. Three hundred and forty-two people, all Catholics, many of them without any connection to the IRA, were arrested in the first raid on 9 August 1971. Within six months, a total of 2,357 people had been interned, again the vast majority of them being Catholics.[14] However, rather than being treated as 'odc's,' the majority were sent to a deserted Second World War air base – Long Kesh – placed in Nissen huts, and were able to operate as if they were in a prisoner-of-war camp. In effect, they had 'political status.'

A much smaller number of 'suspects,' who were arrested and actually processed through the courts, were not placed in these hastily established prisoner-of-war camps. Rather, they were sent to the ordinary prisons and located in cells with no recognition of the political motivations for their 'crimes' – nor of the fact that they were arrested and processed under the *Special Powers Act.* As a result, in mid-June 1972, about thirty republican prisoners who had been tried and convicted went on a hunger strike and, by the fourth week, had gained recognition of their 'special category status.'[15]

Internment and political / special category status created a fundamental contradiction for the British state. On the one hand, Britain prided itself on being the great fountainhead of habeas corpus. And yet, the existence of several thousand untried prisoners was an acute embarrassment. Thus in 1972, Lord Diplock issued his *Report of the Commission to Consider Legal Procedures to Deal with Terrorist Activities in Northern Ireland,*[16] which was an attempt to depoliticize the republican prisoners by encoding them as 'criminals.' A key aspect of this report were proposals to eliminate the system of internment without trial by creating special juryless, single-judge courts that would, with the benefit of a 'modified' common law of confessions coupled with a shift in the burden of proof, be able to process 'suspected terrorists.' The agenda was to reassert the supremacy of the rule of law over the politicization of law. Diplock's recommendations were put into effect in the *Northern Ireland (Emergency Provisions) Act, 1973*, in effect creating a conveyor-belt criminal process.[17]

But it was soon realized that the Diplock process of criminalization did not go far enough in delegitimizing the political integrity of the republican prisoners because once convicted they were entitled to 'special category status,' which had been gained by the hunger strike of 1972. As a result, Lord Gardiner (a former lord chancellor) was called upon by the British government to prepare a report that would further 'rationalize' the program of criminalization. He duly obliged and, in a report published in January 1975, proposed that 'special category status' would not be available to those who were convicted of crimes committed after 1 March 1976.[18]

Central to the project of the removal of 'special category status' and its replacement with a program of 'criminalization' and 'normalization' were the elements of cellular rather than group confinement, and the wearing of prison uniforms. When the first post–March 1st prisoner was given his uniform in September 1976, he refused it and therefore, being without clothes, took refuge in his prison blankets. So began the 'blanket protest.' The response of the British state was to treat this as a breach of prison rules, and, therefore, the prison governor imposed harsh penalties: 'a complete removal of remission; twenty-four-hour lock-up; deprivation of mental stimulation of any sort – reading material, newspapers, books, television, radio, games, hobbies or writing material. This was combined with very intimate body searches'[19] and the reduction of visits to one half hour per month. By September 1977 there were about 160 republican prisoners 'on the blanket.'

This situation continued with a hardening of positions through to April 1978. At this point, in response to further 'disciplining' in relation to washing, as well as 'internal searches of the body, deprivation of letters, removal to punishment cells and beatings of young prisoners,'[20] the prisoners refused to wash or cooperate in any way with the prison staff. But the spiral did not stop with this 'no wash protest.' As part of their policy of non-participation, the prisoners refused to slop out their chamber pots.

These pots, in turn, became part of the contested process in that they were frequently kicked over by prison guards in the course of the ongoing searches. To prevent this from happening, and specifically to avoid the soaking and soiling of their floor-based mattresses, the prisoners threw the contents of the pots out the windows and under the doors of their cells, but these were slopped back in by the prison guards. In turn, by the end of 1978, this led to the 'dirty protest,' in which the prisoners spread their own maggot-infested excrement on the walls of their cells. By 1979 there were approximately 370 prisoners on the 'dirty protest.'

As all the accounts of the hunger strike and the events prior to it indicate, it was clear that it was the prisoners themselves who were setting the agenda.[21] And while there was a significant mobilization on the outside to publicize the conditions, this was not generating sufficient pressure to force the British government to change its agenda of total criminalization. In the face of such ox-like indifference of the British government, as 1980 wore on, the prisoners decided that in pursuit of political status they would resort to a hunger strike to force the government to recognize their claims. However, the Army Council of the IRA objected to this intensification of the protest, and Gerry Adams, as vice-president of Sinn Féin,[22] communicated that the leadership of that organization was 'tactically, strategically, physically and morally opposed to a hunger strike.'[23] But in spite of these objections, on 10 October 1980, the protesters announced a strike demanding 'as of right, political recognition and that we be accorded the status of political prisoners.'[24] On 27 October, seven prisoners went on hunger strike. Bobby Sands was not one of them as he was given the position of OC in the camp. As the weeks progressed, despite the facade of intransigence on both sides, a series of secret negotiations proceeded through intermediaries.[25] The result was that, as one of the strikers seemed about to die prematurely on the fifty-third day, the British government appeared to acquiesce to the prisoners' demands by issuing a thirty-four-page document which seemed to suggest a step-by-step de-escalation process that would in effect reinstate 'special category status.' The strike was called off. However, as became apparent over the next month, the demands were not met and the prisoners felt outmanoeuvred and totally betrayed.

Thus, in January of 1981, Sands took the initiative and announced that a new strike would commence. But on this occasion there was a shift away from the focus on 'political status' to what became known as 'The Five Demands': the right to wear their own clothing at all times; exemption from all forms of penal labour; free association with each other at all hours; the right to organize their own recreational and educational programs; and full restoration of remission. It was thought that this change in the rhetoric would provide the British government with greater space to compromise.[26] The second hunger strike began on 1 March 1981, and the rest is history. Ten prisoners died before a solution was reached. But in the course of the fast, Sands – 'the criminal' – was elected to the British Parliament; Sinn Féin garnered remarkable local political support; and world attention was focused, not just on the strike, but on the intransigence of the British attitude generally to Ireland.

An Interpretation: Fasting as (An)other Jural Claim

The last several pages have attempted to provide a historical narrative of events leading up to, during, and after the hunger strike. This section provides an interpretation of these events, drawing on some of the insights of postmodernism and deconstruction.

Deconstruction argues that the hierarchical construction of relationships is central to logocentric thought. Derrida posits that all oppositions invoke 'a violent hierarchy. One of the two terms controls the other (axiologically, logically, etc.), or has the upper hand.'[27] This is particularly pertinent for an understanding of the politics (and pretensions) of law. The point of logocentrism is to attempt to render that which is contingent, incontrovertible. Thus, within the dominant jurisprudential conception, law is conceptualized as both different from and hierarchically superior to politics in that the latter is acknowledged to be contaminated by vulgar interests, but law is said to be beyond the contingencies of politics.

Thus, in relation to the hunger strike, one reason why the British government was so keen on the program of 'criminalization' of the prisoners was to draw on the logocentric legitimacy of law, so as to put the issue of nationalist claims for self-determination beyond debate, to enforce closure by juridical fiat. Thatcher made much of this on a visit to Belfast after the deaths of several of the prisoners: 'Now what I am saying is we will uphold the law ... I cannot pull solutions out of a hat. I will not depart from upholding the law ...'[28]

As Michael Ryan reminds us, 'the authority of the sovereign's law depends upon the establishing of unambiguous proper meaning for words.'[29] In Northern Ireland during the hunger strike era, the contested terms were 'law' and 'criminal.' The republican prisoners, however, refused to acquiesce in this totalizing trope of criminalization and attempted to destabilize and invert this hierarchical move by demonstrating the inherently political and partisan nature of the legal machinery. They called into question the rationalistic and progressive self-image of law, to tell a different story.

One example illustrates these strategies of resistance that sought to undermine the British state's logocentric ambitions, and law's 'elective self-image.'[30] It was the prisoners themselves (and contrary to the IRA leadership's traditional policy of political abstentionism) who came up with the idea of proposing Sands as a candidate for the British Parliament.[31] His election by over thrity thousand voters not only legitimized the demands for political status but also gave notice to the Thatcher regime that a political consciousness cannot simply be re-encoded by politico-juridical relabelling. Moreover, and seemingly learning nothing, when Sands died, the government hurriedly passed the mendaciously entitled *Representation of the People Act*, so as to prohibit any further prisoners from fulfilling their democratic mandate in 'the mother of all parliaments.' But this also failed because in Sands place his election agent increased the margin of victory by 786 votes. In sum, the British government attempted to use the law to privilege one ideological perspective; the prisoners resisted such a move by asserting a contradictory claim, thereby shearing law of its metaphysical privileges. As Derrida posits, 'to deconstruct the opposition ... is first to overthrow the hierarchy.'[32] Viewed in this light, deconstruction helps us to destabilize hierarchical conceptions of the relationship between law and politics, confirming that law is always and already constituted by politics.

This is not to say, however, that law is just politics. Rather, law is a particular kind of politics, one that commingles express exercises of power with implied normative visions. To elaborate. Most of the conventional reviews of hunger striking in Ireland trace back only as far as the practice had been adopted by the republican movement.[33] Such a historical account identifies the hunger strike with the political ideology of republicanism. However, this is only a partial account. Hunger striking is not a recent phenomenon in Ireland. It is not reducible to republicanism. On the contrary, its roots can be traced back to an ancient, pre-Christian, Celtic legal code, the Brehon Laws,[34] and the practice of *cealachan* or *troscead*, that is, fasting. *Cealachan/troscead* is a component of the ancient Irish Law of *Athgabhail/Athgabal*, which, in common law terms, one could consider to be analogous to distraint.[35] *Athgabhail* 'is a general name for every coercion (lit. binding) through which each person enforces his [legal] interest'[36] invoked, as Ginnell points out, so that 'advantage is obtained after disadvantage ... truth after untruth, legality after illegality, justice after injustice ... right after wrong.'[37] *Troscead* (fasting) is the performative act that triggers the action in distraint. Stated simply, if a person had been wronged by another who was more powerful – for example, a chieftain, brehon, bard, king, or bishop[38] – having given appropriate notice, the wronged party was entitled to claim distress by fasting at the door of the wrongdoer. Responsibility for ending the fast vested in the perceived wrongdoer. If the latter allowed the plaintiff to starve to death, then the wrongdoer was held responsible for the death and had to compensate the victim's family.

A central proposition advanced by this essay is that, building upon not only the political tradition of previous republican hunger strikes, but also upon the *legal* tradition of the Brehon Laws, at the margin of the British state in the H-Blocks, the prisoners rediscovered and reconstituted an almost silenced countervailing legal regime. The hunger strike, then, was not simply a last ditch desperate propaganda stunt, which has been the dominant interpretation. Rather, it was an irruption of an alterior juridical regime, the espousal of a cultural difference, the exposition of a jural other, the assertion of a legal right.

It is important to note how this came about. The agenda of the British state was to eliminate the foundations of Irish identity, to totally erase locations of resistance. It realized that internment and the Diplock courts served to strengthen the integrity and legitimacy of the republican cause. It recognized that by taking activists from their communities, by imprisoning them through the ideological trope of criminalization, they could perhaps silence the nationalist 'other.' But, at the same time, it was understood by the government that by continuing with 'special category status,' they were allowing the persistence of two contradictions within their policies. First, 'special category status' was simply a euphemism for 'political status' and therefore a discordant acknowledgment that there may be a certain legitimacy to the republican liberation struggle. Second, and just as important, 'special category status' acknowledged the military structure of the IRA and allowed free association and control over the recreational and educational processes within Long Kesh to accrue to the military command of the IRA. In other words, the British government realized that internment and 'special category status,' though they temporarily divorced the IRA from the nationalist community, would have the effect of facilitating the emergence of what Sands would later describe as the 'politically educated armed guerilla fighter who will not only use his [*sic*] political mind to guide his weapon, but to guide and teach his politically undernourished countrymen to steer their own destiny ...'[39]

Consequently, it was determined by the British that the repression would have to be intensified. First, in order to undermine the process of political radicalization fostered in Long Kesh, the 'Republican University,' it was necessary to rethink the architecture of coercion so as to undercut the groupist solidarity that the traditional military-type cage structure engendered. As a result, there emerged the idea of H-Block compounds. These were blocks of prison cells constructed in the shape of an *H*, with the four wings connected by an administrational cross-bar. Each block was capable of containing approximately eighty prisoners, each prisoner to be held in an eight-foot by ten-foot cell. Second, de-radicalization required that both the nationalist community and the prisoners themselves cease accepting the code/signifier of 'prisoners of war' and instead adopt the penal bureaucratic argot of 'odc' (ordinary decent criminal) or 'hac' (honest average criminal).[40] It was this quest for the penal construction of 'the criminal' that generated the Gardiner Report's emphasis on uniforms, prison work, discipline, and the curtailment of opportunities for association and education.

But at the margins of the British state, almost absented from the dominant discourse, almost delegitimized within the nationalist communities, the prisoners continued their resistance. First, drawing on the significant increase in the educational aspects of republican tradition in the last years of 'special category status,' the H-Blocks became both a conduit for the dissemination of Irish history and a school for reflection on leftist-inspired revolutionary strategies.[41] Second, and of crucial importance to this process of consciousness raising, was the switch to the use of Irish language. This was required because the new cellular structure required that if the prisoners sought to communicate with each other, they would have to shout. But shouting in English would, obviously, render their communications accessible to the prison guards. The solution was to encode the conversations in a modified version of the Irish language that the prisoners with an earnest humour called 'jailic.'[42] Third, this translation, in turn, engendered a greater consciousness of Irish history. Of particular significance was the interrogation of the legal basis of British colonialism and the rediscovery of the ancient Irish Brehon Laws and, most notably for the purposes of this essay, the practice of *troscead*. Thus, having disinterred what might be called 'a juridical unconscious,'[43] the prisoners could identify Brehon law as a different legal culture.

Consequently, when the announcement of 10 October 1980 claimed that the hunger strike was based on 'a right,' it was not simply rhetoric. Not only did the prisoners base their claim on the terrain of political struggle, or the republican tradition of self-immolative martyrdom,[44] which are the two conventional interpretations. It was also a profound juridical claim premised upon a subordinated, and therefore ex-centric but not eliminated, legal culture. Indeed, a recently published interview with a former prisoner of the hunger strike period indicates this:

With the Gaelic you begin to get back in touch with political and ideological concepts. For instance *cealathan*, where in the Brehon laws to express a grievance against an injustice a guy sat outside the wrongdoer's house and starved himself to death. Now *cealachon* [*sic*] had a whole moral import to it that it wasn't a hunger strike as a protest weapon; it was the legal assertion of your rights. The hunger strike was a legitimate and moral means for asserting those rights, and it had legal precedents dating back to antiquity. You found that there was a literature that was untranslatable from the Gaelic that could never be expressed in the cold English.[45]

The peculiarity is that rather than formulating their claim in some formalistic and bureaucratic cause of action – a form of encoding or translation that severs the plaintiffs from their claim – the fasting prisoners reconstituted their bodies as a jural template so that their claim was, literally, one of life or death.

To recap. The essentially rehabilitative claim that I have advanced is that not only is law politically manipulatable, but also that law is, in a strong sense, culturally contingent; that it is 'local knowledge, not placeless principle.'[46] The hunger strike of 1981 represents and signifies a collision of incommensurable legal cultures in which one – the Brehon tradition of the disempowered fasting against the empowered – because of its marginalized status was not encoded or intelligible ('untranslatable') as such because of the hegemonic ascendency of the common law juridical psyche. Through the deconstructive supplementary logic of reversal and displacement, I wish to rehabilitate this almost erased ethico-juridical other, to reconceptualize fasting as a practice of juridical decolonization, and to posit that the response of the British state in refusing to recognize this other legal culture is but another form of violence.

The Political Ambivalences of Postmodernism

The purpose of this section is to further this interpretation of legal practices, legal institutions, and legal structures through the grid of postmodernism and deconstruction, and to consider the adequacies of these modes of analysis, not just as interpretive techniques, but as potential juridico-social theories.[47] Moreover, I propose to consider Derrida's recent claim that deconstruction is 'revolutionary,' in the sense 'that it assumes the right to contest, and not only theoretically, constitutional protocols ... the right to contest established law in its strongest authority, the law of the State.'[48]

Although postmodernism as political philosophy and deconstruction as critical method[49] do not share an identity, there are certain elements of homology, continuity, and overlap that are of interpretive value. Given its complex and portmanteau character, postmodernism is notoriously difficult to get a handle on. This is because it spans a variety of cultural and academic fields, has advocates who frequently adopt profoundly incompatible perspectives, revels in its ephemeral, splintered, and fractured dynamism, and – as a result of its predilection for being 'post' – is reluctant to construct any determinative or homogeneous self-image. Nevertheless, in spite of its slipperiness, I do think that it is possible to provide an account (though not a definition) of postmodernism in which a few common motifs[50] relate to my discussion.

Of particular importance to this essay, especially in connection with its relation to deconstruction, are the politico-epistemological propositions associated with postmodernism. First, and perhaps most importantly, postmodernism's embracement of alterity and 'otherness'[51] has meant that 'reality' is deprived of its objective foundations, and is re-understood as flimsy, fragmentary, unstable, heterogeneous, and plural.[52] In this light, 'authenticity' and 'reality' are re-encoded as 'fabrication' and 'simulation.'[53] Second, and closely related, because our relationships with reality are socially mediated and constructed, knowledge too is said to lack any objective non-contingent foundation. Such an interpretive approach to knowledge is sometimes called 'perspectivism'[54] or 'antifoundationalism'[55] in that it posits that there can be a plurality of mutually incommensurable perspectives offering equally valid interpretations. Postmodernism dismantles 'Truth,' at least with a capital T.[56] Third, postmodernism is so radical in its disassembly and decomposition of conventional wisdom that it argues that the very idea of 'the individual' or 'the subject' is up for grabs. It posits that so pervasive are the social structures and narratives, that we can no longer be confident of the humanist faith in an essentialist, pre-social, coherent, unified, and autonomous self. Rather, even the self is constructed to the core. Derrida, for example, talks about the 'death' of the subject,[57] and Baudrillard calls for a 'renunciation of the position of the subject.'[58] If postmodernists are accurate in this claim, then they obviously problematize our traditionally received ideas about autonomy, freedom, choice, and agency.[59] Finally, according to Baudrillard, several political consequences emerge from these sociological and epistemological propositions. Most importantly, he argues that power needs to be reconceptualized. 'No more subject, focal point, centre or periphery: but pure flexion or circular inflection. No more violence or surveillance: only "information," secret with virulence, chain reaction, slow implosion and simulacra of spaces where the real effect comes into play.'[60] Indeed, because 'power is no longer present except to conceal that there is none'[61] then '*law and order themselves might be nothing more than a simulation.*'[62] All of which is to say that 'the political sphere (and power in general) becomes empty,'[63] so that 'power pure and simple disappears.'[64] As a consequence of this dispersed conception of power, the idea – indeed the very possibility – of political praxis needs to be reconsidered.

Postmodernism and deconstruction share some political motifs. By highlighting the constructed and necessarily relational nature of that which would be incontrovertible, the deconstructive technique of *différance* endangers and deflates logocentrism. Deconstruction uncovers the plurality of possibilities and demonstrates that what is centralized is dependent upon the repression of alternative contenders by relegating them to the margins. This process of foregrounding contradiction, anomaly, and irrationality is considered to be empowering in that deconstruction creates the possibility for dismantling binary oppositions and revivifying that which has been submerged. Deconstruction creates conditions hospitable to the 'return of the repressed.'

Derrida's concepts of 'marginality, supplementarity, différance and deconstruction'[65] have helped me to better reconsider and explain my own understanding of the hunger strike. In its disinterring and valorization of 'alterity' – the existence and potential legitimacy of otherness – postmodernism also allows space for at least a hearing of alternative and deviant perspectives. There is, then, an intersection between my analysis of the hunger strike, and postmodernism and deconstruction.

However, it would be a mistake to confuse intersection with consensus. There is, of course, an obvious postmodern response to my analysis: that my argument may tend to privilege consciousness and therefore smack of a revivalist and revolutionary voluntarism that is dependent upon an idealistic and nostalgic humanism. Nationalism, after all, is but a by-product of modernity and modernist thinking.[66] More specifically, the postmodernist counter-argument would probably be that the fasting prisoners were but the 'effect,' determination,[67] 'site,'[68] or symptom of the various discourses and structures of Irish republicanism. They were inscriptions of a deviationist subtext, not authors of their destiny. In this section, I want to cautiously and critically relate my analysis to those of deconstruction and postmodernism, especially as they are manifested in the work of Derrida and, more briefly, Baudrillard.

Derrida argues that '... the task [of deconstruction] is ... to dismantle the metaphysical and rhetorical structures which are at work [in the text], not in order to reject or discard them, but to reinscribe them in another way.'[69] A central step in this process is what he calls 'reversal':

I strongly and repeatedly insist on the necessity of the phase of reversal, which people have perhaps too swiftly attempted to discredit ... To neglect this phase of reversal is to forget that the structure of the opposition is one of conflict and subordination and thus to pass too swiftly, without gaining any purchase against the former opposition, to a *neutralization* which *in practice* leaves things in their former state and deprives one of any way of *intervening* effectively. [70]

The reinscription that I have suggested is the reverse proposition that although the hunger strike demonstrated the politics of British law, it also was an indigenously Irish legal claim, the articulation of what Geertz has called an alterior 'legal sensibility,' another 'form of juristical life.'[71] However, from a postmodernist perspective such an argument may be excessively voluntaristic in that it overinflates the 'creativity' of the prisoners.

Derrida has been particularly explicit in his disparagement of 'the subject.' For example, at one point, he argues that 'the subject' is but 'the play of linguistic or semiological différance'[72] and, at another, posits that 'the authority of representation constrains us, imposing itself on our thought through a whole dense, enigmatic and heavily stratified history. It programs us and precedes us.'[73] More expansively:

... the subject (in its identity with itself, or eventually in its consciousness of its identity with itself, its self consciousness) is inscribed in language, is a 'function' of language, becomes a *speaking* subject only by making its speech conform – even in so-called 'creation,' or so-called 'transgression' – to the system of the rules of language as a system of différances, by conforming to the general law of *différance.*[74]

And, with admirable anti-logocentric consistency, Derrida confesses his own lack of agency by denying that he chooses interpretations; rather, 'the interpretations select themselves.'[75]

In relation to something like the hunger strike, this espousal of textual determinism is an attractive thesis in that it seems to explain that which is apparently so eccentric as to be inexplicable: the self-sacrifice of the self in full knowledge of the likelihood of death. However, the problems with an adoption of this deconstructive/postmodernist approach to the question of the subject are twofold. First, it is insufficiently oppositional in its politico-juridical orientation; and, second, it potentially reinforces continued oppression.

The first argument against an excessively thin theory of the subject posits that, in its best light, postmodernism provides little account of how the repressed actually determine their condition, make choices, and resist their oppression. The sort of propositions advanced by Derrida run the risk of oversimplifying the relationship between agency and structure, of merely inverting the humanist hierarchy of agency over structure and therefore simply mimicking it.[76] But perhaps this goes too far and what is required is an intermediary mediation between structure and agency, so that liberal humanism's ontological fetishization of the sovereign, coherent subject is not simply replaced by an excessive and reactive anti-humanism,[77] thereby slipping into an anti-theory of agency. There is a difference between: (a) a sovereign conception of the subject, in which the person is assumed to be unified, rational, and voluntaristic (the liberal humanist position); (b) a concatenated conception of the subject that, because of its deterministic arguments, denies the possibility of self-constitution in any strong sense, and thereby the possibility of oppositional strategies (the postmodernist position); and (c) a situated or embedded conception of the subject,[78] which allows for the possibility of consciousness and self-constitution in the context of the matrix of societal and cultural influences (my position). In other words, what is required is a relational and historicized theory of the subject, a relational and historicized conception of agency. Such an ontology envisions the subject as neither the centre of the universe nor a mere concatenation of social forces, but a subject who is both constituted and constitutive.

There is little doubt that republicanism as a discourse is an important factor in Irish life, but it is not so determinative or constraining as postmodernists might have us believe. Republicanism in the late 1970s and early 1980s underwent a significant transition from its classical political abstentionist and exclusively militaristic form, to a politically participatory and more social movement. Postmodern methodology enables us to track this transition by encouraging us to look at the micro-details of this development. In particular, we would have to analyse the changing subjectivities and emerging ideologies of actors such as Gerry Adams[79] and Bobby Sands[80] – Irish, Belfast-reared, male, working-class, (a)religious – and the differences of opinion within the Army Council of the IRA. Most particularly, we can learn from 'the comms' that were smuggled out of the H-Blocks prior to, and during, the fast. These are perhaps the classic postmodern deviationist micro-texts in that as much as four thousand words[81] could be written with a biro refill tube on one cigarette paper or 'stamped government property toilet roll.'[82] They would then be smuggled to the outside command structures of the IRA through bodily orifices – themselves penetratingly surveilled[83] – but by means of which the prisoners themselves determined the change of direction and future agenda of republicanism.[84] By means of these 'comms,' the prisoners disseminated an alternative political vision for the IRA and even outlined the most appropriate strategies of mobilization, from massive postering campaigns to the standing of fasting prisoners as election candidates.[85]

To elaborate. As the late 1970s wore on, it became increasingly apparent to the prisoners that, despite some outside support, their various protests were not going to change the British state's determination to impose criminalization, nor generate further support for political status in the nationalist community. The terrain of struggle was significantly enlarged when the prisoners – against the wishes of the Army Council – decided that by means of a hunger strike there could be the galvanization of the nationalist community around republicanism. In other words, it was determined by the prisoners that the traditionally sanctified unidimensional military campaign on its own would not succeed. But although the first couple of weeks of the fast expanded the support network, still the majority of the nationalist community remained leery. The key breakthrough occurred when it was decided – once again by the fasting prisoners[86] – that the traditional republican position of abstentionism from political campaigns should be abandoned, and it was proposed to run Bobby Sands as the candidate for the British Parliament. This strategy forced the issue within the nationalist community as to whether it would split the vote between the republican Sands and the constitutionalist SDLP and thereby let the single unionist candidate win. The constitutionalists backed down, thereby giving the full political stage to Sands. The result was that on 9 April 1981, a self-confessed IRA volunteer was elected to the British Parliament with 30,492 votes, in effect inverting the criminalization agenda of the British state. Boomerang.

Furthermore, the election of two more fasting prisoners in a general, election in the Republic of Ireland was crucial to the defeat of the governing party, Fianna Fail.[87] Finally, the strike and the events around it confirmed that the traditional republican stance of political abstentionism in deference to militarism was misconceived and served as a catalyst for Sinn Féin to participate in subsequent local, general and European elections, obtaining between 10.2 per cent and 13.4 per cent of the overall vote, or between 25 per cent to 40 per cent of the nationalist vote in Northern Ireland.[88] The prisoners negated the negation. Resistance though marginal, suitably engendered, can erupt in phenomenal ways.

My apprehensions about the progressive political utility of deconstruction and postmodernism are intensified when I review some of the more explicitly 'political work' of Derrida, for he is equivocal as to the political ramifications of his own project. Because of his anti-theory of the subject, Derrida seems to be insufficiently attuned to what I would describe the noisy agency of the subjugated, but not totally erased, subject.

At first blush, it would seem unfair to complain about Derrida's political progressivism, given that in 1983 he wrote a short essay which challenged not only apartheid but also the West's complicity in its perpetuation.[89] Moreover, apparently in reply to those who have voiced concerns about the political significance of deconstruction, he has argued (with uncharacteristic clarity) that

what is somewhat hastily called deconstruction is not, if it is of any consequence, a specialized set of discursive procedures, even less the rules of a new hermeneutic method, working on texts or utterances in the shelter of a given and stable institution. It is also, at the very least, a way of taking a position, in its work of analysis, concerning the political and institutional structures that make possible and govern our practice, our competencies, our performances. Precisely because it is never concerned only with signified content, deconstruction should not be separable from this politico-institutional problematic and should seek a new investigation of responsibility, an investigation which questions the codes inherited from ethics and politics. This means that too political for some, it will seem paralyzing to those who only recognize politics by the most familiar road signs.[90]

While this seems to be an unequivocal articulation of the political ramifications of deconstruction, it is, in my opinion, vitiated in two ways. First, the comment lacks any specificity as to what might qualify as a desirable 'position' or constitute an appropriate act of 'responsibility.' The abstraction of the argument renders it indeterminate and therefore potentially as supportive of oppressive political practices as liberationist political practices. Second, on what basis are we to justify any 'position' that we might 'choose' – or is it that such positions might 'choose' us? – if decon-struction has as its primary purpose displacement and the proliferation of multiplicity?

Indeed, despite these claims as to the political relevance of deconstruc-tion, on other occasions Derrida has also expressed reservations: 'I must confess that I have never succeeded in directly relating deconstruction to existing political programmes.'[91] But he then proceeds to argue that this does not require inaction or non-commitment:

But the difficulty is to gesture in opposite directions at the same time: on the one hand to preserve a distance and suspicion with regard to the official political codes governing reality; on the other, to intervene here and now in a practical and *engaged* manner whenever the necessity arises. This position of dual alle-giance, in which I personally find myself, is one of perpetual uneasiness. I try where I can to act politically while recognizing that such action remains incom-mensurate with my intellectual project of deconstruction.[92]

And to be fair to Derrida, it must be acknowledged that Derrida the inter-ventionist has taken some progressive political positions. So, for example, in 1981 he visited Prague to meet with some dissident intellectuals. For his troubles he was arrested and jailed for three days. But what did Derrida the deconstructionist philosopher make of his experience? As one com-mentator reports, Derrida 'insisted on the difficulty there is in making an ethico-political gesture (supporting the resistance of the Prague philoso-phers, who demand respect for human rights ... and articulate that with a philosophy of the subject, the person, individual liberty etc) coincide with a philosophical labour governed by the necessity of deconstructing pre-cisely such philosophemes.'[93] Viewed in this light, political prisoners in British-occupied Northern Ireland could expect little in the way of intel-lectual support from deconstruction.

Nor is Derrida alone in his quietism, in the retreat from the discussion of praxis. Baudrillard, too, has suggested that given the pervasiveness of hyper-reality and hyper-conformity,[94] then 'withdrawing into the private could well be *a direct defiance of the political*, a form of actively resisting political manipulation.'[95] For him 'indifference,' inertia, and non-partici-pation are the only available 'counter-strategies':[96] 'This revolution by involution ... proceeds by inertia and not from a new and joyous negativ-ity. It is silent and involutive – exactly the reverse of all speechmaking and consciousness raising. It has no meaning, it has nothing to say to us.'[97]

Yet again, events in the H-Blocks problematize the validity of such asser-tions. It is not that the prisoners have 'nothing to say'; rather, it is that they have had 'no say.'[98] As pointed out previously, one reason why the British government chose the cell system of incarceration was to undermine the collectivism and solidarity fostered in the dormitory-type cages of Long Kesh. The H-Blocks were originally designed to accommodate one prisoner per cell, and prisoners, on entering, for the first year or so, were subjected to a rigorous regime of silence: communication with their colleagues was prohibited.[99] Such a strategy of isolation and individualization was tailored to reinforce the project of criminalization. But the prisoners resisted, both instrumentally and structurally. Instrumentally, they began to communicate to each other by tapping on the heating pipes, exchanging 'comms' at the weekly mass (one of the few opportunities for interaction), and by gradually reviving the Irish language. Structurally, because of the nature of the 'dirty protest,' it meant that in order for the prison authorities to periodically clean the cells to prevent diseases, one of the arms of the *H* had to be kept vacant, so as to shift the prisoners to that section while the other was being cleaned.[100] This, in conjunction with the very high imprisonment rates generated by the Diplock court system, created an overpopulation problem for the prison administration, which was 'solved' by putting two prisoners in most cells and thereby undermining the original plan for a regime of silence. It was this reconsolidation of collectivism that engendered the group solidarity necessary to sustain the 'blanket,' 'no wash,' and 'dirty' protests and, eventually, to plan and pursue the hunger strike. It was only during the fast itself that the silence re-emerged, for, as one ex-prisoner has put it:

The slagging and practical joking stopped during the hunger strike. I minded Bobby [Sands] saying the joking shouldn't decrease. But it was dead artificial. There was no fucking singsongs. We tried but it wouldn't work. Bobby had asked us not to get into the silence. We were all in mourning for the duration.[101]

Thus to summarize my first criticism of postmodernism's thin theory of the subject, I would argue that at the level of theory its conception is so emaciated (and there is no pun intended) that it is incapable of bearing the explanatory weight that is imposed upon it. Therefore, it is proposed that we should see agency and discourse as mutually constitutive. However, we can only understand the degree and extent of that mutuality by actually studying specific situations in particular politico-historical conjunctures. This is what I have attempted to do by focusing on the fast.

The second problem with the postmodern process of the 'aestheticization of politics'[102] – that it may be complicit in the continuation of oppression – relates to the potentially legitimizing function that the espousal of 'hyper-reality' and 'simulation' may accrue to the benefit of those who wield the predominant political power. Two aspects of Baudrillard's analysis are worth noting in this respect.

First, Baudrillard, in his celebration of the politics of silence, characterizes the masses as 'dumb like beasts,'[103] but, as I have pointed out, the imposition of the regime of silence was a central component of the criminalization project of the British state. It was through the articulation of their humanity, identity, and integrity that the prisoners resisted such silencing. Second, by portraying the hunger strike as merely a particular manifestation of hyper-reality, by interpreting it as yet another manifestation of 'ubiquitous simulacra, pseudo-events,'[104] Baudrillard may trivialize the commitment and political consciousness of the subject hunger strikers. Death through starvation for over sixty days is more than simulation; it is more than game playing; it is more than a spectacle in the politics of illusion. Death, I would argue, is a powerful act of resistance in which agency draws on its final resource to transgress against a pseudo-hegemonic politico-juridical regime.[105] In other words, postmodernism unmodified may suggest too much complicity and not enough critique, an inability to distinguish between domination and resistance.[106] It may be accurate to argue we cannot know what the fasting prisoners sought was true in any transcendental sense, but that means neither that 'truth ... [has] ceased to exist,'[107] nor that we should consider subjects as paralysed by 'the spell of indecision,'[108] nor that we have 'nowhere to go.'[109]

In order to escape the relativizing drift and political quandary that postmodernism's embracement of a radical anti-humanism might impose, I would suggest that we can draw on, but adapt to the present context, the work of the sociologist Margrit Eichler. In relation to issues of gender, Eichler argues that in a world based upon (male) domination we cannot know what (gender) equality might look like, and consequently we should refocus our sights on what we do know, inequality, and make our task one of modifying and minimizing these inequalities.[110] Similarly, it can be argued that although we cannot know what an authentic reality might look like, we can know those things that are manifestly untrue and so our task becomes one of minimizing the pervasiveness of these untruths. And, as I have argued, it is clearly untrue that the fasting prisoners were nothing but ordinary criminals. The motivations for their alleged crimes were political; the modes of their arrests and interrogations were the product of exceptional powers; their alleged confessions were obtained under precisely tailored conditions; their trials were specially constructed through the Diplock process; and their treatment in prison was politically motivated, particularly the beatings.[111] How else is one to explain the fact that between 1969 and 1980 the prison population increased by almost 500 per cent,[112] except by acknowledging – as both a former Northern Ireland premier (Major Chichester Clark) and British secretary of state (Reginald Maudling) have done – that the Northern Irish and British states are at 'at war' with the IRA?[113] In short, there is a radical discordancy between the juridical construction of the prisoners as 'odc's' and the incontrovertible existence of a specifically tailored legal process that simply cannot fit within the frame of that legal construct. Thus, it seems to me that if we reorient our inquiry from the quest for truth to the minimization of untruths, then we can adopt the postmodern virtue of self-reflexivity and self-consciousness without necessarily being forced to embrace its vice of being self-undermining.[114] As Bernstein, echoing Habermas, points out, 'violence and distortion may be uneliminable, but they can be diminished.'[115]

For some of those who subscribe to postmodernism and deconstruction, my foregoing reflections on law, agency, truth, and death will be understood as being premised upon a vision – the identity politics of Irish nationalism – that is subject to the withering gaze of deconstruction.

To elaborate. It might well be argued that insofar as my conception of jurisprudence converts a 'conception of identity into a ground of politics'[116] it is necessarily subject to the deconstructive insight that such a strategy is dependent on a point of contradiction: in this case, the British law. Deconstruction, I am likely to be reminded, demands more than a mere reversal of hierarchy, for that merely reproduces binarism without subverting the very concept of hierarchy; displacement engenders a multiplicity that cannot be reduced to (nationalist) identity. Thus, the valorization of identity – an Irish jural other – reinforces and perpetuates the very system of domination that it seeks to transgress – British juridical colonialism – achieving what Schlag suggests is only a 'suicidal reinscription of precisely the sort of hierarchal dualities ... that deconstruction seeks to subvert and displace.'[117] Identities constrain, and therefore what is required is 'a liberation from identity.'[118] Moreover, given postmodernism's commitment to anti-essentialism and its embracement of the social constructionist thesis, the very idea of an Irish identity is but a delusive artifact, a quaint ethnocentric sentimentality, and therefore incapable of bearing the juridical weight that I would wish to impose upon it.

In response to these charges, three points might be made. First, I would want to argue that although I recognize that identity politics are necessarily incapable of having an essentialist base, that does not mean that they are unhelpful, and certainly not irretrievably reactionary. Rather, we can recognize the inevitably artifactual nature of a perspective – and can even countenance the dynamic nature of such identities – but still operate in a self-reflexive way on the basis of such identities. Irish republicanism of the 1970s and 1980s illustrates this. As I have indicated previously, in the 1970s and particularly within the 'republican university,' Long Kesh, republicanism underwent a significant transition from being exclusively militaristic and abstentionist in its orientation to being politically participatory and self-consciously socialist. This transformation of identity was confirmed at the Ard Fheis (Annual Conference) of Sinn Féin in 1985, when the political and ideological leadership of the organization was transferred from the conservative purists of the south of Ireland to the leftist pragmatists of the north of Ireland. To argue that identity has no natural, essential, or absolute significance, to accept the impossibility of 'a rigorously pure self-identity,'[119] does not necessarily commit one to the paralysing and indifferent claim that identity politics is misconceived. It simply allows us to recognize that difference and identity are constitutively interlocking, to be conscious of the inevitability of political change, and to forewarn us not to expect or impose closure.

Second, and more important, to accept the relentless postmodern position that the subject is concocted to the core leads, potentially, to a radically individualized politico-ontology. If so, this might well have the effect of marginalizing the group aspects of our identity, thereby, though perhaps inadvertently, fostering singularity rather than solidarity. As a consequence, postmodernism may devalue that aspect of ourselves that many value highly: our group membership.[120] And for the subordinated, this experience of group identity may act as a form of empowerment and solidarity. Once again the H-Blocks provide an example of how solidarity is achieved through what one commentator has described as 'the solidarity of collective vocality,'[121] that is, Gaelic.

Third, and this is a more negative and clearly strategic argument, it is not as if identity politics is the 'chosen' terrain of struggle by the disempowered. In common with many forms of oppression – for example, sexism or racism – those who oppress on the basis of nationalism do so, in part, because of the 'identity' of the other. The 'criminalization' project of the British government was very much driven by the question of identity; its aim was to efface the nationalist liberation justifications for the prisoners' alleged acts in order to 'identify' them as 'criminals.' The protests and the fasts were an attempt to reassert their identity and their legal rights as prisoners of war on the basis of that identity. In short, identity is a terrain of political struggle that the oppressed simply cannot afford to abdicate.

(In)Conclusion

I find myself in a curious situation in this essay. On the one hand, I find that postmodernism and deconstruction through their critiques of hierarchy, subordination, and oppression open up the space for the emergence and even possible valorization of different voices. Yet, on the other hand, at the very same moment, they may undermine such perspectives by arguing that they are but an interpretation with no necessary connection to reality, truth, or justice, or at least no connection that would make a difference. I only want to go halfway, to acknowledge that postmodernism can be a form of resistance[122] but without having to purchase its unrequited guardedness. I want to employ its strategies as a mode of politico-juridical analysis in order to deconstruct Britain's juridical hegemony, in order to facilitate a reconfiguration of Anglo-Irish relations. As Linda Hutcheon says of feminist encounters with postmodernism, 'exposition may be the first step; but it cannot be the last.'[123]

To maintain this position, to avoid this sense of one step forward, one step back, it will be necessary to draw a distinction between postmodernism as a political philosophy and deconstruction as a method of interpretation, to argue an embracement of the latter as a mode of empowerment does not require a commitment to the former with its eschewal of political practice and its predilection for relentless sceptical indifference.[124] However, deconstruction, too, will have to be revised, dereified, and deflated. It must be shorn of its pretensions to be 'a general law,'[125] a generalization 'without present or perceptible limit,'[126] or a canonized cognate of 'justice.'[127] Regardless of what Derrida – the author – might say,[128] deconstruction itself is probably best understood as a rigorous[129] methodology that enables us to critically interrogate those propositions that aspire to be universal, authoritative, and logical; to demonstrate how they are, in fact, contingent, ambiguous, and arbitrary. Subject to this not insignificant revision, I therefore agree with Derrida when he quips, 'The fact that law is deconstructible is not bad news. We may even see in this a stroke of luck for politics, for all historical progress.'[130]

NOTES

1 This paper has greatly benefited from conversations with Alexandra Z. Dobrowolsky.
2 F. Nietzsche, *The Will to Power*, trans. W. Kaufmann (New York: Random House, 1967), 202.

3 Quoted in L. Hutcheon, *The Poetics of Postmodernism* (New York: Routledge, 1988), 96.

4 The primary focus of much of my scholarship over the last several years has been a negative critique of the relationship between law, state, and violence in the self-satisfied Western liberal democratic societies. See, for example, 'Nomos and Thanatos [Part B]: Feminism as Jurisgenerative Transformation or Resistance through Partial Incorporation?' (1990) 13 *Dal. L. J.* 123; 'Nomos and Thanatos [Part A]: The Killing Fields: Modern Law and Legal Theory' (1989) 12 *Dal. L. J.* 298; and 'Law's Centaur: A Preliminary Theoretical Inquiry into the Nature and Relations of Law, State and Violence' (1989) 27 *Osgoode Hall L. J.* 219. In this essay, however, I seek to move beyond critique to reconstruction through the legitimization of anticolonial juridical claims.

5 C. Douzinas, R. Warrington, and S. McVeigh, *Postmodern Jurisprudence: The Law of Text in the Texts of Law* (New York: Routledge, 1991), 51.

6 See, for example, D. Cornell, *Beyond Accommodation: Ethical Feminism, Deconstruction, and the Law* (New York: Routledge, 1991); N. Wakefield, *Post-Modern-Ism: The Twilight of the Real* (London: Pluto, 1990).

7 See, for example, J. Habermas, 'Modernity versus Postmodernity' (1981) 22 *New German Critique* 3; A. Callinicos, *Against Postmodernism* (New York: St Martin's Press, 1989).

8 R. Cover, 'The Supreme Court, 1982 Term: Forward, Nomos and Narrative' (1983) 97 *Harv. L. Rev.* 4 at 16.

9 P. Bishop and E. Mallie, *The Provisional IRA* (London: Corgi, 1987), 48–53.

10 Ibid. at 55–8.

11 F. Burton, *The Politics of Legitimacy: Struggles in a Belfast Community* (New York: Routledge and Kegan Paul, 1978), 69; C. Keena, *Gerry Adams: A Biography* (Dublin: Mercier Press, 1990), 38.

12 Bishop and Mallie, supra n. 9 at 81–8, 108; Keena, supra n. 11 at 26, 36.

13 Bishop and Mallie, supra n. 9 at 143.

14 A. Feldman, *Formations of Violence* (Chicago: University of Chicago Press, 1991), 86.

15 The government insisted on this term rather than 'political status.' In effect, however, it meant that prisoners did not have to wear prison uniforms or engage in prison labour and were entitled to free association and political education.

16 Cmnd 5185, Dec. 1972, HMSO.

17 K. Boyle, T. Hadden, and P. Hillyard, *Ten Years in Northern Ireland: The Legal Control of Political Violence* (London: Cobden Trust, 1980).

18 *Report of a Committee to Consider, in the Context of Civil Liberties and Human*

Rights, Measures to Deal with Terrorism in Northern Ireland (1975) Cmnd 5847, HMSO.

19 D. Faul and R. Murray, 'H Block and Its Background' (Nov. 1980) *Doctrine and Life* 482 at 483.

20 Ibid. at 484.

21 L. Clarke, *Broadening the Battlefield* (Dublin: Gill and Macmillan, 1987), 84–5, 105, 107, 119, 121, 137; T.P. Coogan, *On the Blanket* (Dublin: Ward River Press, 1980), 95, 118, 224; Keena, supra n. 10 at 86, 89, 100–2; Bishop and Mallie, supra n. 8 at 288, 295; Feldman, supra n. 13 at 161–4, 222, 230, 300; D. Beresford, *Ten Men Dead* (London: Grafton Books, 1987), xi, 20, 25, 37, 208, 251, 266–7; T.P. Coogan, *The IRA* (London: Fontana, 1987), 623–7.

22 Sinn Féin is the unprescribed political wing of the IRA.

23 Clarke, supra n. 21 at 121.

24 Ibid. at 123.

25 Beresford, supra n. 21 at 3–5.

26 K. Kelley, *The Longest War* (Dingle, Co. Kerry: Brandon, 1988), 332–3.

27 J. Derrida, *Positions*, trans. A. Bass (Chicago: University of Chicago Press, 1981), 41.

28 Beresford, supra n. 21 at 179–80.

29 M. Ryan, *Marxism and Deconstruction* (Baltimore: Johns Hopkins University Press, 1982), 3.

30 C. Norris, *Derrida* (Cambridge, Mass.: Harvard University Press, 1987), 80.

31 Clarke, supra n. 21 at 140.

32 Translator's Introduction to J. Derrida, *Of Grammatology*, trans. G. Spivak (Baltimore: Johns Hopkins University Press, 1976), lxxvii.

33 See, for example, G. Adams, *The Politics of Irish Freedom* (Dingle, Co. Kerry: Brandon, 1986), 70; Coogan, *Blanket*, supra n. 21 at 14–30; Clarke, supra n. 21 at 107–8; Feldman, supra n. 14 at 218.

34 For an overview of the Brehon Laws see, for example, R. Grimes and P. Horgan, *Introduction to the Laws of the Republic of Ireland* (Dublin: Wolfhound Press, 1987), 17–21.

35 See, generally, L. Ginnell, *The Brehon Laws* (Littleton, Co. Colo.: Fred B. Rothman, 1993), 161–4; Sophie Bryant, *Liberty, Order and Law under Native Irish Rule* (New York: Encyclopedia Press, 1923), 259–87; D.A. Binchey, 'Distraint in Irish Law' (1973) 10 *Celtica* 22; F. Kelly, *A Guide to Early Irish Law* (Dublin: Mount Salus Press, 1988), 177–88.

36 Binchey, 'Distraint,' supra n. 35 at 29.

37 Ginnell, supra n. 35 at 158.

38 D. Binchey, 'Irish History and Irish Law' 15 *Studia Hibernica* 7 at 24–7 and F. Robinson, 'Notes on the Irish Practice of Fasting as a Means of Distraint,' in

S. Williams, ed., *Putnam Anniversary Volume* (New York: G.E. Stechert & Co., 1976), 557.

39 B. Sands, *Skylark Sing Your Lonely Song* (Dublin: Mercier, 1982), 149.

40 Coogan, *Blanket*, supra n. 21 at 6 and 13.

41 Beresford, supra n. 21 at 60; and Sands, *Skylark*, supra n. 39 at 149–50.

42 Clarke, supra n. 21 at 80.

43 This idea is culled from F. Jameson, *The Political Unconscious* (Ithaca, N.Y.: Cornell University Press, 1981).

44 S.F. Moran, 'Patrick Pearse and Patriotic Soteriology: The Irish Republican Tradition and the Sanctification of Political Self-Immolation,' in Y. Alexander and A. O'Day, eds., *The Irish Terrorism Experience* (Aldershot: Dartmouth Pub. Co., 1991), 9.

45 Feldman, supra n. 14 at 214.

46 C. Geertz, *Local Knowledge* (New York: Basic Books, 1983), 218.

47 Derrida seems to aspire to such a project for deconstruction when, replying to two of his critics, he argues:

> But one thing at least I can tell you now: an hour's reading ... should suffice for you to realize that *text*, as I use the word, is not the book ... it is not limited to the *paper* which you cover with your graphism. It is precisely for strategic reasons ... that I found it necessary to recast the concept of text by generalizing it almost without limit, in any case without present or perceptible limit, without any limit that *is*. That's why there is nothing '*beyond* the text.' That's why South Africa and apartheid are, like you and me, part of this general text, which is not to say that it can be read the way one reads a book. That's why the text is always a field of forces ... That's why deconstructive readings and writings are concerned not only with library books, with discourses, with conceptual and semantic contents. They are also effective ... interventions, in particular political and institutional interventions that transform contexts without limiting themselves to theoretical or constantive utterances ... That's why I do not go '*beyond* the text,' in this *new* sense of the word text, by fighting and calling for a fight against *apartheid* ... the strategic reevaluation of the concept of text allows me to bring together in a more consistent fashion ... theoretico-philosophical necessities with the 'practical,' political, and other necessities of what is called deconstruction. (J. Derrida, 'But Beyond' [1986] 13[1] *Critical Inquiry* 163 at 167–8)

48 J. Derrida, 'Force of Law: The "Mystical Foundations of Authority"' (1990) 11 *Cardozo L. Rev.* 919 at 995.

49 C. Norris, *Deconstruction: Theory and Practice* (New York: Methuen, 1982), 31.

50 Following A. Megill in *The Prophets of Extremity* (Berkeley: University of Califor-

nia Press, 1985), 273, it may be more appropriate to talk of 'motifs rather than themes' in that the former has stronger artistic and literary connotations and therefore is closer to the postmodern mindframe.

51 As Derrida posits, 'deconstruction is, in itself, a positive response to an alterity which necessarily calls, summons or motivates it. Deconstruction is therefore a vocation – a response to a call': (R. Kearney, ed., *Dialogues with Contemporary Continental Thinkers* [Manchester: Manchester University Press, 1984], 118).

52 S. Lash, *Sociology of Postmodernism* (New York: Routledge, 1990), 15.

53 Baudrillard argues in a famous passage that 'the very definition of the real has become *that which it is possible to give an equivalent reproduction* ... the real is not only that which is reproduced, but *that which is already reproduced* ... The hyperreal transcends representation only because it is entirely in simulation' (J. Baudrillard, *Simulations*, trans. P. Fossi, P. Patton, and P. Beitchman [New York: Semiotext[e], 1983], 146–7).

54 F. Nietzsche, *On the Genealogy of Morals*, trans. W. Kaufmann and R.J. Hollingdale (New York: Vintage Books, 1969), 119.

55 R. Rorty, *Philosophy and the Mirror of Nature* (Princeton: Princeton University Press, 1979); K. Baynes, J. Bohman, and T. McCarthy, eds., *After Philosophy: End or Transformation?* (Cambridge, Mass.: MIT Press, 1987).

56 H. Lawson and L. Appignanesi, *Dismantling Truth: Reality in the Postmodern World* (London: Weidenfeld and Nicolson, 1989).

57 J. Derrida, *Of Grammatology*, trans. G. Spivak (Baltimore: Johns Hopkins University Press, 1976), 69.

58 J. Baudrillard, *In the Shadow of Silent Majorities* (New York: Semiotext[e], 1983), 107.

59 See, for example, P. Schlag, 'Normative and Nowhere to Go' (1990) 43 *Stan. L. Rev.* 167 at 173–4.

60 *Simulations*, supra n. 53 at 53–4.

61 Ibid. at 40.

62 Ibid. at 38.

63 Ibid. at 128.

64 J. Baudrillard, *Forget Foucault* (New York: Semiotext[e], 1987), 43.

65 H.J. Silverman ed., *Derrida and Deconstruction* (New York: Routledge, 1989), 4.

66 See, for example, G. Bennington, *Lyotard: Writing the Event* (New York: Columbia University Press, 1988), 52–3.

67 Derrida, for example, posits that consciousness is 'a determination' or an 'effect' in J. Derrida, *The Margins of Philosophy*, trans. A. Bass (Chicago: University of Chicago Press, 1982), 16.

68 L. Ferry and A. Renaut, *French Philosophy of the Sixties: An Essay on Antihuman-

ism, trans. M.H.S. Cattani (Amherst: University of Massachusetts Press, 1990), 209.

69 Translator's Introduction, supra n. 32 at lxxv.

70 Derrida, *Positions,* supra n. 27 at 41.

71 Geertz, supra n. 46 at 175, 215, and 185.

72 J. Derrida, *Speech and Phenomena,* trans. D.B. Allison (Evanston, Ill.: Northwestern University Press, 1973), 146.

73 J. Derrida, 'Sendin: On Representation' (1982) 49 *Social Research* 294 at 304.

74 *Margins,* supra n. 67 at 15.

75 J. Derrida, 'Interview' (1980) 14 *Literary Review* 21.

76 It also suggests a return to a dualistic either/or, which is normally anathema to deconstructive thought.

77 Ferry and Renaut, *French Philosophy,* supra n. 68 at 113.

78 Seyla Benhabib posits that 'vis a vis our own stories we are in the position of author and character at once'; see 'Feminism and Postmodernism: An Uneasy Alliance' (1991) 11 *Praxis International* 137 at 140.

79 In recent years, Adams has become increasingly explicit about the socialist orientation of Sinn Féin: 'we believe that a system of socialism in Ireland should be tailored to meet Irish needs' (Interview, *Magill,* March 1989, Dublin). See more generally, Keena, supra n. 11.

80 Feldman, supra n. 14 at 162–3 and 213 makes some efforts in this direction.

81 Ibid. at 199.

82 'Things Remain the Same – Torturous' in Sands, *Skylark,* supra n. 39 at 131.

83 So creative were the prisoners that they also smuggled in tobacco, biro pen refills, flints, quartz crystal radios, cameras, and even a gun (suitably broken down) via their orifices. The parts of their bodies adapted to these practices of resistance included their ears, nose, mouth, navel, foreskin, pubic hair, and, most commonly, anus. See Bishop and Mallie, supra n. 9 at 276; and Beresford, supra n. 21 at 63.

84 Feldman, supra n. 14 at 161–3, 219–22.

85 See, for example, the 'comm' reproduced in Clarke, supra n. 21, Appendix I at 242.

86 Bishop and Mallie, supra n. 9 at 291.

87 Kelley, supra n. 26 at 341; Coogan, *IRA,* supra n. 21 at 631.

88 For discussions of Sinn Féin's subsequent electoral forays, see Keena, supra n. 11 at 106, 109, 120, 127, 132–4; Clarke, supra n. 21 at 211–19; and Coogan, *IRA,* supra n. 21 at 632–3.

89 J. Derrida, 'Racism's Last Word' (1985) 12 *Critical Inquiry* 290.

90 Quoted in R. Bernstein, *The New Constellation: The Ethical/Political Horizons of*

Modernity/Postmodernity (Cambridge, Mass.: MIT Press, 1991), 186–7.

91 Derrida, in supra n. 51 at 119.

92 Ibid. at 120.

93 T. Keenan, 'Reading Foucault on a Bias' (1987) 15 *Political Theory* 5 at 19.

94 *Shadow*, supra n. 58 at 41.

95 Ibid. at 39.

96 Ibid. at 105.

97 Ibid. at 49.

98 M. Henderson, 'Speaking in Tongues: Dialogics, Dialectics, and the Black Woman Writer's Tradition,' in J. Butler and J.W. Scott, eds., *Feminists Theorize the Political* (New York: Routledge, 1992), 151.

99 Feldman, supra n. 14 at 157.

100 Ibid. at 186.

101 Ibid. at 247. This is not to deny that there may be situations when silence may be the most appropriate and effective way of resisting, for example, during interrogation. See ibid. at 138. But to counsel, as some postmodernists do, the adoption of silence as a strategy would, I believe, be disastrous for progressive political practice.

102 C. Norris, *What's Wrong with Postmodernism* (Baltimore: Johns Hopkins University Press, 1990), 17.

103 Baudrillard, supra n. 58 at 28.

104 I. Hassan, *The Postmodern Turn* (Columbus: Ohio State University Press, 1987), xvi.

105 To be clear, my suggestion here is not a euphoric valorization of sacrifice and death, as Baudrillard occasionally verges on in both his 'Symbolic Exchange and Death,' in *Jean Baudrillard: Selected Writings*, ed. M. Poster (London: Polity Press, 1988), 119–48, and his discussion of the Tasaday peoples of the Philippines in *Simulations*, supra n. 53 at 13–17. Rather, my point is that agency counts.

106 L. Hutcheon, *The Politics of Postmodernism* (New York: Routledge, 1989).

107 Baudrillard, *Simulations*, supra n. 53 at 6.

108 On this latter point, see ibid. at 127; and F. Moretti, 'The Spell of Indecision,' in C. Nelson and L. Grossberg, eds., *Marxism and the Interpretation of Culture* (Urbana: University of Illinois Press, 1988), 339.

109 Schlag, 'Normative and Nowhere to Go,' supra n. 59.

110 M. Eichler, 'The Elusive Ideal – Defining Equality' (1988) 5 *Can. Hum. Rts. Y.B.* 167.

111 For an account of the beatings, see Bishop and Mallie, supra n. 9 at 279. For a close documentation, see Feldman, supra n. 14 at 147–217.

112 Coogan, *Blanket*, supra n. 21 at xi.

113 J. Feehan, *Bobby Sands and the Tragedy of Northern Ireland* (Dublin: Mercier Press, 1983), 68–9.

114 Indeed this shift of focus parallels, to some extent, Christopher Norris's recent attempts to argue that Derrida cannot be lodged in the same camp as the levelling and relativistic postmodernists, because in certain selected passages in his work Derrida does posit that there are certain standards of interpretive truth such as argumentative rigour and consistency. See C. Norris, 'Afterword' in *Deconstruction*, rev. ed. (New York: Routledge, 1991), 145–58.

115 Bernstein, supra n. 90 at 205.

116 J. Butler, 'Gender Trouble: Feminist Theory and Psychoanalytic Discourse,' in L. Nicholson and N. Fraser, eds., *Feminism/Postmodernism* (New York: Routledge, 1989), 327.

117 P. Schlag, '"Le Hors de texte, c'est moi": The Politics of Form and the Domestication of Deconstruction' (1990) 11 *Cardozo L. Rev.* 1631 at 1649.

118 N. Fraser, 'False Antithesis: A Reply to Seyla Benhabib and Judith Butler' (1991) 11 *Praxis International* 166 at 175.

119 Ryan, supra n. 29 at 10.

120 I.M. Young, 'Policy and Group Difference: A Critique of the Ideal of Universal Citizenship' (1989) 99 *Ethics* 250 at 251.

121 Feldman, supra n. 14 at 216–17. For accounts of the importance of group solidarity in maintaining the 'dirty protest,' see Clarke, supra n. 21 at 78–83, 122.

122 H. Foster, *Re-Codings: Art Spectacle, Cultural Politics* (Port Townsend, Wa.: Bay Press, 1985), xii, 121. See also Lash, supra n. 52 at 37 and 52, distinguishing between 'mainstream' or 'reactionary' postmodernism, and 'oppositional' or 'progressive' postmodernism.

123 Hutcheon, supra n. 106 at 152–3.

124 I can gain some support for this strategy in the work of C. Norris, See *Postmodernism*, supra n. 102 at 52; and *Deconstruction*, supra n. 114 at 148–56.

125 Derrida, *Margins*, supra n. 67 at 15.

126 Derrida, supra n. 47 at 167–8.

127 Derrida, supra n. 48 at 945.

128 Consider, for example, that Derrida, in faithful reified deference, argues that 'deconstruction ... has never presented itself as a method ...,' (supra n. 47 at 168).

129 C. Norris, *The Contest of the Faculties* (London: Methuen, 1988), 18.

130 Derrida, supra n. 48 at 943–5.

Rights and Spirit Dancing: Aboriginal Peoples versus the Canadian State[1]

CLAUDE DENIS

Now you try and say what is involved in seeing something as something. It is not easy.

Ludwig Wittgenstein[2]

Prologue

'Ruffians' at the Gate

'We are not like you,' writes Ralph Akiwenzie,[3] chief of an Ojibway band that lives on the Bruce Peninsula – a strip of land between Lake Huron and Georgian Bay. The latter body of water was so named after the English king, George IV; 'huron' is an archaic French word that refers to a hirsute hairstyle or to an ill-mannered person, a 'ruffian,' and was used as a nickname by French colonists to speak of the members of the aboriginal Wendat confederacy.[4]

Framed by this colonial nomenclature, Chief Akiwenzie goes on: 'Our customs are different, our religion is different, our language is different, our history is different.' This blunt affirmation of cultural difference is not a mere statement of fact, for its utterance provides part of the foundation for the political claim of aboriginal self-government, which is a centre-piece of the current Canadian constitutional debate. The other part of the foundation is historical: aboriginal peoples were on this continent first, they were self-governing societies, and they never gave up that sovereignty. Hence the contemporary claim by aboriginal peoples that the Canadian state should recognize their *inherent* right to self-government.

When the federal government released its constitutional proposals in

September 1991, such recognition seemed a very long way off.[5] But only six months later, after a tortuous consultative process and strong pressures from aboriginal organizations, it had become accepted wisdom that 'inherent right' should be recognized, and indeed it was well on its way to being included in the constitution.[6] Not all was settled though. While the principle was now being recognized, governments and aboriginals were arguably no closer to agreement on the next crucial issue, that of the implementation of the right: to what extent would aboriginals be able to govern themselves independently of federal and provincial oversight?[7]

According to the main aboriginal organizations, recognition of inherent right should mean that aboriginal peoples would be able to govern themselves without limitations by Canadian laws of general application. Aboriginal self-government would not, for instance, be subject to the *Canadian Charter of Rights and Freedoms*,[8] unless aboriginals voluntarily decided to adopt the *Charter* for themselves. A number of aboriginal women's organizations have called for self-government to be subject to the *Charter*, but this has been a minority position. The dominant position is that of the Assembly of First Nations, and was expressed by its national chief, Ovide Mercredi. As reported in the *Globe and Mail*, Chief Mercredi's comments are first paraphrased by the reporter, then quoted:

Aboriginal people want their own charter of rights, he said. Moreover, Mr Mercredi said, the individual rights in the Canadian Charter should not be allowed to interfere with the collective rights that natives hope to gain in self-government.

'No one in our organization denies the importance of respecting individual rights. The question is how it should be done,' he said. 'Why would we want to rush into the imposition of a charter that's based not on the values of our people, but white society's values?'[9]

No matter what the future relationship between aboriginal self-government and the *Charter*, the general point is that '... to be equal, native people must be different':

[Chief Akiwenzie]: You created your laws to meet your needs ... They reflect your culture. We too, had laws and ways of dealing with those who harmed their neighbours. Those ways met our needs, *and they will again.* (Emphasis added)

Some People Are More Different than Others

In present-day Canada, aboriginals are being heard to an unprecedented degree. Which is not to say that their problems are over. But when issues of cultural difference arise today in Canada, the claims of aboriginal peoples resonate so powerfully that even the central controversy of the country's cultural politics – the relation between French and English, Quebec and 'the Rest of Canada' – becomes destabilized.

Indeed, the very fact that I, a Québécois and a sociologist who works on Canadian society, would come to investigate issues of aboriginal difference is living proof of this destabilization. I was not, and am not, a specialist on aboriginal issues; my investigation of such issues is entirely framed by their interpellation of 'Canadian society.'[10] What do they mean and, more importantly, *how* do they mean,[11] for Canadian society?

Since 1991–2, much of my intellectual energy has been focused on Canada's constitutional crisis and on its underpinnings. I have been working on the constitutional debate partly out of intellectual interest, but also because of a sense of political obligation: this is *my* country that is on the verge of falling apart, as a result of its inability to deal with the aspirations of *my* people, the people of Quebec. I feel that this situation concerns me, personally. All the more so, because – as strange as this may sound to many English-speaking Canadians, and it may even seem offensive to the much worse-off aboriginals – the 'Québécois' difference has yet to be empowered in Canada.

In the Meech Lake and Charlottetown rounds of constitutional negotiations, aboriginal claims have been something of a joker in the established Quebec-Canada deck of cards. In the main, there is an antagonism being set up between the claims of Quebec and the claims of aboriginals, with the latter being used in English-speaking Canada to undermine the former. This antagonism, I believe, is not a necessary one, and it must be bracketed, in the mind's eye, if one is to engage each claim with a view to understanding it and doing it some justice. Indeed, some of the language used by aboriginal leaders, claiming for themselves phrases otherwise associated with Quebec ('distinct society' and the idea of self-government as a 'full box'),[12] points to *some degree* of commonality between Quebec and aboriginal claims. But the fact that this commonality is expressed as an antagonism rather than as an alliance does speak to the construction of solidarities today in Canada, and to the process of empowerment of difference.

Differences, then, do not all carry the same weight. Some are recognized and given corporate expression within the state, others are not. Some provide the basis for a country's defining political polarities, others do not. In a word, some differences are *empowered*, others are not. To these two types of differences, a third should be added, which could be called the *stigmatized* difference: a difference that is inscribed in the state, but to the great detriment of its bearers   being black in South Africa under apartheid would be a good example.

There is, in other words, a social *adjudication of difference.* I use adjudication here in the sense that, as my legal dictionary would have it, a bankrupt s debts are adjudicated: a hierarchy, or priority, of claims is established, decided upon, whereby certain creditors will be reimbursed and others will not.[13] In society, differences are adjudicated so that there is a hierarchy in the recognition and salience of difference. Some people are more different than others: this formulation can be taken literally, innocuously it may also be given more substance, of Orwellian texture.

Until now in Canada s history, the aboriginal difference, far from being empowered, has been both stigmatized and targeted repeatedly for erasure: sometimes physically through wilful genocide, as with the extermination of the Beothuk people completed in the early nineteenth century;[14] sometimes through legal means, and most recently in 1969, when the federal government proposed a *White Paper on Indian Policy,* whose goal was for Indians to relate to their governments as individuals precisely the way that other citizens did ... Indians, as Indians, would disappear; Indians would become just another element in a multicultural Canada. [15]

It is only in the 1980s that the aboriginal difference has acquired the prominence that will allow it to be empowered. As Chief Akiwenzie wrote, aboriginal ways met our needs, and they will again. But to what extent it becomes empowered remains a wide open question: Mary Ellen Turpel has pointed out that, as empowered as the aboriginal difference may become through recognition of inherent right, this very reliance on the rights paradigm would make the practice of aboriginal ways subsidiary to an occidental frame of reference.[16] This brings me at last to the task I am setting for myself in these pages.

Prospectus: Spirit Dancing and the Adjudication of Difference

Consideration of the radicality of the aboriginal-occidental difference raises the issue of the presence of irreconcilable or irreducible elements of human relations. [17] This issue is particularly important in its specific crystallization in the oppression of aboriginal peoples, the pain and rage they must live with, and *my* situation of being outside aboriginal life, looking in.

But I want to get beyond generalities about irreconcilable differences.

I want to see, in the concreteness of life in Canada, where oppressed aboriginals live among 'whites,' in what ways we can think of the empowerment of their difference. I want to explore Michel Foucault's yearning to *penser autrement qu'on ne pense et percevoir autrement qu'on ne voit.* For Foucault, this is a quest that defines philosophical practice today: '... au lieu de légitimer ce qu'on sait déjà, [la philosophie aujourd'hui ne consiste-t-elle pas] à entreprendre de savoir comment et jusqu'où il serait possible de penser autrement?'[18]

Some of the corollaries to this quest are questions such as these: To what extent is communication possible between cultures? To what extent can cultures coexist without domination? What happens to social solidarity when cultural borders are erected? How can *I*, a white male Canadian and Québécois intellectual committed to equality and democracy, deal with the tensions and contradictions involved in this situation?

Also, can we expect that, once the aboriginal difference is finally empowered, no substantial difference will remain stigmatized, dis- or unempowered in Canada? Have we reached the last link in an ever longer chain of differences? Is there a *finite* number of differences, somehow inscribed in the nature of things, that would allow us to see the end – even if there are a few more after the aboriginal claim (the claim of people of colour, perhaps)? Is adjudication of difference (that is to say, the hierarchy of differences and the making of hierarchy) inescapable, or can it be expected to disappear?

These are some questions that I wish to *explore* in this essay. My entry point into this domain is Canada's current constitutional debate. I will, then, continue to focus on the aboriginal affirmation of difference and its associated political claim. Specifically, I will analyse the story of a lawsuit that was disposed of by the British Columbia Supreme Court in the winter of 1992, which dealt with the aboriginal ritual of 'spirit dancing.'[19] The object of my analysis will be principally constituted by two texts emerging from this suit: a newspaper report on the court's decision and the decision itself.

It is important to underline here the nature of this corpus: my reading of the conflict embodied in the *Thomas* v. *Norris* lawsuit is filtered through the institutional accounts of the courts and the media. The voices of the plaintiff and of the defendants will only be heard through those of Justice Sherman Hood and Robert Matas of the *Globe and Mail,* and only to the extent that the judge and the reporter found them relevant. This does not mean that I am relying on secondary sources: to a large extent, this paper presents an analysis of the judicial and mediatic filters in the relationship between David Thomas, on the one hand, and Daniel Louie Norris et al., on the other.

First Reading – Indian v. White

The Supremacy of English Law

I am a (recovering) political junkie. For people like me, intense political controversies mean frenetic newspaper reading and TV-news watching. Thus, during Canada's 1989–92 constitutional debate, I would begin most of my days by running to the front door and grabbing the *Globe and Mail* – Canada's self-styled 'national newspaper' and de facto newspaper of record. Before I did anything else, I had to know whether anything significant had happened overnight in the Meech Lake/Charlottetown story. It was to be expected that an article called 'Native Rite Ruled Subject to Law'[20] would catch my eye, and that I would read it in a constitutional frame of mind.

The newspaper article reported the decision of the British Columbia Supreme Court in a civil suit for assault, battery, and wrongful or false imprisonment. The defendants were seven members of the Coast Salish aboriginal nation (located in what is now the Canadian province of British Columbia). The plaintiff, David Thomas, was also a member of the Coast Salish nation. He was initiated, against his will, into his people's Long House through the ceremony of spirit dancing. As reported in the *Globe*:

Spirit dancing, which was illegal in Canada from 1880 to 1951, is a native ritual involving fasting and confinement until an individual hears 'the song of his guardian spirit,' which leads to the initiate dancing and singing a song. Individuals are grabbed for the ceremony *with or without their consent*, the court was told. (Emphasis added)

The issue, beyond the facts of the case, was whether or not the initiators could act without the initiate's consent, on the basis of an aboriginal right to conduct traditional ceremonies. The defendants' lawyer put the question to the trial judge, who duly noted it in his decision: 'Are the individual rights of aboriginal persons subject to the collective rights of the aboriginal nation to which he belongs?'[21] The defence answered its own question in favour of aboriginal collective rights, by appealing to section 35(1) of the *Constitution Act, 1982*, which states that 'the existing aboriginal and treaty rights of the aboriginal peoples of Canada are hereby recognized and affirmed.' Justice Sherman Hood disagreed with the defence's contention. He ruled that

assuming that spirit dancing was an aboriginal right, and that it existed and was practised prior to the assertion of British sovereignty over Vancouver Island, and the imposition of English law, in my opinion those aspects of it which were contrary to English common law, such as the use of force, assault, battery and wrongful imprisonment, did not survive the coming into force of that law ...[22]

There is no ambiguity in the court's decision to affirm 'the supremacy of English law to the exclusion of all others,' and thus the 'paramountcy of common law to the alleged aboriginal right.'[23] Hood J. found for the plaintiff and awarded him damages of $12,000. This is the exercise of cultural authority at its most self-assured – where *cultural authority* is defined as

... the authority which one culture is seen to possess to create law and legal language to resolve disputes involving other cultures and the manner in which it explains (or fails to explain) and sustains its authority over different peoples.[24]

The *Globe and Mail* paraphrased the ruling in these terms, which are partly a quotation from Justice Hood, himself quoting the defence's key question: 'The freedoms and civil rights of an *aboriginal Canadian* are not subject to the collective rights of the aboriginal nation to which he belongs' (emphasis added).

The reporter caught very well the spirit of the ruling by referring to the plaintiff as an 'aboriginal Canadian.' In the introduction to his decision, Hood J. had identified the plaintiff, David Thomas, as 'an "Indian" within the meaning of the *Indian Act*, R.S.C. 1985, c. I-5, and ... *of course*, a Canadian citizen.'[25] This 'of course' had been a good indication that the court would consider the plaintiff as a Canadian first and foremost. Aboriginal rights, whatever they may be or amount to, must function *within* that framework:

Placing the aboriginal right at its highest level it does not include civil immunity for coercion, force, assault, unlawful confinement, or any other unlawful tortious conduct on the part of the defendants, in forcing the plaintiff to participate in their tradition. While the plaintiff may have special rights and status in Canada as an Indian, the 'original' rights and freedoms he enjoys can be no less than those enjoyed by fellow citizens, Indian and non-Indian alike. He lives in a free society and his rights are inviolable ... His freedoms and rights are not 'subject to the collective rights of the aboriginal nation to which he belongs.'[26]

The central conflict narrated in the court's decision was indeed that between aboriginal rights and 'individual civil rights.' The presence of this polarity in *Thomas* v. *Norris* was made possible by the existence in Canadian law of dispositions relating to both these rights – if aboriginal rights were nowhere mentioned in at least one area of Canadian law, no defence in front of a Canadian court challenging the rules of the game would have been thinkable. The defence would have been reduced to arguing about facts. Was there an assault, battering, or false imprisonment? Was there consent?

But as things stand in Canada, the aboriginal difference is very much inscribed in law: in sections 25, 35, and 37(2) of the *Constitution Act, 1982*; in treaties and court decisions; and in the *Indian Act*, 'the principal instrument by which the federal Government and, indirectly, the provincial governments have exercised control over the lives of Indian people.'[27]

If a lawsuit was to be fought, then, over David Thomas's misadventure, there existed a whole set of textual-legal resources for it to be fought over Indian v. white, aboriginal right v. civil right, on terms defined and dictated by the 'white' side of the relationship. Within the current Canadian legal framework, it was easy to bring a suit of civil wrong, it was possible to mount a constitutional defence based on s. 35, and it was easy for the court to proclaim the supremacy of English law – to assert the cultural authority of the Occident over aboriginal peoples.

But all this does *not* mean that if we are to *understand* the battle that was waged here, we are bound to stay within its Indian v. white framework. In order to expand our perspective, it will be useful to look at how the issue of difference between Indian and white is being constructed in the suit's narration. I am not trying to dismiss this framework, nor am I suggesting that some *real* conflict in this story lay elsewhere. Rather, I am trying to get at how the Indian v. white conflict is constructed in discourse; at what it is that we are given to understand of the suit by its various storytellers; and at what *additional* issues may be embedded in the Indian v. white framework.

A Clash of Cultures?

After outlining the decision's affirmation of the supremacy of British law, the *Globe and Mail* article presents two more narratives. The first is a description of the circumstances that led to the suit, recounting testimony documenting (a) the initiate's lack of consent to the initiation and (b) the physical injuries and humiliations that he sustained: (a) he was 'forcibly taken' to the Long House, 'imprisoned', and 'forced to undergo the initiation ceremonies'; he 'did not authorize anyone to have him initiated as a spirit dancer and was not interested in learning about his people's culture'; and (b) the initiators 'took turns digging their fingers into his stomach area and biting him on his sides,' causing superficial injuries whose existence was confirmed by the physician who treated David Thomas upon his escape; '... he was stripped naked, forced to walk backwards into the water and submerge himself three times, he told the court. He said he was then beaten with cedar branches'; during these four days, he was given no food and very little water.

Other features of the initiation's circumstances could have been identified by the reporter in his attempt to provide readers of the *Globe* with an understanding of the events. But the two features he did highlight firmly anchor David Thomas's claim to have been wronged in one of modernity's fundamental tenets, at least as it relates to men (more on this below): the autonomy of the bodily self. Thus, any modernist account of these events would have to focus on the 'facts' that David Thomas was denied the exercize of his free will, and that the autonomy and integrity of his body were violated.

Now, there are some circumstances in which modernity will allow such denials and violations, such as with convicted criminals – who, arguably, are *rightfully* imprisoned. Foucault has shown that modernity has involved, for the 'authoritative culture' itself, a severe restriction on the infliction of pain and suffering for socially normative purposes.[28] One would not expect that the authoritative culture would tolerate it coming from the oppressed culture. As Justice Hood put it, David Thomas 'did in fact suffer injuries, both physical and mental,' and he 'did experience pain and suffering during his *ordeal* and for sometime thereafter.'[29] Hence the award of compensatory damages.

So far as we can tell from the *Globe*'s article (and also from the court decision itself), David Thomas had not done anything to deserve such treatment. But this is also where the reporter's account turns bizarre: almost as an afterthought, he writes that Thomas's then common-law wife, Kim Johnny, 'had requested that he be initiated as a way of dealing with marital and other problems,' according to the testimony of an elder, who was also a defendant. He then repeats the information, as supplied by the now married wife herself, who 'told the court she felt the initiation would help their relationship. However, the incident made matters worse,

she added.' Still, they did get married in the interval between the initiation and the trial – which resulted in the trial judge referring to Kim
Johnny as Mrs Thomas.

The initiation, a four-day ritual involving fasting and injuries, none of
which David Thomas consented to, is to be justified on the grounds of
'marital and other problems'?! Could any modern reader of the *Globe and
Mail* feel anything but solidarity with Mr Thomas? Could any such reader
conclude anything other than that he was *wrongfully* imprisoned?

In the story of the initiation of David Thomas as told by the *Globe and
Mail*, there is no doubt where the sympathies of the reader are meant to
reside: with David Thomas, against his initiators, and, most importantly,
against a culture that would allow a man to be subjected to such an – in
the words of Judge Hood – 'ordeal.'[30] We will see below that there were
alternatives to this way of telling the story. But, as it is, the newspaper
reader is placed in a position where he or she has to choose sides; and
where the party to be sided with is us, 'civilized,' modern society, against a
'primitive,' 'barbaric' practice.

This is a morality tale, then, which makes us moderns feel good about
ourselves, about our respect for human rights, and which at the same
time undermines our ability to respect aboriginal cultures. Most of all it
allows us, when we hear the word 'Indian' or 'aboriginal,' to displace concerns, from *our* domination of them to *their* 'barbarity.' At work here is
what Dominick LaCapra calls 'the scapegoat mechanism – a mechanism
that generates purity for an in-group by projecting all corruption or pollu-
tion onto an out-group.'[31]

There was no inevitability in the writer presenting the story in this way.
But it is not so simple as to call for 'the other side' to be heard – for,
indeed, 'the other side' is heard in the report, through the (interviewed)
voice of the defendants' lawyer. In fact, presenting two sides in this way,
constructing 'binary oppositions' (LaCapra), is part of the difficulty, inas-
much as it is a forceful invitation to take sides. We will come back to the
lawyer's comments below, but for now the point is this: in order to provide us with an alternative story, the reporter would have had, not to
present the claims of 'the two sides,' but rather to do something that the
court would not: take seriously the motivations of the initiators.

In assessing damages, the court easily came to the conclusion that the
intentions of the defendants were good, that 'they honestly and sincerely
believe in the Dancing Tradition, that they were helping the plaintiff ...'[32]
As a result, they were not assessed punitive damages. But these good
intentions were of no help in getting either the suit dismissed or a favour-

able judgment. In deciding the case, as far as the trial court was concerned, 'the motives of the defendants are irrelevant.'[33]

I will come back to this issue of why the defendants (and Kim Johnny) did what they did, but I first want to turn to how the cultural difference was constructed by the defendants and their lawyer – how 'the other side's' case is made in the *Globe*. This brings me to the final narrative in the article, consisting of excerpts from an interview with the defendants' lawyer, herself an aboriginal. These excerpts provide the article with the 'balance' that the rules of contemporary reporting call for, in this case outlining an aboriginal cultural and political critique of the judgment. The first excerpt immediately follows the account of the court's decision:

Native leaders on Vancouver Island greeted the judgement with a great deal of anger, lawyer Vina Starr said yesterday in an interview. 'They see it as a complete denial of their constitutionally protected rights.'

Canadian judges, who have been indoctrinated in the Western European tradition of individual rights, have difficulty conceptually in putting collective aboriginal rights in the proper perspective, Ms Starr said.

This aboriginal narrative is then interrupted by several paragraphs describing the contentious spirit-dancing initiation. Then, the article concludes with a comparatively long excerpt of the lawyer's interview:

Ms. Starr maintained that Mr. Thomas's civil rights against assault, battery and false imprisonment are subordinate to the collective rights of the aboriginal nation, protected by Section 35(1) of the Canadian Constitution, which confirms aboriginal and treaty rights.

She said in an interview that most ceremonies involve voluntary participants because they consider the ritual to be an honour. But according to tradition, members of a family may request that a relative be initiated involuntarily in order to help with personal problems, such as drinking, drug abuse or other social illnesses.

The native people do not believe an individual is an island in this world, she said; an individual is part of a family and the family is responsible for the welfare of its members.

Contrary to the reporter's own construction of the suit, which is based on the trial judge's narration of testimony, Vina Starr places herself[34] and her people outside modernity, and finds it cold and unappealing. First, she presents it as oppressive of aboriginal rights specifically; second, she portrays it as obsessed with the isolated individual and his or her rights, and uncomprehending of collective rights in general. This broad outline of a critique of 'white' society sounds some familiar complaints about contemporary occidental societies: there is an excess of individualism; the family is in crisis. But whereas whitestream[35] critics of our times target excesses or specific ills of our societies (e.g., individualism is good, but too much of it is bad),[36] this aboriginal critique takes aim at the whole 'Western European tradition of individual rights.'[37] On the other hand, the spirit-dancing ritual is presented as an honour, and the native family as caring and nurturing. This echoes the defence's submission to Justice Hood, which he quoted in his reasons for judgment: '... the primary reason for a Coast Salish family to request that one of their members be initiated is to enhance the quality of the life of the initiate and to honour him.'[38]

Problems of the individual that may warrant intervention by the family, says the defence lawyer as quoted in the *Globe*, are such things as 'drinking, drug abuse or other social illnesses' – problems, by the way, whose sources are strongly associated with the oppression of aboriginals by whitestream society. Two things are remarkable here: first, whereas the circumstances of the Thomas initiation are narrated specifically (*this* thing happened to *this* man), the justification for initiating without consent is presented as a general statement, which may or may not apply to this case; second, this statement of justification comes at the very end of the article, well after reader sympathies have been established – and, indeed, after many readers will have moved on to some other article, for few newspaper articles are read to the end.

In reporting as it did, even as it followed accepted rules of 'balance,' the *Globe and Mail* made itself an auxiliary of the court, and contributed to the reproduction of the domination of aboriginal cultures by whitestream practices. This is best seen by the reporter's neglect of the initiators' motivations, in conformity to the court's finding them irrelevant. There may be reasons of law (in this case, constitutive of cultural authority) that would lead the court to take this stance, but these are not binding on newspaper reporting.

The notion that the initiation without consent was justified by vague marital problems was not only surreal enough to raise further questions, but it was also undermined by contradictions in testimony (more on this below). Further journalistic investigation would have seemed in order, which would have brought the reporter to consider facts and issues beyond what the court found relevant; that is to say, he would have come in contact with Coast Salish culture. But he did not and consequently deprived his readers of the cultural context within which the initiators acted. As a result, the narration of the 'two sides' was utterly unequal: readers were presented with those facts of the Thomas initiation which the court judged relevant, and they were to make sense of those facts either on the basis of the modern cultural context with which they are utterly familiar (as water is familiar to fish), or of an aboriginal context which appeared not even as a cipher but as a void.

Second Reading – an Attempt to Think Otherwise: Approaching Aboriginal Justice

The first line of defence for the initiators of David Thomas was stated thusly by Judge Hood: 'The defendants deny that they assaulted, battered or falsely imprisoned the plaintiff.' Three more grounds of defence follow: 'first, lack of intention on their part to inflict harm on the plaintiff, second, consent or acquiescence on the part of the plaintiff, and third, a constitutional defence' based on their aboriginal rights.[39]

Given what we know about the facts of the initiation, the first defence can seem quite incomprehensible. The same goes for the second defence, about the lack of intent. And both certainly were quickly dispatched by Justice Hood:

I do not propose to deal at length with ... the tort issues. I am fully satisfied on the evidence that the plaintiff was ... assaulted ... A battery was committed ... He was falsely or unlawfully imprisoned ... There is simply no evidence before me which would support the assertion of necessary intent, or the defense of justification ... The plaintiff has proven, beyond any question, almost continuous assault, battery and wrongful or false imprisonment during his ordeal ...[40]

But it is crucial to realize that these defences do not merely assert statements of facts (no assault occurred, etc.). Rather, they assert an aboriginal *perspective on the facts*: to put it in a nutshell, the dancers did not intend to 'assault,' 'batter,' and 'imprison;' they intended to 'initiate' and 'help.' From their point of view, which is not idiosyncratic or merely self-exculpatory but rather culturally constructed, *they did not* 'assault.' They 'initiated.'

The point here is that 'assault' and 'initiation' are not natural facts, which are directly grasped as such by dancers, judges, and newspaper readers; they are, rather, particular *descriptions* of the world, expressing particular cultures. In claiming that no assault occurred and that there was no intent to assault, the defence was saying that even the most basic tools (such as acts defined in law as 'assault,' 'battery,' etc.) of the Canadian legal system are inadequate for dealing with the events surrounding the initiation of David Thomas. The defence was inviting the court to declare itself incompetent.

But Hood J. did not quite grasp this. He did not, that is, understand that in a situation such as the Thomas initiation, the aboriginal right claimed makes 'assault, battery and false imprisonment' irrelevant descriptions of the world and therefore renders Canadian courts incompetent. This incomprehension is well indicated by his puzzlement at why the defendants chose to appeal to s. 35(1) of the *Constitution Act, 1982*, on aboriginal rights, rather than to s. 25 and common law rights on freedom of religion:

Counsel also advised me that the defendants do not assert the aboriginal right claimed as freedom of religion. She did not elaborate and I am not satisfied that I fully understand her position. While the Charter does not apply to private litigation, the defendants still enjoy their common law right of freedom of religion, as do all Canadian citizens. However, the defendants have chosen to rely solely on the constitutional protection afforded by s. 35(1).[41]

But in the end, Hood J. could afford to not understand, because his description of the world rules over the Coast Salish people's description of the world. It is of no importance to Hood J. that, within this latter description, it is indeed quite possible that nothing other than a proper initiation occurred, and that it was done for perfectly good reasons. This fact, that the propriety of the initiation is (necessarily) ruled irrelevant by a Canadian court, results in exposing its constitutive inability to do justice to aboriginal life. It shows the court's authority to be irretrievably illegitimate. In the words of Mary Ellen Turpel:

... the legitimacy of judging (the knowing and reasoning part) is nothing more than the power of the dominant culture to impose its knowledge-structure and cultural system upon an artificial totality like Canadian 'society.'

The larger significance of cultural difference, in my view, is the extent to which it reveals a lack of interpretive authority in legal reasoning and decision-making and the extent to which it problematizes the rule of law as one particular cultural expression of social life. As a consequence, judging is a problem, not simply an accepted institutional function.[42]

One of the very peculiar features of the *Thomas* v. *Norris* decision is its account of the reasons why the initiation of David Thomas was carried out. Although it is clear how the trial judge's cultural and institutional blinkers would lead him to think these reasons irrelevant, the marginality of the discussion of motivation remains startling. It is almost as though the initiation had been a gratuitous act: in narrating testimony, Hood J. refers to (1) 'marital and other problems'; (2) Kim Johnny, whom he quotes as saying that 'for us, it was the right thing to do – I thought it would help our relationship'; and (3) an elder who, on being told by Kim Johnny that David Thomas was drinking, replied that they would have to have 'more reason than that.'[43]

The question becomes: viewed from an aboriginal perspective, under what circumstances is a forced initiation justified? The defendants in *Thomas* v. *Norris* are not very helpful in answering this question: they were dragged before the court, and they wanted to say as little as possible about their traditions. It is clear, however, that they would not lightly undertake an initiation to which the initiate did not consent. In her comments to the *Globe and Mail*, the defendants' lawyer noted that a family would typically request an initiation if a 'social illness' was involved. The elders were not about to undertake a forced initiation without what they thought of as good reasons; and they did undertake it, which must lead one to conclude that *they thought* that some fairly serious 'social illness' – what sociologists like to call 'deviance' – was involved.

Within Canada's whitestream description of the world, serious deviance is typically defined as 'criminality.' When dealt with by the community, it will typically bring suspects in front of a court and, when convicted, land them in prison – their individual rights suspended often for years at a time. Although Canada's justice system, like that of other liberal democracies, claims to try to rehabilitate convicted criminals, its actual 'redeeming' abilities are – to say the least – limited. The issue of whether a spirit-dancing initiation is an effective means of rehabilitation for those who suffer from a 'social illness' is, thus, not relevant.

Quite apart from issues of criminality, it is also possible, under Canadian law, for family members to have an individual declared mentally incompetent and institutionalized without his or her consent.[44] And the infliction of pain and suffering – say, through electro-shock therapy – has often been part and parcel of 'treatment.' I hope it is clear that I am not endorsing here any such 'treatment': rather, I am outlining some of the suspensions of rights that are deemed acceptable by the dominant occidental criteria.

Within the occidental description of the world, then, there are circumstances in which the suspension of individual rights is deemed legitimate; and this suspension may extend to the infliction of pain and suffering. Presumably, this is also the case within the Coast Salish description of the world. We can expect, then, that initiation ceremonies will be undertaken without the consent of the initiate in such cases when the conduct of the prospective initiate is thought seriously deviant.

Whatever the motivations of the initiators, however, one would have to say that, within the occidental description of the world, David Thomas was neither tried nor convicted of a crime. And no tribunal appears to have ruled him mentally incompetent. These two circumstances, under white-stream standards, would have warranted suspension of rights and/or punishment. On this count, it should first be noted that David Thomas was indeed *not* punished: the override of the individual's consent in the ritual of initiation to spirit dancing strikes me as aiming more at healing a wounded spirit than at punishing a criminal.

To understand the initiation of David Thomas as punishment would be a cultural misreading of the nature of spirit dancing. On the other hand, the theme of healing is central in the accounts given by the aboriginals of their attempts to overcome the devastation that has been wrought in their lives by occidental domination, and which often expresses itself in alcohol and/or drug addiction, prostitution, suicide, and violence against women. This, incidentally, is one important reason why it would also be a misunderstanding to portray the initiation process as an instance of aboriginal 'justice' – where the initiation ritual would be a trial, conviction, and sentence rolled into one. The initiation is, rather, a religious and therapeutic practice, which does incorporate dimensions of social control.[45]

Issues of justice remain, however, central to this story: was it justified for the initiation to take place without David Thomas's consent? On this issue, an occidental perspective would be tempted to claim that *due process* was denied David Thomas. But what we call due process is a culturally specific practice. The circumstances that led to the initiation may be said to represent a Coast Salish version of due process: the initiation would not be undertaken without consent unless the elders in charge of the ritual were satisfied that there were good reasons to do so, as guaranteed by at least one member of the prospective initiate's family. Thus, both in substantive terms and in procedural terms, an initiation without consent is not an arbitrarily conducted event.

In the case of the initiation of David Thomas, then, his lack of consent *may have been* the truly irrelevant issue – as opposed to the motivation of his initiators. But the eventual irrelevance of David Thomas's lack of consent *could not* be established by a Canadian court. Such a court is, by virtue of not being a Coast Salish institution, incompetent. Assuming a process of aboriginal justice, in the event that the initiation had been gratuitous according to aboriginal criteria, I imagine that some kind of recourse would have been available to David Thomas. But the main point is that only a Coast Salish process – whatever it may be – could establish whether the initiation of David Thomas respected (what an occidental description of the world would call) Coast Salish justice.

There is one last twist in the story as told by the *Globe and Mail* and Justice Hood that puts in question the 'grabbing' of David Thomas. As Hood J. narrates it, Thomas

... never authorized anyone to have him initiated into the [dancing] society, and he did not want to be a member of it. He knew very little about the religion of the Coast Somenos people. He was not, and is not, really interested in learning about their culture. He was not brought up in it and lived off the reserve most of the time.[46]

Combined with his submission to the court that his civil rights as a Canadian citizen be affirmed, this strongly suggests that David Thomas took himself out of the aboriginal community that claims him as a member. If this were the case, the legitimacy of his being subjected to the initiation would indeed be facing a strong challenge – although not necessarily a decisive one, for the desire to remove oneself from the community could be seen as 'deviant' and subject to aboriginal ways of social control.

As it happens, several facts can serve in constructing a good argument that Mr Thomas was materially a member of the Coast Salish community, suggesting that, in certain contexts at least, he considered it a good thing to be part of the 'Indian' community. Once he chose to bring a suit in front of a Canadian court, however, it was of course entirely legitimate for him to construct his legal case in the most favourable way possible – in this case, to claim that he was not part of the aboriginal community. Still, by saying that he lived off the reserve most of the time, he suggested that he lived on the reserve *some* of the time; and thus that he had some kind of significant relationship with the people of the reserve. Also, from what can be gleaned from the court's decision, his lifestyle was very much an instance of contemporary aboriginal life in Canada. He further participates in the life of 'his' people at least to the extent that his spouse is a

Coast Salish woman and that their union respects Coast Salish standards of exogamy.[47]

This last feature of David Thomas's circumstances, like many components of the initiation ceremony and the circumstances surrounding it, comes out in Judge Hood's narration as so much anecdotal information. It is detached from its aboriginal cultural context, an at least minimal understanding of which is the only way to realize that, *at least potentially*, the initiation was neither arbitrary, nor an 'assault, battery and false imprisonment,' nor an imposition by a community on someone who is not part of it.

Were aboriginal self-government recognized, a Canadian court presented with David Thomas's suit would be faced with the preliminary issue of whether it could assume jurisdiction over the dispute. In determining the scope of its jurisdiction, one of the things that the court would obviously look to would be whether or not the parties before the court were all members of the aboriginal community. In this case, if it were established that David Thomas were a member of the aboriginal community (all other things being equal), a Canadian court would have to declare itself incompetent to adjudicate the conflict. Were the parties not all members of the aboriginal community, protocols would be required that would define (1) legal obligations between aboriginals and non-aboriginals and (2) the process by which they are adjudicated.

Thus, assuming that aboriginal self-government existed and that aboriginal ways governed aboriginal communities, it is quite likely that the Coast Salish community would have jurisdiction over a number of aspects of David Thomas's life.

Third Reading – Collapsing Oppositions

In this attempt to 'think otherwise,' I obviously do not claim to have produced a Coast Salish version of the initiation of David Thomas. Rather, I have tried to show how *some of the rationale* for the actions of Kim Johnny and the elders is *recognizable* in the terms of the description of the world within which I live. And not only this but, in circumstances of 'serious deviance,' whitestream society does not hesitate to suspend the need for an individual's consent and to inflict various forms of harsh treatment.

Clearly, the two cultures have different ways of dealing with 'deviance.' Still, not only do both exert social control on their members, but there are situations in which both cultures identify the same social practices as unacceptable and subject to some community action upon the individual.

Because there is commonality *and* difference, it is particularly important to be *specific* about what the *difference* entails, and what it does not.

One consequence, up to this point, of my consideration of the *Thomas v. Norris* case is this: contrary to the standard accounts of the cultural difference between the occidental and aboriginal worlds, including the comments of lawyer Vina Starr published in the *Globe and Mail*, this in *not* a conflict between valuing individual or collective rights.

Indeed, some features of the spirit dance make it very clear that a strong individualist streak exists in Coast Salish culture – as is argued, it turns out, in the book that the defendants submitted to the court as a 'learned treatise' whose facts should be treated as prima facie true.[48] Author Pamela Amoss writes that, in Coast Salish culture, 'individualism is most clearly and unequivocally expressed in the beliefs and practices of the guardian spirit complex. The dancer's relations with the supernatural are direct, singular and immediate.'[49]

But, as Vina Starr told the *Globe and Mail*, aboriginal culture does not see the individual as an island, isolated from family and community. Writes Amoss:

A person who was lax in his obligations to his guardian spirit or who invited the retaliation of ghosts by a neglect of their legitimate demands was no asset to the community in which he lived. He would be subject to criticism and even to ostracism. A person who was careful to fulfill his obligations to spirits and ghosts would be rewarded by social approval. Relations with the supernatural order were individual, private, and secret; but because they determined each person's success in his role as a productive member of society, they were of general social concern.[50]

As I understand it, then, the relationship between individualism and collectivism in Coast Salish culture is dialectical: they feed on each other. This is also the case in occidental culture – at least as individualism is constructed in philosophical and ethical systems. This dialectic of individual, family, and community is, for instance, at the heart of hellenistic individualism.[51] It is also crucial in the genesis of modern individualism.[52]

But, within the contemporary occidental description of the world, there is a widespread malaise, typically associated with conservatism, regarding the excesses of individualism, especially in North American society. This was emblematically expressed by Christopher Lasch in his denunciation of 'narcissism'; in *The True and Only Heaven*,[53] he further developed this critique with a paean to the virtues of community and a call to revive individual responsibility so as to counterbalance our obsession with rights. Now, responsibility appears to be a concept, or a paradigm, that characterizes aboriginal cultures.[54]

The construction of occidental individualism by aboriginal critics develops much the same themes, but paints them as inherent to Western culture, rather than as excesses and perversions of a worthwhile outlook – which is what Charles Taylor argues in *The Malaise of Modernity*. The offered alternative, a caring, nurturing, community-oriented aboriginal outlook and ethic of responsibility, is all the more convincing because it speaks quite well to the discontents of many in the West. The Occident's receptivity to this kind of critique is nothing new, as Jean-Jacques Rousseau's 'bon sauvage' will attest.

In turn, the malaise about individualism and the claimed aboriginal difference of community-oriented values make it easy for all concerned to construct the cultural-constitutional debate as one of individual rights versus collective rights. I have tried to show that this opposition is in fact a hindrance when one tries to understand the issues raised by something like the *Thomas* v. *Norris* case. Paradoxically when it is invoked by aboriginals, it ends up comforting the ignorance and the will to ignorance of whitestream Canadians about aboriginal ways. And it buttresses in the eyes of those Canadians the legitimacy of the Canadian state's cultural authority over aboriginal peoples and ways.

Fourth Reading – Differences, Seen and Unseen

Another disquieting feature of the centrality of the individual rights versus collective rights opposition is that it tends to mask other polarities in aboriginal life – as it does in Canadian whitestream life. I am talking here of the relations between women and men in aboriginal communities, an issue made explosive on the political scene by the demand of native women's organizations that aboriginal self-government be subject to the authority of the *Canadian Charter of Rights and Freedoms*.[55]

Although traditional aboriginal culture is often presented as strongly favourable to women, the facts of life for aboriginal women are that they are probably *the* most oppressed group in contemporary Canada. It is indeed quite possible that the oppression of aboriginal women stems entirely from the combination of the West's oppression of aboriginals in general and its imposition of patriarchy. Still, they are victims of, mainly but not exclusively, the men in their communities.

A hint of all this is offered in the marginalization and humiliation of women in the *Thomas* v. *Norris* affair. But, contrary to the Indian versus white narrative, which was in the foreground of the court decision and of the newspaper report, this tension between women and men is only written in the background of the story as told by Hood J. and the *Globe and Mail*. Without the benefit of several readings, it is very much in danger of going unseen.

It is quite remarkable that women are *both* central and peripheral in the story of the initiation of David Thomas. That is, two women played absolutely key roles in the events, but, at various junctures, they are either written out of the story or their part in it is denigrated. The two women are Kim Johnny, then common-law wife of David Thomas, and Helen Kumai, his aunt.[56] To a degree, in fact, they contribute in writing themselves out of the story.

It is, after all, Kim Johnny who set the events in motion: she went to the elders of the spirit-dancing tradition to ask that her common-law husband be initiated. At which point, narrates the trial judge, the elders requested the authorization of a family member. Raymond Peters, an elder and a defendant, testified that

... 'before we could do anything she would have to get permission from someone in the family.' He suggested that she obtain permission either from the plaintiff's brother Gordon, or from his aunt, Mrs. Helen Kamar.[57]

Another elder and defendant, Ernie Rice, also testified that they required Kim Johnny to 'have the consent of the plaintiff's family,' and that she may go to *either* his brother or his aunt.[58] But wasn't Kim Johnny herself a *close* family member? Why should someone else's permission be needed? For some reason (perhaps because, according to the testimony of Raymond Peters, they did not know her at the time), the elders dismissed the possibility that *she* may grant authorization.

So, Kim Johnny sought Helen Kumai's authorization. But Ms Kumai, herself a dancer, removed herself from the events by making her authorization conditional on that of David Thomas's brother Gordon – which made *her* authorization redundant. Asked what effect the matter had on her family, Ms Kumai testified that 'it was not too much, that she stayed at home most of the time, and did not really associate with the family.'[59] This is something of a rebuke to Vina Starr's claim in the *Globe and Mail* that this case could be properly understood only by starting from the notion that, in aboriginal life, 'the family is responsible for the welfare of its members.'

Kim Johnny did not, apparently, obtain Gordon Thomas's authorization. But she went back to the elders claiming that she had Helen Kumai's. And so the elders went ahead with the initiation. This sequence of events was not challenged by Kim Johnny, in her testimony as narrated by Justice Hood. For reasons that are not made clear in the decision, she seemed reluctant to testify; she repeatedly claimed that she could not remember various events and conversations in which she had taken part. This clearly bothered the trial judge, who narrated at length her claims to a failing memory, making her seem like a fool.

It needs to be pointed out that other witnesses (the elders who had been in charge of the initiation) had been reluctant to testify, especially on the specifics of what the initiation involved. This reluctance of the elders had elicited a degree of understanding on the part of Hood J. In fact, of all the witnesses, only Kim Johnny comes out looking bad in Justice Hood's narration.

With Kim Johnny being dismissed by the elders and discredited by Justice Hood, and Helen Kumai removing herself from the events, the *Thomas* v. *Norris* case became very much an affair *among men* only: David Thomas, the elders and the initiators, the trial judge. But it had, from the start, been *an affair about men.* In whitestream society, it is taken for granted that men are autonomous selves, with control over the integrity of their bodies. But the extent to which *women* are autonomous selves remains an issue, and especially so when it comes to control over the integrity of their bodies.

As such, the fact that David Thomas is a man is certainly not unrelated to this other fact that his forced initiation became *an affair* – an affair that received judicial attention. To him, the override of his consent appeared outrageous, as did the 'ordeal' he was subjected to. So it did to the court and to the *Globe and Mail.* Nobody thought to tell David Thomas that his 'no' really meant 'yes.' But women, and aboriginal women more than others, see their consent routinely violated as they are subjected to treatments far worse than what David Thomas experienced. And, routinely also, these other 'ordeals' do not make their way to court.

Aboriginal women today face a dilemma: now that their lives have been doubly affected (as aboriginals and as women) by Western domination, and that Canadian women have, in their own struggles, been making gains that can be of use to all women in Canada, aboriginal women may try to use a set of whitestream resources (e.g., the *Charter*) in order to mitigate a gender oppression that was induced by Western patriarchy and is mediated in large part by aboriginal men.

My examination of the *Thomas* v. *Norris* case suggests no positive solutions to this dilemma of aboriginals using occidental tools in the process of freeing themselves of occidental oppression. It does, however, allow me to discount two possible claims about the relationship between the *Charter* and aboriginal self-government.

First, aboriginal values themselves are clearly incompatible with the oppression that aboriginal women experience today. Thus, the Canadian *Charter may be* a temporarily useful tool for aboriginal women, but it does not necessarily have to be a continuing ingredient in their liberation – aboriginal cultural resources, in the context of full self-government, may well do better than the *Charter.*

Second, the opposition of collective aboriginal rights to individual women's rights is itself a discourse constructed by the hegemony of the Canadian state over aboriginal life. As such, it is not helpful in understanding either the dynamics of aboriginal life (beyond its being shaped by oppression), or how aboriginal ways could bring an end to the Western-induced oppression of aboriginal women.

In all of this, the issue of *collective* 'right' is only relevant to the following questions. Is a given social unit – say, aboriginal peoples, or Quebec – to have jurisdiction over its own collective life and the lives of its individual members, and if so to what extent? Or is this authority to be exercised by some larger unit – say, the Canadian state – regardless of the specific ways of the smaller unit? Looking at these three units – Canada, Quebec, aboriginal peoples – it is easy to find that all three respect the autonomy of the individual while imposing certain limits upon it.

But, in Canada's current political/cultural debates, *this* issue of 'collective rights' is only problematic relative to Quebec and aboriginal peoples: the collective right of the Canadian state to rule over 'its' people(s) is already established. This latter collective right is taken for granted, allowing the Canadian state and those who identify with it to be ostensibly interested only in individual rights. The question remains: what collectivity has jurisdiction over whose individual rights? It is, then, quite meaningless to oppose individual to collective rights, as though English-speaking Canadians were only interested in individual rights – the fully civilized thing to do – and Quebeckers and aboriginals cared only about collective rights – the tribal and primitive thing to do.

The conflict in *Thomas* v. *Norris*, then, is not one between an individualist culture and a collectivist culture. The main conflict, but not the only one (witness the gender nexus), stems from the assertion by the Canadian state of cultural authority over aboriginal ways. Put differently: faced with allegedly 'deviant' behaviour by an individual, the Canadian state claims a monopoly to the authority to sanction it. More specifically: what the Canadian state could not tolerate in the initiation of David Thomas was less the initiation itself than the fact that social control was being exercised independently of its own authority.

Conclusion: Wither Difference?

Here, then, are a whole series of concepts that seem to be at home both in occidental and aboriginal cultures: individual(ism), family, community, responsibility. The concept of right would appear to be a different story: Turpel writes that rights are deeply associated with private property, which is also foreign to aboriginals.[60] This is, perhaps, a genuine difference. But given the existence of what Amoss calls the importance of personal autonomy in Coast Salish culture, we have the elements that would allow each culture to *recognize* something akin to itself in the other.

Wither difference, then? In some sense and to some extent, yes. But I see no reason to jump from a belief in radical incommensurability to the affirmation of a renewed universalism of unbiased communication, *à la* Habermas. Somewhere in between, the initiation of David Thomas tells me that difficult communication, *weak* communication, is possible. I am borrowing this notion of weakness somewhat freely from the *philosophy of weak thought*, an Italian version of post-structuralism in which 'the use of the adjective "weak" refers to the necessity for "reason" to operate within a dimension of light and shade ...'[61]

There are several layers of philosophical considerations entailed by this stance, which I will have to leave aside, so as to focus my last comments on a question of politics. Does this possibility of *recognition* between cultures undermine the aboriginal claim to a right to self-government? It does not.

The first thing to remember is that my attempt to 'think otherwise,' while aiming at *approaching* an aboriginal perspective, remained firmly anchored within an occidental description of the world. I may be able, within my own language, to make some sense of aboriginal ways, but once I have translated some of their cultural language to my own, I have not produced one single language, one single description of the world. It is as when I began: there are two cultures, two descriptions of the world; not one. To claim otherwise would be to reinstate the exact cultural authority which I have tried to destabilize.

Second, and finally, the key word in the claim to self-government remains *inherent*, which refers not to difference so much as to historical precedence. Aboriginals were here first, with their own (various) ways of governing themselves, and they never gave them up. This alone is sufficient for aboriginals to be entitled, on their own terms, to self-government. Once they achieve self-government, they could very well decide to adopt the exact same institutions as whitestream Canada, but separately. The fact that they are not likely to do so does speak of an enduring and profound difference. Ultimately, Chief Akiwenzie might well have said: 'We are not you.' And rested his case.

NOTES

1 I would like to thank Annalise Acorn, Michael Asch, and David Schneiderman for helpful comments on various parts of this essay. I could not have completed this project without the help of Annalise and David's legal expertise, and their willingness to answer my layperson's questions and to access for me resources I wouldn't know existed. Of course, the responsibility for whatever nonsense remains is mine only.

2 Quoted in Ray Monk, *Ludwig Wittgenstein: The Duty of Genius* (London: Vintage, 1991), 514.

3 Ralph Akiwenzie, 'We Want to Do It Our Way,' *Globe and Mail* (hereafter *G&M*), 6 March 1992.

4 See 'Georgian Bay' and 'Huron' in *The Canadian Encyclopedia*, vol. 2 (Edmonton: Hurtig Publishers, 1985); also, 'huron' in *Le Petit Robert 1* (Paris: S.N.L. – Dictionnaire LE ROBERT, 1978).

5 Government of Canada, *Shaping Canada's Future Together* (Ottawa: Minister of Supply and Services Canada, 1991). For an evaluation of these proposals, see the articles contained in (1992) 3(3) *Constitutional Forum* and, in particular, on the issue of aboriginal government, the contributions of Michael Asch, Larry Chartrand, and Claude Denis.

6 See 'Natives Promised Self-government,' *G&M*, 10 April 1992.

7 The whole constitutional process eventually crashed, of course, when the Charlottetown Accord, negotiated by Canada's first ministers and aboriginal leaders, was rejected in the referendum of 26 October 1992. (For a postmortem of the Charlottetown process, see [1993] 4[2] *Constitutional Forum.*) The issues with which the Accord dealt, however, did not become obsolete. Most importantly, it is hard to imagine a future resolution of the debate that would step *back* from Charlottetown's recognition of inherent aboriginal rights. As such, the question of how aboriginal peoples and the Canadian state will relate to each other remains entirely current, both politically and intellectually.

8 *Canadian Charter of Rights and Freedoms,* Part I of the *Constitution Act, 1982,* being Schedule B to the *Canada Act 1982* (U.K.), 1982, c. 11.

9 'Natives Divided over Charter,' *G&M,* 14 March 1992.

10 See on this issue my 'Un sociologue à Oka?' (1990) 12(5) *Bulletin d'information, Association canadienne des sociologues et anthropologues de langue française* 6.

11 To borrow a phrase used by Barbara Johnson at the conference 'Explorations in Difference.'.

12 This was very much in evidence at the aboriginal constitutional conference of 13–15 March 1992; for a synthesis of the conference that includes this discourse, see 'Canada Redefined,' CBC-TV, 15 March 1992.

13 J. Balyette et al., *Dictionnaire juridique \ Legal Dictionary, Français-anglais, English-French* (Paris: Editions de Navarre, 1977), 20 (English-French section).

14 James Frideres, *Native Peoples in Canada: Contemporary Conflicts,* 3rd ed. (Scarborough, Ont.: Prentice-Hall Canada Inc., 1988).

15 J.R. Miller, *Skyscrapers Hide the Heavens: A History of Indian-White Relations in Canada* (Toronto: University of Toronto Press, 1989), 226–7.

16 Mary Ellen Turpel, 'Aboriginal Peoples and the Canadian *Charter:* Interpretive Monopolies, Cultural Differences,' in *Canadian Human Rights Yearbook 1989–1990* (Ottawa: University of Ottawa Human Rights Research and Education Centre, 1990), 3.

17 Ibid. at 13.

18 Michel Foucault, *L'Usage des plaisirs: Histoire de la sexualité, volume 2* (Paris: Gallimard, 1984), 14, 15.

19 *Thomas* v. *Norris,* [1992] 2 C.N.L.R. 139 (B.C.S.C.).

20 *G&M,* 8 February 1992.

21 Thomas v. *Norris,* supra n. 19 at 160.

22 Ibid. at 160.

23 Ibid. The reasoning underpinning the decision is less clear. Relying mainly on three historic decisions (*Delgamuukw* v. *The Queen,* [1991] 3 W.W.R. 97 (B.C.S.C.); *R.* v. *Sparrow,* [1990] 2 S.C.R. 1075; *Saumur* v. *City of Quebec,* [1953] 2 S.C.R. 299), Justice Hood noted that 'just as rights guaranteed under the Charter are not absolute, those guaranteed under s. 35 are not absolute'; he then affirmed that the plaintiff 'lives in a free society and his rights are inviolable' (*Thomas* v. *Norris* supra n. 19 at 161, 162). My purpose here, however, is not to evaluate the internal consistency of the court's legal reasoning; it is, rather, to situate it in its inter-cultural context.

24 Turpel, supra n. 16 at 4.

25 *Thomas* v. *Norris,* supra n. 19 at 140 (emphasis added).

26 Ibid. at 162.

27 Frideres, supra n. 14 at 25.

28 Michel Foucault, *Surveiller et punir: Naissance de la prison* (Paris: Gallimard, Bibliothèque des Histoires, 1975).

29 *Thomas* v. *Norris*, supra n. 19 at 162 (emphasis added).

30 It is interesting that Justice Hood, in referring to the initiation, should use this term, which can carry a meaning of 'a *primitive* form of trial to determine guilt or innocence by subjecting the accused person to fire, poison, or other serious danger, the result being regarded as a divine or preternatural judgment' (*Webster's Encyclopedic Unabridged Dictionary of the English Language* [New York: Portland House, 1989], 1013 [emphasis added]). This evocation, assuredly unintentional on the part of Judge Hood, of a *different* form of judicial process does raise the issue of *why* the defendants proceeded with an initiation despite the likely lack of consent of David Thomas.

31 Quoted in Arnold Krupat, *Ethnocriticism: Ethnography, History, Literature* (Berkeley and Los Angeles: University of California Press, 1992), 19. For an extensive discussion of the use of scapegoating, see the essay by Ross Chambers in this collection.

32 *Thomas* v. *Norris*, supra n. 19 at 162.

33 Ibid. at 159.

34 Although of course she, a practising lawyer in Vancouver, lives very much within modernity. Or, perhaps more accurately, modernity lives within her – as it does for all those whose lives it has been shaping. It is hard to imagine that anyone in Canada, as in much of the world, escapes this fate.

35 I am coining this term by borrowing from feminism's analogous 'malestream.' It is meant to underline the fact that, while Canada is a multi-coloured society, white European cultural codes remain the norm.

36 The work of Christopher Lasch, *The True and Only Heaven* (New York: Norton, 1991), for example, is emblematic of this critique. In the Canadian context, see for example the popular sociological essay by Reginald W. Bibby, *Mosaic Madness: The Poverty and Potential of Life in Canada* (Toronto: Stoddard, 1990).

37 This indictment, only hinted at in the *Globe and Mail*, is developed much more fully by Mary Ellen Turpel in her article, supra n. 16.

38 *Thomas* v. *Norris*, supra n. 19 at 158.

39 Ibid. at 141.

40 Ibid. at 150.

41 Ibid. at 157.

42 Turpel, supra n. 16 at 25.

43 *Thomas* v. *Norris*, supra n. 19 at 145, 146, and 147.

44 See, for instance, A. Alan Borovoy, *When Freedoms Collide: The Case for Our Civil Liberties* (Toronto: Lester and Orpen Dennys, 1988), ch. 9 ('Involuntary Civil Confinement').

45 On this issue, see Pamela Amoss, *Coast Salish Spirit Dancing: The Survival of an Ancestral Religion* (Seattle and London: University of Washington Press, 1978); and Wolfgang Jilek, *Salish Mental Health and Culture Change* (Toronto and Montreal: Holt, Rinehart and Winston of Canada, 1974).

46 *Thomas v. Norris*, supra n. 19 at 142–3.

47 He is a member of the Lyackson Band; she is from the Cowichan Band. On Coast Salish standards of exogamy, see Amoss, supra n. 45.

48 *Thomas v. Norris*, supra n. 19 at 154. The book is Amoss's *Coast Salish Spirit Dancing*; see supra n. 45.

49 Amoss, supra n. 45 at 145.

50 Ibid. at 20.

51 Michel Foucault, *Le Souci de soi – Volume 3: Histoire de la sexualité* (Paris: Gallimard, Bibliothèque des Histoires, 1984).

52 Among a multitude of discussions of this issue, see Charles Taylor's highly readable and concise *The Malaise of Modernity* (Concord, Ont.: Anansi Press, 1991).

53 See supra n. 36.

54 Turpel, supra n. 16.

55 Says Winnie Giesbrecht, president of the Indigenous Women's Collective of Manitoba: 'My biggest fear is that native women are not going to have any rights whatsoever. They will be controlled by the male powers in the native hierarchy' (quoted in E. Kaye Fulton, 'Drumbeats of Rage,' *Maclean's*, 16 March 1992 at 17).

56 In the judgment, Justice Hood refers to her as Helen Kamar. But in preparing this essay, I spoke with Vina Starr, the defendants' lawyer, who noted that 'Kamar' is a misspelling and that the correct spelling is Kumai.

57 *Thomas v. Norris*, supra n. 19 at 145.

58 Ibid. at 147.

59 Ibid. at 146.

60 Turpel, supra n. 16.

61 Giovanna Borradori, '"Weak Thought" and Postmodernism: The Italian Departure from Deconstruction' (1987–8) 18 *Social Text* 40.

Rewriting the Enlightenment: Allegory and *Trauerspiel* in Alejo Carpentier's *El Siglo de las luces*

PAMELA McCALLUM

What happens to the great emancipatory moments of the French Revolution and the Enlightenment when they are inscribed in the different spaces of the New World colonies? What is the effect when the project of liberty announced by revolutionary Paris is transferred to the Creole and plantation societies of Guadeloupe and Martinique? How are the convulsive and changing political alignments of the European countries reproduced in the relationships among their colonies? These are some of the questions which organize and inform the narrative of Alejo Carpentier's novel *El Siglo de las luces*,[1] a title which, translated literally, means 'century of enlightenment.' In the different template of colonial space, the revolutionary transformation of France is both magnified and diminished: on the one hand, a moment which passes almost unnoticed in the streets of Paris – the Convention's abolition of slavery – proposes a whole social transformation for the Caribbean; on the other, a moment which radically shifts Parisian politics – Thermidor and the fall of the Robespierrists – has little effect on the struggles for power in Fort-de-France. Carpentier's narrative never fails to underscore the startling, ironic turns which the unique configurations of the Caribbean can give to the master texts and famous men of the European Enlightenment: a slave ship owned by an admirer of Jean-Jacques Rousseau plies the Latin American trade – its name? *The Social Contract.* There can be little doubt that Carpentier's text constructs and represents a different revolution, a revolution that problematizes the claims of 1789 and offers new directions out of the impasse of a European event which by the end of the century of enlightenment appeared to have veered off course.

Like the novels of Walter Scott, Alessandro Manzoni, and Leo Tolstoy, Carpentier's *El Siglo de las luces* could be said to 'reflect' historical reality in all its concreteness (and therefore would be a historical novel in the sense in which Georg Lukács defines it). In Lukács's discussion of the genre, the historical novelist strives to portray a historical period and to create fictional characters who 'typify' it. As Fredric Jameson remarks,

> For Lukács realistic characters are distinguished from those in other types of liter-
> ature by their *typicality*: they stand, in other words, for something larger and more
> meaningful than themselves, than their own isolated individual destinies. They
> are concrete individualities and yet at the same time maintain a relationship with
> some more general or collective human substance.[2]

This notion of typicality suggests that *El Siglo de las luces* has an obvious resemblance to a Lukácsian historical novel: Victor Hugues would 'stand for' the Jacobin leader, Esteban for the disillusioned intellectual. Such characters really do convey the sense of a whole historical period which extends from the French Revolution through the Napoleonic Empire. They also personify the collective and historical forces which took part in the Great Revolution. Then, too, Carpentier does adhere to Lukács's distinction between the great and powerful figures in the historical drama and the minor and unknown figures in the historical novel. While the depiction of 'dramatic collision' structurally requires eminent historical figures (Buchner, for instance, stages the French Revolution as the conflict between Danton and Robespierre), the historical novelist ('much more closely bound to the specifically historical, individual moments of a period')[3] is compelled to readapt such inflated heroes to the world of everyday reality. Indeed, it might be said that Victor Hugues – 'almost completely ignored by historians of the French Revolution'[4] – has close affinities with the subordinate, anonymous protagonists of Scott. Other familiar Lukácsian themes and motifs are also present: the preference for a detailed Balzacian intensity and an aversion to Zola's abstract schematism, the insistence on the ideal of 'concrete totality' and the championing of a nineteenth-century realist form, the distrust of psychologism and the desire to rehabilitate epic narration. This is the sense in which *El Siglo de las luces* could be easily assimilated to the generic category of the historical novel.

Strange as it might seem, however, Carpentier's novel begins with a modernist, even postmodernist, shard of disembodied monologue. Or rather, to borrow a phrase from Walter Benjamin, 'in the spirit of allegory it is conceived from the outset as a ruin, a fragment.'[5] Readers of *El Siglo de las luces* are confronted with a mysterious opening prologue, which consists of a few paragraphs of solemn meditation, an unidentified scrap of speech. There are so many spectral images, so many obscure and esoteric allusions, that the reader feels he/she has entered a hallucinatory world, a dream world; there are so many enigmas and riddles that everything seems wrapped in an impenetrable secrecy. At first all the reader has in this realm of intangible shadows is a vague impression of the *Máquina*, which has been splintered into the dispersed fragments of its blade, lintel, and uprights. Little by little, however, the bits of fragmentary sensory data become invested with a strangely familiar meaning that derives from the cultural past. Some of the motifs and images recall the classicism of antiquity, the Renaissance, and the Enlightenment: the pure geometry of the architectural shapes in the 'inverted half pediment,' the black triangle, the 'set square'; the starry skies of Kant's *Critique of Pure Reason* in the luminous constellations and Milky Way of the southern sky. Still other motifs and images bring to mind romantic *Naturphilosophie*: 'the continuous, rhythmical and persistent' sound of the waves; the promise of land in a breeze smelling of 'humus, dung, corn and resin'; the inexhaustible profusion of the tropical sea in 'a flash of scales' or 'floating wreath of sargasso.'[6]

But, stylistically, it is surely the nightmarish apparition of the ghostly Plenipotentiary that absorbs the reader's attention. In this cold and disembodied figure 'beside the black rectangle in its inquisitorial cover'[7] there appears the 'motif of the ruler's omnipotence, the leading motif of baroque absolutism.'[8] For the key to the passage is the paradoxical riddle of the baroque tyrant (formerly 'confidant, guide and mentor'; now 'sullen Mandatory')[9] whose Janus-faced emblematic persona comes to embody all the insoluble contradictions of the century of enlightenment. Such extravagant and strange imagery is less reminiscent of classical or romantic mythologies than of the historical/political *Umwelt* of the baroque *Trauerspiel*. Baroque drama does not hinge on the divine fate of a tragic hero who is sacrificed to the gods. Rather it is organized around the earthbound fate of the baroque prince, who represents absolute power and its downfall. Thus side by side the classical and romantic imagery, there takes shape the enigmatic figure of the baroque tyrant-martyr, positioned, in Jameson's words, 'halfway between a tyrant justly assassinated and a martyr suffering his passion.'[10] Here, as the reader might expect in an allegorical construction, the inner antitheses and paradoxes of the image serve as a vehicle to convey the still obscure and incomprehensible hidden meaning. Indeed, this is made explicit in the contrast between the 'confidant, guide and mentor' and the 'sullen Mandatory,' which recurs throughout the novel. From the antinomy between them arises the narrative action of *El Siglo de las luces*. This formal opposition is powerfully reinforced by the juxtaposition of the 'starry skies' and the *Máquina* (or, more appropriately, the guillotine, for the reader will by now have pieced together the blade, crosspiece, and lintel into that grisly instrument of death). Thus the impressionistic fragments of the opening passage turn out to be the heterogeneous raw material of a complex allegory, baroque in inspiration, a set of peculiarly legible, yet still puzzling, signs to be deciphered.

This is not the traditional realism that informs nineteenth-century historical novels. Carpentier's text foregrounds its own representational strategies or, to borrow Linda Hutcheon's phrasing, 'acknowledges its identity as construct, rather than as simulacrum of some "real" outside.'[11] While there can be no doubt that *El Siglo de las luces* contains formal elements of the nineteenth-century historical novel, as outlined by Lukács, it is also clear that these allusions to an older practice of historical fiction are constantly put into dialogue with and interrogated by the allegorizing structures of the novel itself. In this way, its 'constructive' character is much closer to Benjamin's theory of baroque allegory than to Lukács's mimetic representationalism. Certainly, the category of the 'baroque' has proven to be a familiar interpretive model[12] for Carpentier's texts and for Latin American fiction in general. 'La Ciudad de las columnas,' Carpentier's own influential essay in *Tientos y Diferencias*, identifies the layering and exuberance of the baroque with Latin America.[13] Commentators have tended to focus, however, on the stylistic motifs which establish formal affinities with baroque art, architecture, and writing, highlighting what Djelal Kadir calls Carpentier's 'profuse Baroque linguistic plenitude.'[14] It is not my intention to call into question analyses of baroque style in Carpentier's writings. I would suggest instead a complementary strategy of interpretation, one which investigates the novel's affiliation to an 'other' baroque, the seventeenth-century *teatrum mundi* which Benjamin theorizes in his *Trauerspiel* book. With its world of political intrigue, ever-present treacheries, and abrupt changes of fortune, seventeenth-century drama would seem to offer an all too appropriate configuration with the political texture of the French Revolution.

Is it possible that Benjamin's *The Origin of German Tragic Drama* could provide the terms and themes within which Carpentier's text might be read? Such a reading would suggest that *El Siglo de las luces* constructs and represents historical experience in a second-level baroque allegory which is conscious of itself as a 'rewriting' of the Enlightenment. Such a reading would formulate the questions of novelistic creation or formal innovation in terms of a metafiction rather than a 'reflection theory of knowledge.' In this sense, *El Siglo de las luces* – which is formally quite similar to allegory and *Trauerspiel* – can be reread as an exercise in the baroque process of giving form.[15] As Benjamin defines it, 'what is vital is the transposition of the originally temporal data into a figurative spatial simultaneity.'[16] Here the allegorist reinserts the empirical temporal data into a sharply delineated allegorical construction: chronological developments and historical actions are transposed and fixed in a 'spatial image' (*Raumbild*) or allegorical structure. What has occurred in a chronological sequence of actions is then brought out by means of the *Stillstand* of an allegorical emblem (or, what amounts to the same thing, a self-conscious and second-level metafiction). For it is quite apparent that the baroque tyrant – so central to the *Trauerspiel* – is reclaimed and rewritten by Carpentier in terms of Victor Hugues, the Jacobin leader, hero, and protagonist. He becomes an allegorical figure standing for the antinomies of the French Revolution and Enlightenment thought. The story of Hugues is the story of the decline and fall of revolutionary France; it brings to a close the century of enlightenment and ushers in the instrumental reason of the triumphant middle classes. Thus the very employment of allegorical figures in *El Siglo de las luces* points beyond a Lukácsian replica realism. From this perspective, Benjamin's allegorical construct is far better able than the later Lukács's dogmatic realism to articulate the tensions and contradictions of history. By construing the allegorist's activity as 'one of arranging,'[17] by rendering allegory as 'consciously constructed ruins,'[18] Benjamin acknowledges a gap or rift between the text and its referent – a gap which is annulled in Lukács's closed scholasticism of the totality. Or, as Sandor Radnoti says in his reading of Benjamin, 'the internal tension between allegorizing representation and its object becomes its own secret object and the internal unity of the work is born through this fantastic roundabout.'[19]

If we ask what point of departure can be established for understanding baroque allegory, then it must be those melancholic figures who brood over omens and portents, those mourners who – in Benjamin's words – 'ponder over signs and over the future.'[20] The melancholic is oppressed by an acute consciousness of catastrophe, by a world of ruinous devastation and shattered fragments. Wretchedness and despair determine his/her life experience. For nowhere can the melancholic discern or assume anything but a meaningless chaos. The image here is one of helpless desolation before the disasters of history. It is an image which evokes the 'playing and displaying of human wretchedness' of baroque *Trauerspiel* (literally 'play of sorrow'). The melancholic is plunged into an unreliable, arbitrary, inscrutable world in which the force of circumstance reigns, in which names have been divorced from their objects. This is the reason, too, that he/she experiences a painful discontinuity between his/her own 'will to meaning' and the meaningless void which surrounds him/her.

It might seem, therefore, that the melancholic can never encounter anything other than paralysing disappointments in the sordid baseness of a fallen existence. However, we should not overlook the fact that he/she does cherish one pleasure – that is, allegory. As Benjamin puts it,

It is true that the overbearing ostentation, with which the banal object seems to arise from the depths of allegory is soon replaced by its disconsolate everyday countenance; it is true that the profound fascination of the sick man for the isolated and insignificant is succeeded by that disappointed abandonment of the exhausted emblem ... But the amorphous details which can only be understood allegorically keep coming up. For if the instructions are: 'everything [must be] considered in its own right, and the intelligence [will] increase and taste be refined,' then the appropriate object of such intentions is ever present.[21]

No doubt the melancholic's fondness for puzzling and obscure minutiae quickly gives way to a feeling of disillusionment and exhaustion. On the other hand, it must not be forgotten that his/her obsession with emblematics and allegory is revived in the isolated and irrelevant details which constantly come into view and captivate his/her attention. This unexpected reversal serves to open up a space for the pleasurable activity of allegorical construction. To insist that the steady gaze of the melancholic allegorist depletes existing phenomena of their meaning is not only to say that it makes visible a dead and alien world; it is also to acknowledge that his/her infatuation with the faded traces or ruined memorials of the past stimulates a delight in the construction of allegorical emblems. This is how the pain of the outsider passes over into the pleasure of the allegorist (still, to be sure, threatened with the return of anxiety and suffering).

Benjamin's theory of allegory is based on the distinction between symbol and allegory as it is found in German neoclassical aesthetics. Goethe and Schopenhauer both privilege symbolic art, which is dominated by an experience of positivity – an experience of beautiful wholeness, divine reconciliation, natural plenitude, future fulfilment, and so on. According to their neoclassical prejudices, the symbol is a concrete universal; in

Goethe's words, 'whoever grasps the particular in all its vitality also grasps the general without being aware of it.'[22] Whereas the symbol apprehends the supreme value of the universal in the most individualistic and particular moments, allegory shockingly imposes an abstract meaning on the abundance and multiplicity of life. Whereas the symbol is the incarnation and vehicle of the Idea, allegory is said to be 'the trifling amusement of carving a picture to serve at the same time as an inscription, as a hieroglyphic.'[23] For this reason, Goethe and Schopenhauer claim that allegorical representation is unable to express the profound immanence of the perfect individual, the 'beautiful soul'; rather, it remains within the framework of an excessively schematic and artificial formalism. That is, to put it briefly, for Goethe and Schopenhauer allegory turns out to be little more than 'a mere mode of designation.'[24]

Against this tradition of neoclassical aesthetics, Benjamin argues for the priority of allegorical form. Allegory, he maintains, is 'not a playful illustrative technique, but a form of expression, just as speech is expression, and, indeed, just as writing is.'[25] As Benjamin sees it, the flawless classicism of the symbolic artwork is not suited to the catastrophes and disasters that were the subject matter of baroque *Trauerspiel* (or, in more concrete terms, the Germany of the Thirty Years' War). He puts it in quite explicit terms when he says, 'It is only thanks to this [allegorical] structure that the *Trauerspiel* can assimilate as its content the subjects which contemporary conditions provide it.'[26] For Benjamin, what is compelling about allegory lies in its capacity to represent the surprisingly sudden breakdowns and collapses which overcome a prostrate historical world. In the beautiful illusion of the symbolic artwork there is no place for a creaturely human existence shot through with disorder and decay; in the formed completeness of the symbolic artwork there is no place for the chronic unease and political intrigue of a transient historical world. In a much-quoted passage, Benjamin makes the following observation:

Whereas in the symbol destruction is idealized and the transfigured face of nature is fleetingly revealed in the light of redemption, in allegory the observer is confronted with the *facies hippocratica* of history as a petrified, primordial landscape. Everything about history that, from the beginning, has been untimely, sorrowful, unsuccessful, is expressed in a face – or rather in a death's head. And although such a thing lacks all symbolic freedom of expression, all classical proportion, all humanity – nevertheless, this is the form in which man's subjection to nature is most obvious and it significantly gives rise not only to the enigmatic question of the nature of human existence as such, but also of the biographical historicity of the individual. This is the heart of the allegorical way of seeing, of the baroque, secular explanation of history as the Passion of the world; its importance resides solely in the stations of its decline. The greater the significance, the greater the subjection to death, because death digs most deeply the jagged line of demarcation between physical nature and significance.[27]

This enables us to appreciate how the baroque conception of allegory exceeds the serene classical perfectionism of the symbol. It also allows us to arrive at an understanding of the way in which baroque allegorical form is able to incorporate as its content the fallen domain of history. Here the very image of the passing of time – 'history as a petrified, primordial landscape' – shows the enormous difference between the allegorical impulse of the baroque and the ideal of classical beauty. For the element of uniformly objective classical symmetry is almost wholly lacking in Benjamin; nothing in his new interpretation of baroque allegory and *Trauerspiel* is designed to preclude the contradictions and vicissitudes which make up history. Seen in this way, the 'jagged line' of baroque allegorical construction refuses to abolish 'man's subjection to nature' in the harmonious proportions of the symbolic artwork. Indeed the dissonant, and problematic, form of baroque allegory is able to come to terms with a 'fallen nature which bears the imprint of the progression of history.'[28] Nature is not made to appear in 'bud and bloom' but in 'over-ripeness and decay,'[29] so that the allegorical image becomes endowed with the special ability to convey the disharmony and corruption of the profane world. Within this representational frame, the baroque emblem of the death's head captures 'everything ... that ... has been untimely, sorrowful, unsuccessful' about creaturely history. Thus, in opposition to the finished forms of the classical symbol, which excludes the waste and ravages of time, the death's head attests to the eerie, grotesque paradoxes of a tormented earthly history.

In Benjamin's view, allegorical structure presents an immanent set of antitheses or, more properly, a system of contradictory oppositions. This dialectical principle informs what he calls 'the antinomies of the allegorical'[30] and is formulated as follows:

Any person, any object, any relationship can mean absolutely anything else. With this possibility a destructive, but just verdict is passed on the profane world: it is characterized as a world in which the detail is of no great importance. But it will be unmistakably apparent, especially to anyone who is familiar with allegorical textual exegesis, that all of the things which are used to signify derive, from the very fact of their pointing to something else, a power which makes them appear no longer commensurable with profane things, which raises them onto a higher plane, and which can, indeed, sanctify them. Considered in allegorical terms, then, the profane world is both elevated and devalued.[31]

In this passage, the antinomies of the allegorical can be observed in the interplay of two opposed terms: the devaluation of existing natural phenomena and the allegorical sanctification of the dead object. The first moment involves a destructive act that discards the natural details and living entities of a fallen and meaningless, world. The second moment involves a sanctifying act that confers new meaning on the now deadened and emptied objects of this profane world. If 'any person, any object, any relationship can mean absolutely anything else,' to follow Benjamin, then it is clear that the inanimate and dead object can be seized as the raw material of an allegorical understanding. Precisely because the object is dead and meaningless, the allegorist is free to invest it with a new and sanctified meaning 'no longer commensurable with profane things.' Accordingly, the isolated and unimportant fragments acquire their fresh and unexpected allegorical significance from 'pointing to something else' (here Benjamin follows traditional usage in drawing on the etymological root of allegory – 'speaking otherwise'). Such, then, is the inner contradictory structure of allegory: on the one hand, natural organic life is divested of its sensuous content, which leaves it an empty husk; on the other hand, this deadness is sanctified or redeemed by a new allegorical meaning which fills the void and heralds salvation. As Bainard Cowan notes, 'in becoming a world of allegorical emblems, the profane world is robbed of its sensuous fullness, robbed of any inherent meaning it might possess, only to be invested with a privileged meaning whose source transcends this world.'[32]

I said earlier that Carpentier employs the mannered and ornamental motifs of baroque allegory in his text. As a guiding thread through the discrete details and episodes of the century of enlightenment, he makes reference over and over again to the transformation of Victor Hugues, the principled leader, into a cynical opportunist (here Carpentier transposes the motif of the tyrant-martyr from the storehouse of baroque literature to the novel). This formal affinity between baroque structural elements and Carpentier's novelistic practice will become clearer as I now try to summarize briefly the whole course of action in *El Siglo de las luces*.

Carpentier opens his novel in eighteenth-century colonial Cuba. The story-line begins with a family of three young people (Carlos, Esteban, and Sofia) whose father's death signifies the end of authority. In this idyllic interlude, the three live together in a disordered and unrestrained anarchic freedom. The arrival of Victor Hugues, the French trader from Port-au-Prince, a freemason and a democrat, restores order to the upside-down, playful existence of the wayward youths: he saves the family business from the disastrous manipulations of the executor; he assembles scientific instruments from their jumbled pieces; and he reorganizes the untidy scattered furniture of the house. A progressive who believes all men are equal, Victor will temper the naïve and utopian dreams of the young people by acquainting them with the rationalist values of the Enlightenment and the political struggles of the French Revolution. Victor and Esteban sail to France and the intoxicating atmosphere of revolutionary Paris. Even so, bit by bit they grow apart. The disillusionment of the intellectual is portrayed by the melancholic Esteban, whose obsessive reflections on the disastrous course the Revolution had taken force him to conclude it has been betrayed. The central action, however, consists in the career of Victor Hugues, whose decisive, principled leadership is succeeded by the cynical indifference and vacillation of the opportunist. The climax of illusion and disillusionment – the fall of Victor, the tyrannical Plenipotentiary – represents the collapse not only of an extraordinary individual but of revolutionary Jacobinism and indeed the Enlightenment itself. From this point on, Victor stands for the counter-Enlightenment and political repression; he no longer embodies the emancipatory values and aspirations of the Age of Reason, but rather their betrayal (illustrated most strikingly by the reinstitution of slavery in the French colonies). The ailing, sickly Esteban is driven to the very edge of despair. Sofia, who had joined Victor in Cayenne, deserts him when she learns of his decision to brutally repress a slave rebellion. Discouraged by the turn of events, she and Esteban seclude themselves in a house in Spain. But they are too much products of the century of enlightenment to retreat into apathy and defeatism. When they hear the tumultuous sounds of the Madrid uprising against Napoleon, they join the people and are killed. The narrative ends with their deaths in a collective/popular struggle, which brings to a close the century of enlightenment and sparks off the Spanish and Latin American wars of independence.

On a literal level, the character of Victor Hugues seems to faithfully render the historical events and forces of the French Revolution in Europe and the Caribbean colonies. On an allegorical level, however, he becomes a figure for the reversal of the Enlightenment and its emancipatory claims. Nothing foregrounds this drastic reversal so well as the scene in which Victor stares fixedly at his old uniform. After having led another meaningless and defeated expedition to recapture escaped slaves, ill and feverish, he concentrates his gaze on the uniform he wore as commissar of the Convention. This is what he says:

I've put on so many costumes I no longer know which is the right one ... But there is one that I prefer to all the others: this one. I was given it by the only man [Robespierre] I've ever looked up to. When they overthrew him I ceased to understand myself. Since then I haven't tried to fathom anything. I'm like those automata who play chess, walk, play the fife or beat a drum when they're wound up ... And he added in a whisper, counting on his fingers: 'Baker, trader, mason, anti-mason, jacobin, military hero, rebel, prisoner, absolved by the men who killed the man that made me, Agent of the Directory, Agent of the Consulate ...' The enumeration which had exceeded the number of his fingers, died away into an unintelligible murmur.[33]

Carpentier's description of the discarded uniform should be understood in connection with the impoverishing process of allegory. For Victor, the uniform had represented the living reality of his authority as a Jacobin leader. Such clothing seemed to enjoy the filled density of a natural phenomenon which sparkled with the pulsating vivaciousness of life. In Victor's hands, however, the once resplendent uniform now becomes drained of the fullness of practical political activity; it is nothing but a dead, empty shell – a museum piece.[34] At the same time, the cast-off uniform begins to speak of something else; it is invested with a new meaning as the allegorical emblem of the French Revolution and the Enlightenment shattered into bits and pieces. Allegorically, the obsolete dress-coat and breeches, 'whose contours [are] no longer tenanted by flesh and blood,'[35] speak of a historical event which has ceased to have any meaning. Here Carpentier is referring (through the figure of Victor) to the 'double character' of the century of enlightenment.[36] On the one hand, it cannot be denied that the utopian discourse of the eighteenth century contained an emancipatory content; on the other hand, the limitations of its revolutionary project became all the more visible with the passing of time. The very tone of Victor's lament – his melancholy, his distress, his grief – forms a sharp contrast with the robust, assertive, all-powerful commissar of the Convention. The allusion is, of course, to the tyrant-martyr of baroque drama. Just as Victor Hugues personifies the double character of the French Revolution (its emancipatory potential and its systematic repression), so he epitomizes the double character of the baroque ruler – part tyrant, part martyr.

This strange image of the baroque tyrant-martyr reminds us of the abrupt appearance of the Plenipotentiary and the *Máquina* in the opening section. Let us return to the baroque riddle-figure that occurs in the cryptic and veiled prologue. In the passage, the reader is able to detect a deliberate spectral distortion of an older commonsense or 'realistic' mimetic representationalism, which is achieved by mannered and hyperbolic baroque conceits. There is, after all, a shadowy unreality about the enigmatic figures in the prologue, whose identity can only be guessed at rather than really pinned down. As I have previously pointed out, Carpentier does not reveal who the speaker is or who the Plenipotentiary is. He even breaks up the image of the *Máquina* into separate and disconnected pieces – all we are provided with is a momentary glimpse of the lintel, supports, blade, and uprights. Nowhere are there definite fully formed figures and representations which could impart an unequivocal and incontestable meaning to the passage. Instead of some clearly defined and easy to grasp symbol, instead of naming the Plenipotentiary and the guillotine, he constructs a hazy, inscrutable allegorical image intended to blur the exact identity of the Plenipotentiary and the grim silhouette of the *Máquina*. The atmosphere of the passage is uncertain and imprecise, is perplexing and undetermined. The unknown speaker seems to gaze forever at the unsolved enigma of the ghostly Plenipotentiary and the lethal *Máquina*, which are enshrouded in the darkness of the night. In its strange dreamlike illegibility, then, the opening prologue borders on an almost indecipherable obscurity. Its dominant atmosphere (so different from a straightforward and recognizable symbolic meaning) is that of mysterious secrecy.

This mood of uncertainty and indeterminacy recurs in the last paragraphs of the novel. It is, of course, quite true that the reader can now identify the speaker as Esteban, the Plenipotentiary as Victor, the *Máquina* as the guillotine. But we once again encounter a riddle-figure in the final passages. For the reader, who never discovers what happens to Esteban and Sofía, is left pondering the mystery of their disappearance: 'no further trace of them or their final resting place was ever found.'[37] Their anonymous deaths intensify the pervasive atmosphere of melancholic sadness, quite in keeping with the baroque plays of sorrow. Notwithstanding this, there is a shift from the esoteric and undefinable to the realistic and graphic in Carpentier's frequent allusions to Goya's paintings. His vivid portrayal of outward events becomes strongly sensory and explicit – indeed, his language becomes charged with turmoil, bloodshed, terror, and brute force. Here Carpentier's much more clearly identifiable scenes make extensive use of Goya's violent tableaux of pitched battles and convulsed death throes: 'The mamelukes, cuirassiers and Polish Guards had fired on a crowd which retaliated with cold steel, men and women throwing themselves at the horses and slashing their flanks with razors and knives' (*The Second of May 1808*); 'the gunners behind a cannon fell ... and frenzied women lit the fuses when there were no more men to do it';[38] 'the streets were full of corpses, and of groaning wounded, too badly injured to stand, who were finished off by patrols and sinister myrmidons ...'[39] Elsewhere the same impression of sensory-graphic concreteness is reinforced when we seem to discover Esteban and Sofia's deaths in the man and woman of 'One Cannot Look at This.'[40] But an even more striking example of a reawakened sensoriness and immediacy is the strong echo of Goya's *The Third of May 1808* in the 'night of the slaughter, of grim mass executions, of exterminations.'[41] The group of French soldiers, 'concerted together in a fearful rhythm,'[42] invert the principles and values of the Age of Reason. At this point Enlightenment turns into counter-Enlightenment, the utopia of the *philosophes* into the 'sleep of reason.' Ostensibly the French soldiers should epitomize the rational content and universal principles of the Revolution – liberty, equality, fraternity. In spite of this, however, they come to be seen as the bearers of a blind obscurantism and an instrumentalized rationality which has been enlisted in the service of naked political force. For as Jean Starobinski says in his chapter on Goya in *1789: The Emblems of Reason*: 'Revolutionary France, source of the light of principle, which Goya had hoped would radiate far and wide in peace, appears as a violent army, leaving murder and mindless rape in its wake. A baneful reversal had substituted darkness for light.'[43] He continues: 'Light ... is linked to the group of victims, especially to the man of the people who will be slain by the salvo about to be fired ... For the beholder the light, though logically diffused from the lantern as its source, seems to emanate from the white shirt of the victim.'[44] In the prologue, Carpentier appealed to the more abstract auditory sense to produce the effect of a mysterious intangibility. In the last chapter, he appeals to the more direct and graphic visual sense to represent the brute reality of the Napoleonic reaction. Thus the extraordinary emphasis on the visual element or the sensory-graphic heightens the effect of what could be called a 'concrete and realistic allegorism.'[45]

Here we see human life in the frenzy of destruction abandoned to its fate as an object; here, too, we are confronted with the favourite baroque themes of crisis, collapse, and disintegration. This intensely expressive visual representation of apocalyptic chaos calls to mind Monsu's *Explosion in a Cathedral*, the baroque painting which gives the English translation of the novel its title.[46] Earlier the melancholic Esteban had assigned a definite allegorical meaning to this painting, which had so much personal resonance for him; its falling columns and sturdy columns seemed to account for both the upheavals of the revolutionary age and the persistence of feudal institutions. Now he himself is dead and the painting 'ceased to have any subject,' so that 'the scattered and falling columns became invisible against a background which, even now that the light had gone, retained the colour of blood.'[47] If the frozen rigidity of the columns on the left side of the picture plane seemed to signify the *ancien régime* and the startling movement of those on the right depicted the revolutionary transformation of France, then Goya's *The Third of May 1808* effects a sombre inversion: here the upheavals on the right side have been replaced by the terrifyingly straight lines of French troops and muskets, while the left side represents the chaotic collapse of wounded and dying Spaniards. Thus the ostentatious turbulence of Monsu's baroque painting, which had depicted the cataclysms of the century of enlightenment, becomes itself empty and drained of any meaning. But at the same time, a curious reversal takes place: the disintegration and deadness which seemed to be the final referent of Monsu's painting begins to speak otherwise. The Spanish and Latin American wars of independence are set against the ossified praxis and 'second nature' of the French Revolution and the Enlightenment. This new twist reverses and restructures the impoverishing action of Carpentier's self-reflexive allegorical construction, his second-level metafiction. More accurately than Monsu's art, Goya's paintings and etchings make imaginable and concrete the horrors of the Napoleonic occupation of Spain. In Carpentier's text, the gruesomely sensory visualizations of the *Dies Irae* assume the form of an allegorical realism which reproblematizes the European century of enlight-enment. The image of the tyrannical Plenipotentiary and the French Revolution is eclipsed by the image of the people and the collective/popular struggles of the nineteenth and twentieth centuries.[48] However, what is noteworthy, and quite unmistakeable, is that the outcome remains more than a little uncertain: the shadowy fragments of dissolution and dying in the final pages suggest that there is no ultimate replenishment in a dogmatic historical metaphysics. Everything is obscure, everything is unstable, everything has become enveloped in the winter twilight. Nothing is visible through the play of light and darkness except the sudden clear perception of the wall, stained the colour of blood, a stark reminder of Goya's painting. Thus if, at the very end, we had expected to experience some fully developed and completed wholeness, a 'metaphysics of presence,' the absence of a fulfilling event plunges us back into the world of baroque doubt and unease.

It would be misleading, however, to conclude that Carpentier's text ends in death and destruction. The moment when Sofia and Esteban join the people is the climax of the novel, for it is a moment in which the past and present are brought together so as to anticipate the future. Such an active political commitment rules out a self-indulgent withdrawal into an empty subjectivism innocent of history. Thus the deaths of Sofia and Esteban no longer express the heroism of individual protagonists but take on the sense of collective history. The privileging of the peripheral Caribbean subplot over the central French main plot in the final pages opens up a space for the new collective energies mobilized by the Spanish and Latin American wars of independence, and ushers in a different revolution.

NOTES

1 Alejo Carpentier, *El Siglo de las luces* (Mexico: Compania General de Ediciones, 1962); translated into English by John Sturrock as *Explosion in a Cathedral* (New York: Harper and Row, 1979).

2 Fredric Jameson, *Marxism and Form* (Princeton: Princeton University Press, 1971), 191.

3 Georg Lukács, *The Historical Novel*, trans. Hannah and Stanley Mitchell (Harmondsworth: Penguin, 1981), 197.

4 *Siglo*, supra n. 1 at 350.

5 Walter Benjamin, *The Origin of German Tragic Drama*, trans. John Osborne (London: New Left Books, 1977), 235.

6 *Siglo*, supra n. 1 at 10.

7 Ibid.

8 Erich Auerbach, *Mimesis: The Representation of Reality in Western Literature*, trans. Willard R. Trask (Princeton: Princeton University Press, 1953), 381.

9 *Siglo*, supra n. 1 at 10.

10 Jameson, supra n. 2 at 70.

11 Linda Hutcheon, *A Poetics of Postmodernism: History/Theory/Fiction* (New York and London: Routledge, 1988), 119.

12 See Marie-Anne Macé, '*Le Siècle des Lumières ou les turbulences baroques,*' in Daniel-Henri Pageaux, ed., *Quinze Etudes autour de 'El Siglo de las luces' de Alejo Carpentier* (Paris: L'Harmattan, 1983), 187–204.

13 Alejo Carpentier, *Tientos y Diferencias* (Mexico: Universidad Nacional Autonoma, 1964).

14 Djelal Kadir, *Questing Fictions: Latin America's Family Romance* (Minneapolis: University of Minnesota Press, 1986), 89.

15 Macé, supra n. 12, establishes some formal resemblances between *El Siglo de las luces* and baroque motifs which she finds primarily in art history (Wölfflin, Dubois, d'Ors). For a perceptive, if rather unthematized, analysis of allegory, see Carlos Santander, 'Historicidad y Alegoria en *El Siglo de las luces* de Alejo Carpentier,' in *XVII Congreso del Instito International de Literature Iberoamericana*, t. 1 (Madrid: Ediciones Cultura Hispanica, 1978), 499–510.

16 Benjamin, supra n. 5 at 81.

17 Ibid. at 179.

18 Ibid. at 182.

19 Sandor Radnoti, 'The Early Aesthetics of Walter Benjamin' (1974) 7 *International J. Sociology* 76 at 118.

20 Benjamin, supra n. 5 at 193.

21 Ibid. at 185.

22 Ibid. at 161.

23 Schopenhauer, as quoted in ibid. at 162.

24 Ibid.

25 Ibid.

26 Ibid. at 216.

27 Ibid. at 166.

28 Ibid. at 180.

29 Ibid. at 179.

30 Ibid. at 174.

31 Ibid. at 175.

32 Bainard Cowan, 'Walter Benjamin's Theory of Allegory' (1981) 22 *New German Critique* 109 at 116.

33 *Siglo*, supra n. 1 at 347–8.

34 Ibid. at 336.

35 Ibid.

36 The classic statement of the double character of the Enlightenment is found in Max Horkheimer and Theodor Adorno, *Dialectic of Enlightenment*, trans. John Cumming (London: Allen Lane, 1973). See also Jürgen Habermas, 'The Entwinement of Myth and Enlightenment' (1982) 26 *New German Critique* 13 for a recent contribution to the discussion.

37 *Siglo*, supra n. 1 at 362.

38 Francisco Goya, 'What Courage,' in *The Disasters of War* (New York: Dover, 1970), 7.

39 'Infamous Gain' in ibid. at 83.

40 Ibid. at 26. For discussion of Carpentier's deployment of Goya's images in a

manner different from my own, see Beatriz Pastor, 'Carpentier's Enlightened Revolution, Goya's Sleep of Reason,' in James A.W. Heffernan, ed., *Representing the French Revolution: Literature, Historiography, and Art* (Hanover and London: University Press of New England, 1992), 261; and Catharine E. Wall, 'The Visual Dimension of *El Siglo de las luces*: Goya and *Explosion en una Catedral*' (1988) 13 *Revista Canadiense de Estudios Hispanicas* 148.

41 *Siglo*, supra n. 1 at 348.

42 Ibid.

43 Jean Starobinski, *1789: The Emblems of Reason*, trans. Barbara Bray (Charlottesville: University Press of Virginia, 1982), 199.

44 Ibid. at 201.

45 I have borrowed this phrase from Erich Auerbach, *Dante: Poet of the Secular World*, trans. Ralph Manheim (Chicago: University of Chicago Press, 1961); compare also *Mimesis*, supra n. 8, ch. 8.

46 Monsu Desiderio is the name given to two French painters, François de Nomé and Didier Barra, who worked in collaboration. The painting depicts the biblical subject of 'King Asa destroying the idols,' and is in the collection of the Fitzwilliam Museum, Cambridge, England.

47 *Siglo*, supra n. 1 at 349.

48 It is crucial that a focus on the opposition of Caribbean colonies to European colonizer does not lose sight of the system of difference signified by race. In Carpentier's narrative, it is often slavery which turns the claims of the European Enlightenment upside down. For an analysis of the role of blacks in the novel, see Roberto Echevarria, 'Socrates among the Weeds: Blacks and History in Carpentier's *Explosion in a Cathedral*' (1983) 24 *Massachusetts Rev.* 545.

Notes on Contributors

Richard W. Bauman is associate professor of law at the University of Alberta and, in 1994–5, a visiting scholar at Duke University School of Law. He has published in Canadian and foreign journals on topics in corporate law and constitutional law, as well as legal and political philosophy, and is author of *Critical Legal Studies: A Guide to the Literature* (forthcoming).

Ross Chambers is Marvin Felheim Distinguished University Professor of French and comparative literature at the University of Michigan. He is the author of numerous books, including *Meaning and Meaningfulness* (1979); *Story and Situation* (1984); and *Room for Maneuver* (1991).

Claude Denis is associate professor of sociology at Faculté St Jean, University of Alberta. He has published articles on political sociology and the Canadian state, and has been particularly active as a commentator on recent Canadian constitutional developments.

The Honourable Jules Deschênes, C.C., is the former chief justice of the Province of Quebec. He has also served as president of the Royal Society of Canada. He has published *The Sword and the Scales / Les Plateaux de la balance* (1979) and *Sur la ligne de feu: Autobiographie d'un juge de chef* (1988). He is currently a judge on the United Nations' International Criminal Tribunal for the Former Yugoslavia.

Richard F. Devlin is associate professor of law at Dalhousie University. In addition to numerous articles on legal theory, he has edited *Canadian Perspectives on Legal Theory* (1991).

Jonathan Hart is professor of English and adjunct professor of comparative literature at the University of Alberta. He is the author of *Theater and the World* (1992) and *Northrop Frye: The Theoretical Imagination* (1994), editor of *Reading the Renaissance* (forthcoming 1995), and contributing editor of *Canadian Review of Comparative Literature / Revue canadienne de littérature comparée*.

Pamela McCallum is professor of English at the University of Calgary. She has written *Literature and Method* (1983) and is a member of the editorial board of *Cultural Critique*. She is also an editor of *Ariel*.

Jennifer Nedelsky is professor of political science and law at the University of Toronto. She is the author of *Private Property and the Limits of American Constitutionalism* (1990).

Sheila Noonan is assistant professor of law at Queen's University, Kingston. She has written articles on abortion, obscenity and the criminal law, and feminist jurisprudence.

Christopher Norris is a professor of English at the University of Wales at Cardiff. He has written numerous articles and books, including *The Deconstructive Turn* (1984), *Music and the Politics of Culture* (1989), and *What's Wrong with Postmodernism* (1990).

Christine Sypnowich is associate professor of philosophy at Queen's University, Kingston. She has written articles on political and legal theory, which have been published in Canada, the United States, and the United Kingdom. She is the author of *The Concept of Socialist Law* (1990).